*The Ethics of Asking*

# The Ethics
# of Asking

## Dilemmas in
## Higher Education
## Fund Raising

*Edited by Deni Elliott*

The Johns Hopkins University Press
Baltimore and London

© 1995 The Johns Hopkins University Press
All rights reserved. Published 1995
Printed in the United States of America on acid-free paper
04 03 02 01 00 99 98 97 96 95  5 4 3 2 1

The Johns Hopkins University Press
2715 North Charles Street
Baltimore, Maryland 21218-4319
The Johns Hopkins Press Ltd., London

Library of Congress Cataloging-in-Publication Data will be found at
the end of this book.
A catalog record for this book is available from the British Library.

ISBN 0-8018-5049-5

*To my son, James, and to all the others
who have taught us about giving*

# Contents

*Contents*

## Appendixes: Codes of Ethics and Statements of Principles

# *Preface and Acknowledgments*

An academic analysis of the ethical problems of higher education fund raising quite literally involves looking a gift horse in the mouth. Development officers have been apt to react with hurt surprise that anyone would ponder their ethical behavior. It is true that the intentions of development officers are almost universally good. The compensation for positions in higher education advancement tends to be lower than the compensation for equivalent jobs in the for-profit world. The work itself encourages one of the finest virtues—beneficence.

The suggestion that attempts to tap the charitable impulse may raise questions of ethics became a topic of discussion among scholars and development officers at Dartmouth College in the mid-1980s. CASE, the Council for Advancement and Support of Education, was also exploring these questions. Dartmouth and CASE joined forces to submit a grant proposal in 1989 to undertake the first comprehensive ethical analysis of higher education fund raising. Funded by grants from the Lilly Endowment and the W. K. Kellogg Foundation, Dartmouth and CASE mustered a task force of thirteen ethical theorists, philosophers, development officers, and university administrators to examine the issues.

Our first task was to clarify what constitutes an ethical problem for development officers. We quickly came to understand that practitioners could find themselves embroiled in ethical problems despite the best of intentions. We did find cases of development officers acting with bad intentions, but these cases were the exception rather than the rule. For instance, we had all heard about the male development officer who preyed on elderly widows and invariably created a sizable gift for himself in addition to one for the university. Similarly, we had heard about the college on the other side of the state that diverted a gift from a program signifying a donor's clearly stated intention to a project that represented a direct contradiction of the donor's wishes.

But we found that we had little to learn from these cases of outright fraud. We decided to focus instead on the ethics problems that confront development officers when they are earnestly trying to do the right thing. We started our project assuming that good people can do the wrong thing even when they have the best of intentions. University and college development officers have a lofty goal: they raise funds so that their institutions can do a better job of educating students, advancing knowledge, and serving the community. Yet, sometimes fund raisers find themselves uncertain what is the right thing to do, for example, in cases such as the following:

- A generous gift is offered by a donor whose identity stands to embarrass the institution.
- A volunteer lies about his level of giving, but classmates believe him and match his purported gift. The development officer wonders whether it is up to her to set the record straight.
- A planned-giving officer feels torn between his desire to make sure that the giver's needs are taken care of and his perceived obligation to get what he can for the institution.
- The development officer is charged with the uneasy task of explaining to a donor the relevant differences between naming an endowed chair and naming the person who can fill the chair. When it comes right down to it, the line between reasonable donor expectations and intrusion seems extremely fine.
- The development officer struggles over whether to disclose some information about the institution that the potential donor would consider relevant in deciding whether or not to make a gift.
- The development officer tries not to push donors too hard or to distort the facts, but she realizes that year-end bonuses are awarded for raising money, not for being a nice person.

We set out to analyze the difficult situations that confront real-life development officers. Those situations gave us the context from which to tease out understandings that could help development officers in similar situations. In the process, we found that we had a wealth of information that potential donors ought to know. We dis-

## Preface and Acknowledgments

covered a broad range of morally relevant considerations that should be of interest to scholars of applied and professional ethics as well.

This volume is one result of our study. Our goal in writing this volume has been to construct a detailed understanding of the foundations and processes of higher education fund raising. Our assumptions are equally straightforward: The unique American tradition of relying on private voluntary activity to promote the common good has important political and social implications. The diversity of thriving causes reflects the plurality of the giving public. Fund raising plays an integral role in promoting and shaping philanthropic activity. We therefore support the role of fund raising in society and consider it an appropriate object for careful study. We also assume that an institution's public policies serve as a direct shield against charges of unethical conduct. A public act is not necessarily a right act, but many ethical problems disappear when all relevant parties have an opportunity to consent to practices and procedures that involve them.

This is not a cookbook for making fund raising ethical. It is a collection of ideas from a small group of people in higher education who have given serious thought to fund-raising practice. We hope that this volume will provide directions for further thought and discussion, particularly in the development offices of higher education institutions throughout the nation.

The acknowledgments that we would like to make would fill a volume. On behalf of the Ethics and Higher Education Fund Raising Task Force and the authors of the chapters in this volume, I would like to thank Dartmouth College for providing a home for the project and Dartmouth's director of foundation and corporate relations, Ken Spritz, for creating the proposal that funded the project. The project was sponsored by the Institute for the Study of Applied and Professional Ethics at Dartmouth College and the Council for the Advancement and Support of Education, and funding was generously provided by the Lilly Endowment and the W. K. Kellogg Foundation. The assistance of all of these organizations is gratefully acknowledged.

The authors also wish to acknowledge the significant contribution of the members of the Task Force who are not authors of chapters in this book: Charles Culver, Professor of Psychology, Lincoln University, Buenos Aires, Argentina, formerly Professor of Psychiatry, Dartmouth Medical School and Adjunct Professor of Philosophy, Dartmouth College; Eugene C. Dorsey, formerly Chairman, Independent Sector; Gary A. Evans, Vice President for Development and College Relations, Lafayette College; Robert L. Payton, former Director and current Professor of Philanthropic Studies, Indiana University Center on Philanthropy; Jerome Schneewind, Professor, Department of Philosophy, Johns Hopkins University; and Adam Yarmolinsky, Regents Professor of Public Policy in the University of Maryland System.

And a very special thank-you goes to Barbara Hillinger, assistant to the director at Dartmouth's Ethics Institute, for nurturing the project and the team from proposal to manuscript, and to Patricia Blandford for shepherding the project through its final year.

*The Ethics of Asking*

# Introduction:
# The Ethical Landscape

Eric B. Wentworth

In the early days, when American colleges and universities reached out to alumni and other donors for contributions, their approach was as simple as crossing a wooden bridge over a country creek. But time has swept us downstream. That country creek has swelled to a mighty river that swirls past industrial parks and power plants, high-rise condominiums and monuments. Institutions reach their donors across huge, heavily traveled spans of steel and concrete. Educational fund raising today is a complex, high-stakes, high-stress enterprise.

Dramatic changes in educational fund raising over the past quarter-century reflect even more dramatic changes throughout the nonprofit sector—and throughout the academic world itself. In today's environment, philanthropy often resembles investment. Larger donations resemble transactions. The trust that was at one time implicit between givers and recipients must now be earned, reinforced, and validated. Fund raising's ethical principles, whose existence was previously taken for granted, now require definition. Once defined, they must be adopted and applied. Nonprofit organizations and institutions have come under increased pressures to be efficient, effective, and accountable to donors, to the government agencies to whom they owe their tax-exempt status, and to the public at large.

Campus populations have exploded. Student enrollments today total 15 million, which is more than double the figure just a quarter-century ago. More than 3,500 American higher education institutions (including branch campuses) were functioning in 1990–91, compared with fewer than 2,200 in 1964–65. By one estimate, they had produced as many as 50 million college and university alumni. Campus production of new knowledge and technology that must be ingested, digested, and disseminated sets a pace inconceivable a generation ago. This explosion has produced enormous growth in campus facilities and equipment as well as in human and fiscal resources.

Annual college and university current-fund spending reached approximately $198 billion in 1993–94, compared with less than $90 billion a decade earlier. Even after adjusting for inflation, the increase is a hefty 53 percent. Federal spending on higher education, including research as well as student aid and other programs, totaled about $26.5 billion in 1991, nearly twice the $13.9 billion in 1965. In sum, higher education has become one of the nation's major industries. Societal and governmental expectations—as well as demands for accountability—have meanwhile burgeoned. Shouldering fiscal responsibilities undreamed of a generation ago, today's college and university decision makers must be astute planners, budgeters, and managers. As cost pressures relentlessly mount, they must pay ever closer attention to revenues, expenses, and bottom-line outcomes.

In these increasingly competitive, financially strained circumstances, educational and humanitarian values long nurtured by the academy are being jostled in institutional executive offices and boardrooms by the hard-edged values of the competitive marketplace. This clash of values has intensified as major institutions, accustomed to growth in the 1960s, 1970s, and early 1980s, have had to confront the painful necessity of "restructuring" in the face of threatened deficits. In some cases entire programs or departments have been axed.

The evolution to more corporatelike campus cultures has come to seem inevitable. Cost pressures have mounted inexorably. While colleges and universities relentlessly raise tuition year after year, they meet with growing resistance and resentment; occasionally there is even talk of government-mandated price controls. Federal financial aid for students has failed to keep pace with their needs. State governments, besieged with budget woes, have trimmed their own campus support.

In this environment, educational fund raising has gained greater strategic importance. At the same time, it has come under intense pressures. As institutional resource needs have soared, so has demand for more private support. Once icing on the cake, annual giving support now represents basic bread-and-butter revenue. Fund drives in recent years have become complex, high-stakes megacampaigns. Consider the following:

- Colleges and universities raised an estimated $10.7 billion in gift support in 1991–92, more than double their 1981–82 total of $4.86 billion.
- By the summer of 1994 eight universities—Stanford, Columbia, Cornell, Pennsylvania, Yale, Michigan, New York University, and Harvard—had undertaken fund-raising campaigns with goals of at least $1 billion dollars each. Harvard's goal, the highest, was $2.1 billion.
- In 1991–92 sixteen universities each raised more than $100 million: Harvard, Stanford, Cornell, Pennsylvania, Yale, Wisconsin-Madison, Columbia, California-Berkeley, Duke, Minnesota, Washington, Johns Hopkins, Indiana University, New York University, the University of Southern California, and Northwestern.

And as of June 30, 1992, fourteen universities had endowments with market values of more than $1 billion each: Harvard, the University of Texas System, Princeton, Yale, Stanford, Columbia, Washington University, MIT, the Texas A&M University System, Emory, Rice, the University of Chicago, Cornell, and Northwestern. Some thoughtful professionals began to voice concern that universities raising and managing such large sums risked being perceived as greedy.

Competition for gift dollars has also emerged as a troubling issue. Higher education fund raising has been the traditional province of private institutions. But in recent years public institutions, from flagship state universities to two-year community colleges, have become aggressive and often effective players. Of the sixteen institutions that raised more than $100 million in 1991–92, five were state institutions. Moreover, higher education is only one of the major competitors in today's philanthropic enterprise. According to Independent Sector's biennial report *Dimensions of the Independent Sector*, in 1990 there were an estimated 983,000 tax-exempt voluntary and philanthropic organizations in this country, up sharply from 793,000 in 1982. *Giving USA* reported in its authoritative annual survey of philanthropy that in 1991 Americans gave an estimated total of $124.77 billion, or 2.20 percent of the gross national product (GNP), to charitable organizations and causes. A decade earlier, in 1981, the total was $55.7 billion, or only 1.84 percent of GNP.

Colleges and universities compete for philanthropic dollars not only among themselves but with hospitals, museums, symphony orchestras, health groups, environmental groups, social service groups, churches and other religious groups, the United Way, and countless other organizations and institutions. Intensifying the competition for private support over the past decade has been the relative decline in government support. This decline reflects a fundamental shift on the part of citizens away from reliance on government to address and solve domestic societal problems and toward greater reliance on the private sector. It also reflects the impact of a relentless federal budget deficit, which has made it increasingly difficult for Washington to afford discretionary investments in education and other domestic priorities. Budget problems have squeezed state spending too. On the other side of the federal budget ledger, attempts to offset the deficit by increasing tax revenues have brought pressures to restrict the tax deductibility of private donations. State and local governments have sought to squeeze revenues from tax-exempt institutions. Moreover, federal and state governments alike have become more aggressive watchdogs, demanding greater accountability from the tax-exempt sector.

In the media, investigative reporters have found the nonprofit sector to be a new frontier for exposés involving such issues as executive compensation. For example, in 1993 the *Philadelphia Inquirer* published a seven-part series by two reporters, Gilbert M. Gaul and Neill A. Borowski, that later appeared as a book, *Free Ride: The Tax Exempt Economy*. Excessive executive compensation was one concern of a congressional subcommittee that planned legislation in the wake of the *Inquirer* series to make nonprofits more accountable. Colleges and universities have come under scrutiny for collecting excessive indirect costs from research grants or for earning tax-free income from activities the government claims are unrelated to their exempt purposes. The Justice Department has even attacked prominent higher education institutions on antitrust grounds, for alleged price fixing in tuition and financial aid practices.

Meanwhile, in the contemporary corporate-campus culture, educational fund raisers are confronting greater pressures and responsibilities than ever before. Fund raising has become too crucial and too sophisticated to be delegated to the folksy former English professor, the gregarious grad, or the burned-out football coach. Large uni-

versities today rely on scores of *institutional advancement officers*—
not only fund raisers but communicators, including those whose role
it is to "market" the institution to various constituencies. Sophisticated alumni programming builds support among graduates of all
ages.

Technology—computerized databases, word processors, tele-
phones and fax machines, rapid air travel—enables today's fund
raisers to identify, profile, contact, and solicit prospective donors
more systematically than ever before. As bottom-line corporate values and practices hold greater sway in nonprofit management, they
may be subtly altering the ethos as well as the practice of philanthropy. Institutions develop fund-raising plans and strategies. They
market themselves to their constituents. They segment and target
donors as well as solicit them. While fund raisers identify potential
donors as "prospects," some also speak of possible donors as "suspects." Just as salesmen "close" sales, so fund raisers "close" gifts. As
such changes occur, the consideration of donative intent sometimes
becomes obscured.

As fund-raising megacampaigns proliferate, dramatic dollar goals
have been attracting more attention than have the intended uses of
those dollars. And, to the extent that total dollars raised becomes
an overriding measure of fund-raising success, debates arise about
incentive compensation for those who do the fund raising. Fund
raisers in education and other philanthropic fields have generally
taken the high road. Despite the trends toward bottom-line corporate
values and preoccupation with meeting dollar goals, they have
moved toward professionalism rather than commercialism. Fund
raisers—consultants as well as those on institutional payrolls—see
themselves as members of an emerging, increasingly demanding
profession that requires training and experience in many technical
and managerial areas. They read books, magazines, and newsletters
about fund raising. They attend conferences and seminars. They pursue formal education toward a professional credential or advanced
degree in fund raising. They form affinity groups in such specialized
fields as proposal writing, prospect research, and planned giving.

In the name of institutional advancement an entire technocratic
hierarchy has sprung up. At the top are senior executives whose roles
in institutional fund-raising operations take them from fine points of
law and accounting through myriad supervisory tasks to the broad

sweep of strategic planning and institutional management. Their staffs include newcomers and mid-level development officers in an ever-expanding array of specialties and subspecialties: annual giving, direct mail, telemarketing, special events, major gifts, planned gifts, prospect research and tracking, gift recording, proposal writing, corporate and foundation relations, and campaign communications, among others.

The Council for Advancement and Support of Education (CASE), in particular, offers a broad array of training programs, publications, and other services for fund raisers, alumni-program executives, campus communicators, and others in what are now known as the institutional advancement professions. At the same time, CASE and other fund-raising organizations have been putting new stress on professional ethics and responsibilities. Professionalism has another side, however. For the new generation of fund raisers, climbing career ladders and attaining personal goals increasingly take equal (or greater) billing with loyalty to particular institutions or even particular causes (education, the performing arts, health care).

"Probably the last of a breed" was how a 1980 *Wall Street Journal* profile described James V. Moffatt, associate headmaster of the Hill School in Pennsylvania. The genial onetime Latin teacher had loyally served one school for four decades, raising money from its wealthy alumni for more than a quarter-century. Today's educational fund raisers no longer typically work for their own alma mater, nor do many stay at a single campus or in a single community for long. Amid great demand and rising pay for top fund raisers, those with ambition and ability move from campus to campus on their own initiative, building impressive track records as they go. They may move out of education into other fund-raising fields for a while, and then move back. Those with well-established reputations may become consultants. Moreover, as in the contemporary corporate world, they can no longer take job security for granted. Campus chief executives have also become a mobile crowd, and new presidents may ease senior fund raisers out to make room for their own team. For that reason too, fund raisers must be mindful of self-interest as well as institutional interest.

As higher education fund raisers become increasingly preoccupied with professionalism, they become more concerned with how others perceive them on their campuses, as reflected in the roles they are invited to play in the campus management hierarchy. Fund raisers seek respect and respectability both on campus and off. They seek a voice in top-level strategizing and goal-setting, at least in their own area of expertise, private support. On the strategy councils of many presidents, they are gradually becoming accepted as full members alongside provosts, deans, and chief financial officers. Yet on other campuses they remain excluded from these deliberations, charged instead with attaining fund-raising goals that they have little voice in shaping.

Professional status in higher education is usually achieved via the academic disciplines. While fund raising advances the interests of the academic community, its tenets have evolved largely from practical field experience. Only recently have fund raisers begun building an academic base through studies of nonprofit management and philanthropy. Another hallmark of professionalism is a code of standards for ethical behavior. Codes alone seldom solve real-world ethical dilemmas, but they offer general guidance on basic issues, raise awareness of the ethical dimensions of any decision or activity, and can reassure larger publics that professional concerns exist.

CASE and other organizations representing fund raisers in the nonprofit community—the National Society of Fund Raising Executives, the American Association of Fund-Raising Counsel, and the Association for Healthcare Philanthropy—have all adopted codes or statements covering ethical conduct that typically have been derived more from the lessons of practical experience than from philosophers, moralists, or ethicists. In November 1993 these same four organizations unveiled a ten-point "Donor Bill of Rights," which delineates what donors should be able to expect from organizations that solicit them for contributions. Among these are truthful information about the soliciting organization (and access to its financial statements), as well as assurance that it will use gifts for their intended purposes. In addition, CASE has established a national clearinghouse for ethics in educational fund raising, with a library of case studies for training development officers. CASE has also led a project to develop standards for fund-raising campaigns. Independent Sector, a national coalition of funding and fund-raising organizations, has also played a leading role in fostering ethical behavior in the nonprofit community, developing a statement entitled *Ethics and the Nation's Voluntary and Philanthropic Community: Obedience to the*

*Unenforceable* and encouraging organizations to undertake ethics audits.

The growing importance of fund raising, with its high stakes, competitiveness, and public visibility, makes it essential that practitioners not only be aware of ethical standards but follow them scrupulously in their work. Ethical behavior not only enhances fund raisers' professionalism but strengthens their credibility—and that of the institutions they represent. Practitioners must take into account both the reality of their behavior and how others perceive it. Public perceptions are especially important, since effective philanthropy depends upon public policy as well as private support: tax exemptions for entities serving desirable public ends and tax incentives for donors who support them. Philanthropy may be well rooted in the American ethos, but federal tax incentives are statutory, not constitutional, and vulnerable to curtailment by policy makers eager to augment tax revenues. Moreover, in the arena of public perceptions, higher education has come increasingly under attack on certain fronts for ethical laxity. Stories of improprieties in intercollegiate athletics, plagiarism and research fraud in the professoriate, diversion or even squandering of taxpayer funds, and extravagant presidential compensation packages have aroused concerns about a perceived lack of responsibility and accountability in today's environment of general fiscal restraint.

Colleges and universities can ill afford scandals arising from their fund-raising practices, whether real or perceived. The risks of subjection to stricter government controls or losing government tax incentives for private support, to say nothing of losing any of that private support itself, are very real. Fostering ethical behavior in fund raising, as in other higher education pursuits, is imperative. Fund-raising ethics should be a concern both for the professionals and for the numerous others who play important roles in the fund-raising enterprise: presidents, deans, and faculty members, for example, as well as trustees and other volunteers. Ethical standards for individuals representing a college or university fall within the larger framework of the institution's own ethics and integrity. The ethics of fund raising also encompasses the behavior of donors—alumni, parents, other individuals, corporations, and foundations—who bring their own values and expectations to the ethical equation.

As fund raising becomes more sophisticated and specialized, specific ethical concerns enter sharper focus. One important set of concerns involves the behavior of individual fund-raising professionals as institutional employees. A fund raiser may, for example, encounter conflicting loyalties when he or she moves from one institution to another. What are the ground rules for taking donors, as well as information about donors, from the old position to the new one, especially when both positions are in the same community? Cannot fund raisers at least take their Rolodexes with them? To what extent is information about donors gained at one institution proprietary—in an ethical as well as a legal sense? Fund raisers can hardly be expected to erase from memory all the facts they learned about donors in a prior position. Similarly, should institutions hire fund raisers not only for their proficiencies but for the donors and donor contacts they might bring with them?

Ethical questions may arise in distinguishing appropriate from inappropriate incentives for job performance. Professionals generally reject commissions or bonuses tied to dollars raised. Salary increases based on performance are usually acceptable unless performance is itself measured in terms of dollars raised. The level of fund raisers' compensation, compared with what faculty and other staff members earn, can have ethical ramifications. Another set of ethical concerns involves fund raisers' freedom to undertake private consulting for other institutions. At what point do conflicts of interest become serious? What if the fund raiser serves as a consultant for an institution that is a competitor of his or her primary employer?

Fund raisers, like other professionals, must always try to balance personal (and family) interests with loyalties and responsibilities to the institution. But should they ever compromise personal standards or beliefs in order to accommodate donors or supervisors? Should they tolerate others' conflicts of interest or call attention to them? When their views on controversial issues are in conflict with the institution's position or with the views of major donors, should they keep them to themselves or express them?

Numerous ethical issues surround the accepting of gifts, because of the donor's character, reputation, or underlying motive; because of the character or source of the gift assets; or because of the donor's explicit or implicit conditions or expectations that accompany the gift. Fund raisers must be sensitive to the donor's mental capacity and judgment, especially if he or she is aged or ill, and must take into account the interests, rights, and welfare of the donor and the donor's family and dependents. Ethical conflicts may erupt if a gift that has been accepted turns out to be tainted by revelations about the donor or the donated assets; if the donor demands quid pro quos that were not mentioned when the gift was made; or if the donor later suffers financial losses or illness that turn an affordable gift into an extreme sacrifice.

As *prospect research*, the gathering and maintaining of information about donors, gains importance in sophisticated and systematic fund raising, it raises a growing list of ethical questions, particularly concerning privacy. Questions may involve the methods of conducting research and the appropriateness of various information sources; the nature of information developed through research, including personal data that perhaps should be off-limits; the protection, management, and use of prospect and donor data; and the honoring of a donor's request for anonymity under all circumstances. The American Prospect Research Association, a relatively new professional group, has developed a code of ethics covering these issues.

Fund raisers may run into sensitive ethical issues in cultivating, soliciting, and recognizing donors. They must draw and observe lines between professional and personal relationships with donors with regard to accepting personal favors, responding to donors' emotional needs, and providing professional advice or services. An elderly widow may think that she has a new personal friend, but the fund raiser, however congenial, must maintain professional detachment. If fund raisers let themselves become too friendly with donors, the donors may try to enlist them as financial advisers, name them as executors of their estates, present them with gifts, or leave them bequests—all of which would cause conflicts of interest. In particular, fund raisers must maintain professional comportment in cultivating or soliciting prospects of the opposite sex.

Fund raisers must balance the needs and best interests of the donor and the donor's relatives with the institution's own needs and best interests. They must refrain from competing for donors' allegiances with fund raisers for other organizations or causes through inappropriate means. Also, they must be careful not to deviate from their institution's own standard donor recognition policies to offer major donors special recognition for their gifts, such as board membership or benefactor status, naming opportunities, academic honors, or special privileges.

Donor recognition is an integral part of fund raising. Membership in gift clubs, opportunities to name a building or endowed professorship or scholarship fund, and various forms of VIP treatment are common ways to recognize generous donors. To qualify, donors normally must give gifts that meet minimum thresholds or other criteria. Occasionally a donor will ask for special treatment that would clash with institutional policy or practice. Granting such treatment could be unfair to other donors or might even threaten the institution's integrity (e.g., presenting a major benefactor with an honorary degree). While there are times when exceptions may be justified, such instances test the ethical wisdom of institutional leaders.

Enthusiasm can sometimes conflict with candor when the institution provides information to donors, funders, prospects, constituents, or the general public about its needs for certain gifts, its capacity to manage and use gifts effectively, and its suitability to receive gifts and serve as their fiduciary. Potential donors have a right to accurate information about the needs their gifts would address and about the institution's fiscal health, overall performance, future course, and ability to put the gifts to effective use. Donors asked to support a particular program or project have a right to know whether their gifts will provide added support for that purpose or simply replace existing support that will then be diverted to other purposes. Equally important are the institution's candor about its actual management and use of gifts, its use of any portion of gifts or gift earnings for discretionary accounts or to cover paying fundraising costs, and its honoring of donor restrictions or conditions regarding the use of gifts.

Planned giving is a relatively new and rapidly growing phenomenon in educational fund raising. Stimulated by the 1969 federal tax law, it involves a variety of arrangements whereby donors place assets in trusts or other instruments that provide distinct benefits for the donors and, in due course, for the institutions. While donors may have bona fide charitable intentions, planned giving engages them in contractual relations with institutions in a more formal and complicated way than more traditional forms of giving do. It may also place the institution's planned giving officer in the position of being concerned with both the donor's financial interests and the institution's fund-raising interests. This can create ethical conflicts for fund raisers, especially when they are being pressured to "close" gifts to meet the goals and deadlines of a major fund-raising campaign.

The reputation of planned giving was threatened when a 1986 tax law led some entrepreneurs, commercial brokers, financial planners, and others to promote charitable trusts to clients as tax shelter investments or retirement plans. They would then "shop" the trusts as gifts to institutions, asking for a "finder's fee" or other remuneration from the intended recipient. Alarmed about a possible backlash, a group of planned giving officers set about developing what in 1991 were published as *Model Standards of Practice for the Charitable Gift Planner*, which stress, among other things, the "primacy of philanthropic motivation" and assert that "finder's fees" or commission-based compensations are "never appropriate."

Fund-raising campaigns with high dollar goals raise the stakes and stresses for everyone concerned with attaining these goals. Particularly when competition is a major factor, these campaigns have intensified concerns about such ethical issues as truth-telling, candor, fairness, and trust. Ethical conflicts may arise in determining the campaign's size, scope, goals, and duration; in packaging and marketing the campaign; in creating and maintaining campaign momentum; in informing faculty and students about the campaign's potential benefits to them; in setting and abiding by guidelines for counting gifts, including planned gifts, especially if the guidelines differ from industry standards or norms; in making exceptions to campaign guidelines in special circumstances; and in responding to a threatened failure to meet campaign goals. One fundamental question is whether the size and purposes of a major campaign truly serve the institution's long-term best interests. Decision makers may be influenced by competitive factors (e.g., the desire to set a higher goal than those of rival institutions) or an unrealistic zeal for prestige. Have they carefully determined that the campaign's purposes address the institution's highest-priority needs?

Institutions differ on what to count toward the goal. A campaign that depends too heavily on bequests and planned gifts may disappoint faculty and students, since assets the gifts represent may not be received for many years. How bequests and planned gifts are counted is another question. One institution may count a bequest if the donor is at least sixty-eight years old; for another, the magic number may be seventy; a third may count *all* bequests, regardless of the donors' ages. Should such gifts be counted at face value or discounted to allow for inflation?

Institutions may likewise differ over whether, and how, to count other gifts, such as life insurance. Institutions differ sharply on whether to count government grants toward campaign goals, especially grants to be matched with private gifts. Today's megacampaign, which seeks funds for multiple purposes within an overall dollar goal, tends to focus attention on the total dollars raised rather than on the special purposes for which they are being raised. The institution may define its campaign purposes broadly enough that most, if not all, of the gifts received during the campaign can be counted toward the overall goal, even those that do not address campaign purposes.

The Campaign Reporting Advisory Group, which has worked since 1990 under CASE's aegis, has developed standards for structuring and managing campaigns and for counting campaign gifts. The group has stressed that success in fulfilling a campaign's announced purposes is far more important than achieving its dollar goal. The group has called for campaign strategists to clearly spell out gift-counting criteria at the campaign outset and not change the rules once the campaign is underway. As these standards are adopted and followed by individual institutions, they, should go far toward assuring that those who undertake campaigns design them responsibly and play by the rules in counting results. Given the public attention that major campaigns have been receiving, the new standards should strengthen the credibility of all educational fund raising.

Another cluster of ethical issues arises when institutions seek grants from corporations and foundations. In these instances too the needs and stakes, as well as the intensity of competition, have grown in recent years. Ethical concerns may arise in connection with how the institution represents its capabilities and resources to fulfill the purposes of the requested grant; its effective management and proper use of the funds once granted; and its reports to the funder regarding the institution's success in fulfilling the purposes of the grant. The potential for hyperbole in each of these areas exists and must be resisted.

Questions may occasionally arise about the institution's integrity in approaching a particular funding source. If an institution divests itself of a corporation's stock over a matter of principle, should it apply to that corporation or its foundation for a grant? Would the institution not be sacrificing principle for expediency and breaking faith with constituents who sought the divestiture in the first place?

While the quest for government funds falls outside the scope of this book, it is important to recognize that ethics issues lurk in that area as well. Aside from whether to count government funds toward a campaign goal, questions may arise about how an institution seeks those government funds in the first place. Is it ethical to lobby for funds in a congressional appropriation that have been earmarked for a campus project—an increasingly frequent practice in recent years—when this may compromise the traditional peer review process, whereby grant recipients are supposedly selected on the basis of merit? There are arguments on both sides.

The academic pork barrel has been growing relentlessly. According to the June 16, 1993, issue of the *Chronicle of Higher Education,* Congress earmarked a record $763 million for projects involving particular colleges and universities in the 1993 fiscal year—up nearly 12 percent from the prior year. Is it ethical to hire a lobbyist to obtain earmarked funds? For that matter, is it ethical to "cultivate" key lawmakers with gifts, honorary degrees, special treatment for family members in admissions decisions, or other special favors? After all, some would argue, business lobbyists fly these lawmakers to golf resorts. Others vehemently insist that educational institutions must hold themselves to the highest standards.

This leads us to still another consideration: Are holier-than-thou institutional leaders and fund raisers unethical if they put their own needs for purity above the best interests of the institution they serve? Are there times when they should rise above principle if doing so were best for the institution? The ethics of being too ethical—that raises a different set of issues!

Few of these questions have obvious right answers or lend themselves to textbook solutions when they are encountered in the rough-and-tumble of the real world. Likewise, codes of ethics, while often important starting points, seldom suffice to resolve daily dilemmas. To address the ethical issues raised here and throughout this volume, institutional leaders should develop and articulate clear policies that draw upon their institution's fundamental values—values such as respect for truth and fairness. Such policies can at least mark the channels of ethical behavior for fund raisers and donors alike and thus provide frames of reference in which decision makers can ask the right questions, weigh all the relevant factors, and work their way toward responsible judgments.

# Social and Moral Foundations

# Law and Regulation
## Bruce R. Hopkins and Deni Elliott

Through seeking and accepting donations, educational institutions create a trust relationship with donors, a legal as well as a moral relationship. But while the moral aspect of that trust relationship may be obvious, the legality of compelling promises on either the donor's or the institution's part was a point of contention in the nation's early years.

## The Historical Perspective

The restrictions that donors put on their gifts are delicately negotiated by development offices and then carefully monitored for compliance. This has not always been the case. In fact the idea that a gift created, by its restrictions, an obligation on the part of the institution receiving the funds was a point of debate in the U.S. courts for two hundred years.[1] The ultimate outcome is that charities are not allowed to divert gifts away from their donors' intentions.

Nor was it clear at first that the promise of a gift created legal obligations on the prospective donor. Such promises were not considered binding under English common law, which did not consider them to be "contracts." According to one scholar of English law, "A promise to contribute money to charitable purposes is a good example of the class of promises which, though they may be laudable and morally binding, are not contracts."[2] But through case law that emerged in the nineteenth and twentieth centuries, the states ultimately rejected that common-law doctrine.[3] It was decided that donors could be held liable for their promises of donations, particularly when educational institutions acted on those promises by beginning to build or to create programs that relied on the donors' pledges.

In addition to compelling donors and institutions to keep promises to one another, the United States has used its tax laws to determine what legally counts as a gift. The tax-law exemption for charitable contributions was the government's way of encouraging individual voluntary contributions to the common good. But the government has determined that unless *donative intent*, which it defines as disinterested and dispassionate giving, is present, and unless the donor receives nothing of value in return, the transaction is, at least in part, something other than a gift.

Only recently have state and federal governments begun to consider what constitutes appropriate *requests* of gifts. Fund-raising regulation and legislation has developed since the mid-twentieth century, mostly in response to pseudo-charities and coercive solicitation procedures that exploited an unsuspecting public. When one considers the vast amount of wealth that U.S. educational institutions have amassed through fund raising (which Eric Wentworth describes in the introduction to this volume), it is surprising how little litigation literature involves these institutions.

The federal and state governments first addressed the matter of fund raising in the mid-1950s. North Carolina was the first state to enact a law regulating fund raising. Other states soon followed, generating a series of laws that came to be known as *charitable solicitation acts*. New York was the second state to pass one of these laws, and the New York law became the prototype for the many that were to follow.

The New York law and its progeny involved a statutory scheme based upon registration and reporting. Charitable organizations were required to register in advance of solicitation and report annually;[4] bond requirements came later. Subsequently, forms of regulation involving professional fund raisers and solicitors were developed. Exceptions evolved, often including religious organizations and sometimes educational institutions as well. These first laws were basically licensing statutes. They gave the states essential information about the fund raising to be conducted so that they would have a basis for investigation and review should abuse be suspected.

With the passage of time, some states responded to abuses by affirmatively regulating charitable solicitations and by developing forms of regulation that applied to professional fund raisers and solicitors. Some of the states included provisions regulating disclosure and the requirement that fund raisers act as fiduciaries, and some even defined what counted as (illegal) deception in fund raising. Structurally, the typical statute about charitable solicitation originally had nothing to do with the relationship between the donor and the institution or between the donor and the fund-raising professional. Its requirements were based on the submission of written information (registration statements, reports, and the like) by charitable organizations and their fund-raising advisers, bond requirements, and enforcement authority granted to the attorneys general, secretaries of state, or other governmental officials charged with administering and enforcing the law. Later, however, new laws were written to more affirmatively regulate what some people had considered "ideal" fund-raising behavior. These laws went beyond registration requirements, filing deadlines, and accounting principles and entered the realm of telling fund raisers how they could and could not conduct solicitation.

## Federal Law Regulation

Fund-raising regulation at the federal level is universal, with nearly all federal fund-raising regulation administered by the Internal Revenue Service (IRS).[5] It is interesting to note that in 1988, a year in which the IRS took a directive from the U.S. House of Representatives to put charitable organizations under greater obligation for determining how much of an exchange could be counted as a tax-exempt gift, the U.S. Supreme Court limited the states' ability to regulate fund-raising practice. And while the states have been slow to change the language in their charitable solicitation acts to conform to the Supreme Court ruling, the federal government moved in 1993 to enact into law the IRS directive of 1988.

In general, the IRS regulates the practice of fund raising for charitable purposes in the following ways:

- It requires a charitable organization to summarize its fund-raising program at the time it applies for tax-exempt status.[6]
- It requires an organization to report the receipts of its fund-raising activities, as well as its fund-raising expenses, annually.[7]

- It applies the rules concerning private inurement in such a fashion as to discourage fund-raising compensation arrangements that are based on percentages or otherwise involve commissions.[8]
- It interprets and enforces the rules involving deductible charitable contributions.[9]
- It engages in a program of education and examination of charitable organizations that engage in fund raising in order to encourage them to disclose the portions of payments that are not considered "charitable gifts."[10]

These means of regulation are generally quite technical, with the last point constituting the one exception. The IRS has been concerned since 1967 that taxpayers were taking greater charitable deductions than were warranted and that charitable organizations were doing little to inform their donors that only part of their donation might be tax-deductible. In that year the IRS issued guidelines directing charities to advise donors of circumstances in which their "gifts" were not deductible at all (the donor received something from the charity whose value approximated that of the payment) or were only partially deductible (the donor received something in return for the gift whose value was less than that of the gift).[11]

In 1988 a congressional committee expressed dismay over the continuation of, if not an increase in, these practices and demanded that the IRS act to resolve the problem. The IRS commissioner sent all charitable organizations a clarification of what counted as tax-deductible, along with a note stating that the IRS would be working to figure out "the extent to which taxpayers are furnished accurate and sufficient information concerning the deductibility of their contributions."[12]

In 1993 the Omnibus Budget Reconciliation Act became law. While it made the taxpayer responsible for claims of charitable contribution, the law also created affirmative obligations for charitable organizations. Specifically, "no income tax charitable deduction will be allowed for a contribution of $250 or more unless the taxpayer has a written receipt . . . from the donee organization for the contribution." In addition, the charitable organization had to make clear what part of the gift could be counted as tax-deductible. If the charitable organization gave the donor nothing of value, that information was to be included on the donor's receipt; a good-faith value of any goods or service provided had to be described and deducted from the donated amount.[13]

The IRS is intent on ferreting out instances of abusive fund raising.[14] Under this the IRS includes the following:

- "[M]isleading statements in solicitations literature that imply deductibility of contributions, where none probably exists."
- "[C]ontracts with professional for-profit fund raisers, who themselves use questionable fund raising methods to solicit funds from the general public."
- "[S]ituations where other expenses, such as administrative and fundraising costs [,] constitute an unusually high portion of the solicited funds or noncash contributions."
- "[F]und raising activities that result in other tax consequences, i.e., generating taxable income, resulting in additional filing requirements, etc."

The federal government thus cast a bright light on the hazy area of how educational institutions thank their strongest supporters. When the thank-you involves "admissions or other privileges or benefits . . . received in connections with payments by patrons of fund-raising affairs . . . the presumption is that the payments are not gifts."[15]

For example, the IRS ruled that contributions to athletic scholarship programs are not completely deductible as charitable gifts if the donors are provided with special opportunities to purchase tickets or to get preferred seating.[16] Those contributions are deductible only at a rate of 80 percent. More recently, the IRS held that payments by corporate sponsors of college and university bowl games are not charitable gifts to the bowl game associations but must be treated by the association as forms of unrelated business income because the corporate sponsors received a valuable package of advertising services.[17] This led to the issuance of more general guidelines for donor recognition in order to help educational institutions and other charities distinguish between instances of "mere recognition" and instances in which payers are provided a substantial return benefit.[18]

These federal expectations for fund raisers created a new complexity for educational institutions at which development activities are rewarded by special recognition or dinners or receptions are offered as true expressions of appreciation, something no one could gain through intended purchase. With the 1993 law, if donors have a reasonable expectation of receiving some benefit, the cost of the benefit must be determined and deducted by the charitable organization. It may be difficult for educational institutions to inform out-of-town alumni that they must subtract the cost of an event from their gift when there this little or no chance that they could take advantage of the benefit. In response to some of these complexities, some development offices give donors an opportunity to formally decline all benefits, thus making their donations 100 percent deductible.

Despite the tightening of regulations through the tax laws, federal decisions also limit state regulation. For example, the U.S. Supreme Court decided in 1980 that states could not use the level of a charitable organization's fund-raising costs as a basis for determining whether a charity might lawfully solicit funds in a jurisdiction.[19] Four years later, in 1984, the Court held that the principles of free speech apply despite the presumption that costs in excess of a specific ceiling are "excessive."[20] In 1988 the Court held that these free-speech principles applied when the limitation was not on a charity's fund-raising costs but on the amount or extent of fees paid by a charitable organization to professional fund raisers or solicitors.[21] Subsequent litigation suggests that the courts are consistently reinforcing the legal principles so articulately promulgated by the Supreme Court during the 1980s.[22]

Despite these rulings, as of late 1993 many states still had such requirements on the books. The laws in Arkansas, Connecticut, Illinois, Massachusetts, Ohio, Tennessee, and Utah all contained questionable language. For example, the provisions of the Illinois law probably requires that professional fund raisers or solicitors must disclose to those being solicited the percentage of their compensation in relation to gifts received.[23] And one Arkansas law makes the failure of a person soliciting funds to "truthfully" recite, upon request, the percentage of funds raised to be paid to the solicitor an "unlawful practice."[24]

## State Law

The states continue to provide the lion's share of fund-raising regulations. The application of constitutional law to charitable solicitation acts motivated state regulators to strengthen state laws to regulate the process by which charitable organizations solicit funds. The registration and annual reports became more extensive. Other states tried, with limited success, to force charities and solicitors into various forms of disclosure at the time of solicitation; some states even dictated the contents of telephone solicitors' scripts.

By the end of 1993 all but four states—Delaware, Idaho, Montana, and Wyoming—had some form of statutory structure for regulating the fund-raising process.[25] Thirty-two of these states, as well as the District of Columbia, formal charitable solicitation acts.

The various state charitable solicitation acts generally contain the following features:

- Procedures by which charitable organizations register or otherwise secures a permit to raise funds for charitable purposes in the state.
- Requirements for reporting information (usually annually) about organizations' fund-raising programs.
- A list of organizations that are exempted from some or all of the statutory requirements.
- A process by which professional fund raisers, professional solicitors, and/or commercial co-venturers register with and report to the state.
- Record-keeping requirements for charitable organizations, professional fund raisers, professional solicitors, and/or commercial co-venturers.
- Rules concerning the contents of contracts between charitable organizations and professional fund raisers, professional solicitors, and/or commercial co-venturers.
- A list of so-called prohibited acts.
- A provision for reciprocal agreements between the states concerning coordinated regulation.
- A summary of the powers of the governmental official having regulatory authority (usually the attorney general or secretary of state).
- A statement of the various sanctions that can be imposed for failure to comply with the law (e.g., injunctions, fines, and imprisonment).[26]

As noted, many of the states exempt one or more categories of charitable organizations from the ambit of their charitable solicitation statute. The basic rationale for these exemptions is that the exempted organizations are not part of the problem that gives rise to the objective the state is endeavoring to achieve through this type of regulation, namely, the protection of its citizens from fund-raising fraud and other abuse.

Twelve states, including the District of Columbia, exempt certain types of educational institutions, including colleges and universities, from their charitable solicitation acts.[27] This exemption usually applies only to accredited educational institutions. The more common practice is to exempt educational institutions from only the registration or licensing, and reporting, requirements. Nineteen states have adopted this approach,[28] which is typified by the provision of the law in North Carolina that exempts from that state's charitable solicitation act's licensing requirement "any educational institution, the curriculum of which in whole or part, is registered, approved or accredited by the Southern Association of Colleges and Schools or an equivalent regional accrediting body."[29]

Nine states, either as an alternative to or in addition to the foregoing approach, exempt from the registration and reporting requirements educational institutions that confine their solicitations to their "constituency."[30] Thus, for example, the law in Virginia provides an exemption from registration for an "educational institution confining its solicitation of contributions to its student body, alumni, faculty, and trustees, and their families."[31] Three states exempt solicitations by educational institutions of their constituency from the entirety of their charitable solicitation laws.[32]

Many colleges, universities, and other educational institutions undertake some or all of their fund raising by means of related "foundations." Thirteen states expressly provide exemption, in tandem with whatever exemption their laws extend to educational institutions, to these supporting foundations.[33] Five states exempt alumni associations from the registration requirements,[34] and one state, Mississippi, exempts them altogether, as long as the fund raising is only among the membership.

The rationale for exempting educational institutions from coverage under these laws is that they do not solicit the general public, they have not abused the fund-raising process, they already adequately report to state agencies, and their inclusion under the charitable solicitation act would impose an unnecessary burden on the regulatory process.[35]

## Law and Regulation

Some states provide other affirmative obligations for fund raisers. Most of the states' charitable solicitation acts contain a list of one or more acts in which a charitable organization (and perhaps a professional fund raiser or solicitor) may not lawfully engage. These may include some or all of the following:

- A person may not, for the purpose of soliciting contributions, use the name of another person (except that of an officer, director, or trustee of the charitable organization by or for which contributions are solicited) without that person's consent.
- A person may not, for the purpose of soliciting contributions, use a name, symbol, or statement so closely related or similar to that used by another charitable organization or governmental agency that it would tend to confuse or mislead the public.
- A person may not use or exploit the fact of registration with the state in a way that would lead the public to believe that the registration in any manner constitutes an endorsement or approval by the state.
- A person may not by any manner, means, practice, or device represent to anyone or mislead anyone to believe that the organization on behalf of which the solicitation is being conducted is a charitable organization or that the proceeds of the solicitation will be used for charitable purposes when that is not the case.
- A person may not represent that the solicitation for charitable gifts is for or on behalf of a charitable organization or otherwise induce contributions from the public without proper authorization from the charitable organization.

The Illinois law states that all solicitations must "fully and accurately" identify the purposes of the charitable organization to prospective donors. The use of more than 50 percent of funds for "public education" must be disclosed under this law. And every contract with a professional fund raiser must be approved by the charitable organization's governing board.[36] In New Hampshire it is a "prohibited act" to represent that a charity will receive a fixed or estimated percentage of the gross revenue from a solicitation in an amount greater than that identified to the donor.[37] In Virginia it is a "prohibited act" for an individual to solicit charitable contributions if the individual has been convicted of a crime involving the obtaining of money or property by false pretenses unless the public is informed of the conviction in advance of the solicitation.[38]

In Connecticut it is a prohibited act for a charitable organization (or, in some instances, a person acting on its behalf) to misrepresent the purpose of a solicitation; to misrepresent the purpose or nature of a charitable organization; to engage in a financial transaction that is not related to the accomplishment of the charitable organization's exempt purpose;[39] to jeopardize or interfere with the ability of a charitable organization to accomplish its charitable purpose; or to expend an "unreasonable amount of money" for fund raising or management.[40]

Some states—New Hampshire, for example[41]—make violation of a separate law concerning "unfair or deceptive acts or practices" a violation of the charitable solicitation act as well. This list of prohibited acts reads like an ideal standard to which all fund raisers should aspire, in that some of those precepts are difficult to enforce as law.

Many of the state charitable solicitation acts require that the relationship between a charitable organization and a professional fund raiser or solicitor be evidenced in a written agreement. This agreement must be filed with the state soon after it is executed. These types of requirements are clearly law and are not particularly unusual. However, a few states have enacted requirements that dictate to the charitable organization the contents of the contract. In Connecticut, for example, a contract between a charitable organization and a fund-raising counsel must contain sufficient information "as will enable the department [of Consumer Protection] to identify the services the fund raising counsel is to provide and the manner of his compensation." Another provision of the same law mandates that the agreement "clearly state the respective obligations of the parties."[42] The law in Maryland requires a contract between a charitable organization and a fund-raising counsel to contain provisions addressing the services to be provided, the number of persons to be involved in providing the services, the time period over which the services are to be provided, and the method and formula for compensation for the services.[43]

In Massachusetts every contract between a professional solicitor or a commercial co-venturer and a charitable organization must include a statement of the charitable purposes to be described in the solicitation, as well as a statement of the "guaranteed minimum percentage of the gross receipts from fund raising which will be utilized exclusively for the charitable purposes described in the solicitation."[44] This type of law seems predicated on the assumption that charitable organizations are not quite capable of developing their own contracts and tend to do so impetuously.

Other states seek to govern the nature of the relationship between charitable organization and donor. Illinois, like a half-dozen other states, imposes on the individual who raises funds for a charitable organization the responsibility to deal with contributions in an "appropriate fiduciary manner."[45] Thus, such individuals owe an explicit legal fiduciary duty to the public, and they are subject to a surcharge for any funds not accounted for or wasted. The position of fiduciary should not be assumed lightly. It is one thing to impose some responsibility on those who temporarily hold "charitable" dollars as these moneys make their way to charitable purposes; to cause them to be "fiduciaries" is to impose a much heavier burden of duty.

## The Relevance of Law to Fund-raising Ethics

To "obey the law" is a prima facie moral duty, but the phrase expresses a minimum standard for behavior. It is expected that fund raisers in educational institutions will comply with the law, but this book is written with the assumption that fund raisers have set their sights higher than the legal expectations. In tightening up the tax regulations, for example, the federal government is expressing the expectation that charitable organizations will provide their donors with the kind of information they need in order to be in compliance with tax-reporting requirements. With or without the law, it would be inconsistent for educational institutions to seek to hide such information from their donors. The special social role of educational institutions carries with it a basic assumption of honesty. The trust relationship between institutions and donors upon which successful development depends requires that development officers protect their donors' interests as though they were the institution's own. They often are.

# 2

# The Moral Context
# of Fund Raising
## Deni Elliott and Bernard Gert

The moral context of fund raising provides the foundation for establishing what fund raisers ought to do and what they ought not do.[1] That foundation is based on the universal agreement that it is wrong to cause other people to suffer harms, to deceive, or to break a promise unless one has sufficient reason. In addition, fund raisers have special responsibilities based on the nature of their job and on the nature of the institution that employs them. The moral foundation provides criteria for determining which actions are morally prohibited, which are morally required, which are morally permitted, and which are morally ideal for fund raisers in institutions of higher education.[2]

It is as important to be clear about the moral context of fund raising as it is to be clear about the social and legal contexts. Although moral and legal dictates often coincide, there are two relevant differences between them. The first is a difference in accountability. No matter how ill-conceived one might judge a federal or state law relating to the solicitation, acceptance, or recording of donations, the fear of accountability in terms of fines or other penalties keeps all but the most recalcitrant institution or fund raiser in line.

Accountability for moral infractions is of a different and more diffuse sort. The institution that treats prospects or donors in ways that are immoral but not illegal will suffer a loss of trust, credibility, and ultimately donations. But unless the immoral act is also illegal, no one will go to jail. The law proscribes a very narrow scope of activities that are almost always morally as well as legally prohibited. That is why it is almost always morally required that people obey the law. But the scope of moral prohibitions is far larger than the scope of law. It is generally wrong to act deceptively, but the law holds people accountable for only certain acts of deception, for example, deceiving the IRS.

Another important difference between law and ethics is the way they define compliance. Laws are straightforward. Institutions, fund raisers, and donors may sometimes search for loopholes in the law, but the laws are written, and precedents are established, in an attempt to make the minimal legal requirements increasingly more clear. The law holds in a very exacting way regardless of context.

Moral imperatives, while clear on the surface—"Don't cheat," "Don't deceive," "Keep your promises"—require interpretation and application for individual situations. Behavior that is morally permitted or even encouraged in a poker game, for example, is morally prohibited in most occupational relationships, including the relationship that exists between fund raisers and potential or actual donors. Even though the moral rules prohibiting deception, cheating, and breaking a promise are universal, whether a specific act counts as deception, cheating, or breaking a promise is determined by context. Moral problems in fund raising cannot be treated as isolated, as though their solutions will not have implications for all other moral problems. The moral imperatives of fund raising exist within a system of morality that extends to all other questions of applied and professional ethics.

Morality is a public system that applies to all moral agents. By *moral agents* we mean persons who are held morally responsible for their actions. Such persons must know at least some of the rules that everyone is morally prohibited from violating and be able to control their actions with respect to those rules; this includes almost all adults of near normal intelligence and above, as well as most children above the age of ten and even many below that age. They all know certain general facts, for example, that all people have only limited knowledge; that they do not want to suffer any harm or evil, namely, death, pain, disability, or loss of freedom or pleasure, unless they believe that someone, either they themselves or someone else, will avoid at least a comparable harm or gain some comparable benefits, namely, abilities, freedom, or pleasure. Further, such persons themselves want to avoid acting in a way that will cause them to suffer any harm unless they have such beliefs about someone benefiting. Acting in such a way is to act irrationally. Although all of us probably act irrationally at one time or another, for example, when we get very angry, most people would like this never to be the case.

All the persons to whom a public system applies—those whose behavior is to be guided and judged by it—understand it; that is, they know what behavior the system prohibits, requires, and encourages. And it is not irrational for any of them to accept being guided or judged by it. The clearest example of a public system is a game. The rules of the game are part of a system that is understood by all of the players, they all know what kinds of behavior are prohibited, required, and encouraged by the rules of the game, and it is not irrational for players to use the rules to guide their own behavior and to judge the behavior of other players by those rules. Morality is a public system that applies to all moral agents; people are subject to morality simply by virtue of being rational persons with sufficient knowledge to be held responsible for their actions. None of this is surprising. The high degree of consensus as to what counts as a moral question or an ethical violation goes unnoticed because we make so many moral judgments based on commonly understood and shared rules.

Is it morally acceptable for fund raisers to steer prospects to nonprofits rather than to the educational institution that employs them? Should fund raisers use sex or power to obtain gifts? Should educational institutions seek gifts under false pretenses? The answers to these questions are obvious, and obviously not what we are addressing in this book. There is not always a unique correct solution to every moral problem, but it does not follow that all solutions are morally acceptable. It may be that people cannot agree on a single correct solution but will agree that a number of solutions would be simply immoral.

Although most people use the same moral system when they think seriously about making a moral judgment or deciding how to act when confronting a moral problem, they probably are not conscious of doing so. Grammar provides a useful analogy. Most speakers cannot explicitly describe the grammatical system; they all know it in the sense that they use it when speaking themselves and in interpreting the speech of others. Although there are some variations in the grammatical system, no one should accept a description of the grammatical system that rules out speaking in a way that they regard as

## The Moral Context of Fund Raising

acceptable or permits speaking in a way that they regard as unacceptable to those who are competent speakers of the language.

Similarly, a moral system that promotes acting in a way that conflicts with one's considered moral judgments should not be accepted. However, recognition of the systematic character of morality may demonstrate some inconsistencies in one's moral judgments in much the same way that careful grammatical analysis can uncover a speaker's error in sentence construction. Making the moral system explicit, including making clear which facts are morally relevant and which are not, may reveal that some moral judgments are inconsistent with the vast majority of other moral judgments. Thus, one may come to see that what one accepted as a correct moral judgment is mistaken.

In this book we point out the morally relevant facts and use a systematic approach to analyze specific cases and actions. For example, how gifts and donors are recognized by educational institutions is a morally relevant fact in determining the ethics of gift exchange. In chapter 7 Holly Smith and Marilyn Dunn provide criteria for deciding what kind of recognition is morally permitted and what makes some types of recognition morally prohibited.

Most of the moral judgments fund raisers make will be noncontroversial. Their understanding of what it means to act in morally permitted ways, combined with their special role-related responsibilities, provides the scope for determining they ought and ought not to do. Some of what appears as guidelines for ethical fund raising throughout this book should appear obvious to practitioners in the field.

We can think of the role of the university fund raiser in a nested way. The primary job responsibility for fund raisers is to raise money. The moral responsibility that surrounds them stems from their role as part of the institutional advancement team. Therefore, along with other advancement officers, they share the duty of promoting the university's interests. Still more broadly, fund raisers are administrators in their institutions of higher education. Thus, they also share the responsibility of actualizing the mission and operating philosophy of the institution.[3] In chapter 4 James Donahue provides a detailed analysis of the aspects of the fund-raising role that create moral responsibilities.

What counts as a role-related responsibility for fund raisers is important because fund raisers, like everyone else, are morally required to do their jobs. Specifically, fund raisers are morally required to bring in money in a way that reflects an understanding of the institution's mission and promotes the institution's interests. It is immoral to neglect one's duty, to fail to meet one's role-related responsibilities, but except in unusual cases it is also immoral to fulfill this duty through a process that involves causing harm, deception, cheating, or breaking one's promise. Fund raisers are morally required to raise money, but not at any cost. Their meritorious goal of bringing in money cannot justify deceiving prospective donors, violating a prospect's privacy to get information, or violating tax laws to help a donor.

## Reasonable Expectations and Moral Permissibility

An explanation of the relationship between the fund raiser and the donor can clarify some of what is morally permissible for fund raisers. The nature of the relationship between the fund raiser and potential or actual donor provides the basis for determining what the prospect or donor can reasonably expect from the fund raiser. Knowing what to expect from a business or professional relationship protects people from being too vulnerable. For example, it is reasonable to expect salespeople to withhold information about the positive qualities of competitors' products and the negative qualities of their own. This is a convention of the sales business that most of us have come to expect. Consider what happens to customers who do not understand this convention and think that salespeople will give them all the pertinent information. Those customers perceive themselves to be less vulnerable than they really are. Because of their mistaken expectations, they are depending on the salesperson as their sole source of information.

It is more difficult to clarify the conventional expectations for fund raisers than it is to describe the conventional expectations for salespeople. Like sales personnel, fund raisers have a primary responsibility to their employer; however, unlike sales personnel, they are expected to develop trust relationships with actual and prospective donors. "Buyer beware" is the conventional standard for sales; there is no parallel "giver beware" in charitable solicitations.

It is important that fund raisers define and be able to describe the reasonable expectations that donors have of them. This sets the rules of the game. Then if fund raisers violate expected standards of behavior, they are acting in an unfair way; we may even regard it as cheating. What is it reasonable for actual or prospective donors to expect in their relationships with higher education fund raisers? The following understanding emerges from the literature and practice of conscientious fund raising:

> Philanthropy is a social relation between the donor and the recipient organization in which giving is a voluntary act. Fund raising is in service to that relationship and act.[4]

The relationship between a fund raiser and a prospective or actual donor differs in important ways from that between a salesperson and a customer. The fund-raising relationship begins with the assumption that the potential donor wants to provide a gift specifically to the recipient organization. A sales relationship begins with the assumption that the customer needs or wants to buy some product or service that can be found in various stores. Givers do not often approach a charitable organization with the view that they have a certain number of dollars to give away and that maybe they will give it to that charitable organization, and maybe they will not. The reasons that lead a donor to give to a specific charitable organization are far more complex than those that lead a buyer to purchase goods from a particular store.

Philanthropic giving is an expression of the donor's values and world-view. It is also an expression of ideal rather than required behavior. While one may want to encourage all people to give of themselves in some beneficent way, the giving of a particular gift to a particular institution is not a moral requirement for any donor. By bestowing gifts, donors act in a way that is morally ideal rather than morally required. It is morally permissible for donors to do any number of other things with their money or to give it to any number of worthy causes. The fund raisers exist to facilitate gift giving to the educational institutions that employ them.

Philanthropy scholar Robert Payton and colleagues state the facilitative role of the fund raiser succinctly: "We believe that fund raising for social purposes engages fund raisers in the lives of other people for their benefit or for some larger public benefit as well as for the benefit of the fund raisers themselves. Intervening in the lives of others for their benefit is a moral action."[5] These are laudable goals, but the fund raiser's intervention is a moral action only if the process of fund raising is as exemplary as its goal. Since giving is a voluntary act, any morally permissible methods of fund raising will be accompanied by the assumption of explicit or implicit consent on the part of the potential donor.

One can think of any number of beneficial actions that, if done without consent, would be immoral rather than moral actions. Rational adults are allowed to make incorrect decisions, to act in ways that are not necessarily in their benefit or in the public's benefit. No matter how strongly a fund raiser believes that alumni owe something to the college, taking their money in a way that circumvents their will is not permissible.

Except in rare, justifiable cases, it is immoral to deprive anyone of the opportunity to make choices. Being so deprived is a harm that any rational person normally wants to avoid. One might be justified in depriving an adult of the freedom to make choices through involuntary commitment when it is clear that the choices that person is making are likely to cause him serious harm; or one might be justified in imprisoning someone who has harmed others. But when we are speaking of an action such as giving money to one's alma mater, there is no justification for depriving the donor, by deception or other immoral means, of the freedom to give or not to give. Donating one's extra money to a worthwhile cause is itself a morally exceptional act, rather than one that is morally required, and the freedom to decide whether and how to give is critical to the ethical nature of the relationship.

The relationship between the donor and fund raiser is based on trust, with the fund raiser working as a conduit between the donor and institution. The following reasonable expectations extend from that trust relationship:

1. Donors reasonably expect fund raisers to protect their gifts by understanding and safeguarding the donative intent.
2. Donors reasonably expect fund raisers to give them pertinent information to assist them in making decisions about whether and how to give.
3. Donors reasonably expect fund raisers not to deceive them as they make determinations relative to their donations.

Thus, it is reasonable for donors to expect their beliefs, concerns, and desires to be important features of their relationship with fund raisers. This is not to say that every belief, concern, or desire of every donor must be condoned. If the prospective donor's offer or conditions for the gift's use are inconsistent with the institutional mission or interest, the gift ought not to be accepted. The acceptance of a gift assumes that the donor's gift and conditions and the institution's acceptance reflect a shared understanding of institutional mission and interest. Consider how these reasonable donor expectations unfold.

## Protection of the Gift

It is morally unjustifiable for an institution to fail to respect the donor's intent, just as it is morally unjustifiable for the fund raiser and the institution to fail to protect that intent. As time passes and the understanding of a donor's intent fades, preserving that intent may not be an easy task. It is unfair for fund raisers to fail to solicit, comprehend, and carry out the donor's wishes to the best of the institution's ability. The willingness of development staffs to regard such stewardship seriously long after the actual donation will be favorably noticed by other alumni who are concerned about the future of their gifts in perpetuity.

## The Requirement to Tell

The disclosure requirement of fund raisers requires that they share all information that donors would consider relevant in the decision process. This clarifies the limits of deception in higher education fund raising: a lie is always morally unacceptable, that is, unless it is otherwise justified,[6] but omitting or withholding information is only sometimes morally unacceptable.

While it is not deceptive for fund raisers to fail to reveal details of their personal lives to prospective donors, there is some information that fund raisers have a moral obligation to reveal, namely, information that donors would reasonably consider relevant to their determination of whether to give. The fund raiser, as facilitator, has a good-faith obligation to find out what the prospective donor considers relevant and to provide that information even if the prospect might withhold the gift in light of the information.

In chapter 6 Judith Gooch provides an example of a donor who proposes to fund an endowed chair in a department that will soon announce the hiring of a new faculty member with views antithetical to the funder's. Gooch clarifies why not telling the donor that information should count as deception.

## Respect for Donors

Telling prospective donors information that they would consider relevant to the making of their gifts is one important way that fund raisers show respect for donors. Another way is through the collection and retention of information concerning the prospective donor. One of the standard tenets of the profession is that information that the prospective or actual donor might consider embarrassing or damaging should not be intentionally collected or retained by the institution.[7] As discussed in detail in chapter 5, this rule shows respect for donors by allowing them and their sensibilities to control the information that is known about them. It acknowledges the freedom that the donor has in choosing to maintain a relationship with fund raisers and with the institution.

## Morally Unacceptable Actions in Fund Raising

Causing pain, depriving freedom or opportunity, deceiving, cheating, or breaking the law are the kinds of action that require justification. The moral rules that prohibit such actions are not absolute, and all of them have justified exceptions. Most people would agree that even killing is justified in self-defense, for example. Further, one finds almost complete agreement on the features of justified exceptions. The first of these is *impartiality*. When all of the relevant features are the same, if a violation of a moral rule is justified for any person, it is justified for every person.

Simple slogans like the Golden Rule, "Do unto others as you would have them do unto you," and Kant's categorical imperative, "Act only on that maxim that you could will to be a universal law," serve as heuristic devices for people who are contemplating the violation of a moral rule: "Consider whether you would be prepared to impartially favor that kind of violation no matter who is doing the violating and to whom."

It is also generally agreed that there is some kind of *publicity* requirement, that is, that everyone know that this kind of violation is allowed. The publicity requirement guarantees genuine impartiality. It is not sufficient to justify allowing everyone to violate the rule in the same circumstances. One must also be willing to advocate the violation publicly. Consider a fund raiser who deceives a prospective donor in a situation in which failure to receive the donation would result in the loss of great benefits to the institution but the donor would suffer no harm other than being deceived and no one would become aware of the deception. This would be a justified violation of the rule "Do not deceive" only if everyone, including all fund raisers and all donors, knew that it was a justifiable exception. But logically, no one would favor everyone's knowing that this kind of deception was allowed. If everyone knew it, the kind of trust that is essential in the relationship between fund raiser and donor would be destroyed. And if no one favored publicly allowing this kind of deception, then practicing it would involve arrogance; that is, one would be making special exceptions for oneself, which is clearly immoral.

We do not claim that everyone agrees *which* violations satisfy these conditions, but no violation is justified unless it has satisfied these conditions. The proper attitude toward moral rules, therefore, is as follows: *Everyone is always to obey the rule unless an impartial rational person can advocate that violating it be publicly allowed.*

There are justifiable exceptions to the rules. For example, most people would consider it justifiable to cheat or deceive a hostage-taker if such behavior were likely to lead to the release of his hostages, especially if everyone, including potential hostage-takers, understood that that was how law enforcement officers were likely to react toward hostage-taking. If hostage-takers knew that they could not trust law enforcement officers to do what they said in a hostage-taking situation, the hostage-takers' power would be gone. Part of what makes this exception to the rule "Do not deceive" justifiable is that the law enforcement officers are deceiving those who have acted immorally by depriving innocent people of their freedom. It is far easier to justify deceiving those who are acting immorally than it is to justify those who are not. Many would favor deceiving hostage-takers even when everyone, including the hostage-takers, knew that such deception was allowed. Indeed, one point of having everyone know that deception is allowed in these cases is to establish future uncertainty on the part of would-be hostage-takers that law enforcement officers would meet their demands. But publicly allowing deception in fund raising would create an uncertainty that no one in the field of fund raising wants.

In order to avoid the kind of uncertainty that can arise if it is not clear what counts as deception, the rules of the fund-raising game must be made public. Throughout this book, authors refer to the need for institutions to set public policy. Many activities that give rise to charges of unfairness or unethical behavior can be avoided by making policies public. In chapter 10, for example, Richard Seaman and Eric Wentworth argue that before the beginning of a major fund raising campaign, institutions should adopt written rules for how to count various types of gifts. Publicly adopting such rules and sticking with the rules throughout the campaign allows all the players—donors as well as volunteers and development officers—to set reasonable expectations for the conduct of the campaign.

It is very difficult, if not impossible, for fund raisers to justify actions that are usually morally unacceptable, because the act that forms the basis of the relationship between fund raiser and prospect or donor is an act of philanthropy. Donors act on moral ideals when they give. Giving is not morally required. It is morally permissible for donors to refuse to give, to give elsewhere, or to give less. There is no basis from which to argue that it is ever morally acceptable for fund raisers to deceive, cheat, deprive prospects or donors of their freedom of choice, or otherwise cause them harm in the process of raising funds.

Two faulty justifications that are sometimes offered for morally unacceptable actions on the part of fund raisers are (1) that the donor is not acting out of meritorious donative intent and (2) that the institution has a desperate need for the money. Neither justification holds. It is very difficult to fully know the donor's intent. Motivations for giving vary from the psychological to the economic to the social.[8] The so-called charitable impulse is present as a theme in all the various conscious and unconscious motivations to give. Even if it were possible to determine with absolute certainty that a donor was providing the donation for some purely nonphilanthropic reason, fund raisers would not be justified in treating that donor in a morally unacceptable way. Whatever the purpose, intent, or motivation, the donor's act is still a morally good one.

Fund raisers' guesses that a prospective donor's motivation is nonphilanthropic are irrelevant unless the donor's motivation or gift conditions conflict with the institutional mission or interests. The sleazy donor is neither a problem for the fund raiser seeking to act in morally permissible ways nor a justification for morally prohibited behavior on the part of the fund raisers. If the donor's goals are inconsistent with the institution's mission or interests, then no gift ought to be accepted. On the other hand, if the donor's goals for the gift are consistent with the institution's mission, then fund raisers are morally required to do their job without engaging in actions that might cause the donor to suffer harm.

Nor is the desperation of the institution a justification for acting in morally unacceptable ways toward prospective or actual donors. Several years ago, at a seminar for Ivy League prospect research officers, a participant justified an unacceptable technique for obtaining information in the following words: "Don't you understand? This is about survival!" The school's multimillion-dollar endowment made the claim especially ironic, but this justification is morally lacking even in times when the institutional doors might really have to close.

The rule suggested in allowing the desperate situation of an institution to justify morally unacceptable behavior is that it is morally permissible to engage in actions that might cause individuals to suffer harm if those actions will bring about a good result for one's institution. This rule describes a world in which Robin Hood is the model fund raiser. The rule also would not stand up under the public scrutiny that is required for behavior that is generally morally unacceptable. That is, the fund raisers in this example would need to let everyone know that they are willing to deceive donors when the institution is in desperate need of funds. This obviously is not a practice that could be made known to donors, because then donors would never know whether or not to believe fund raisers. If fund raisers take Kant's categorical imperative—"Act only on that maxim that you could will to be a universal law"—as their guide, their proper moral

*Social and Moral Foundations*

behavior is to act only in those ways that they would be willing to be publicly allowed. This means never causing harm, deceiving, cheating, or breaking promises unless one would be willing for everyone to know that violating a moral rule in these kind of circumstances was allowed for everyone.

# 3

# The Language
# of Fund Raising

## Allen Buchanan

The working hypothesis of this chapter is that an evaluation of fund raising should not be restricted to determining whether particular actions of fund raisers comply with or violate moral rules such as "Don't deceive," "Respect people's privacy," or "Do not breach confidentiality." Framed more positively, a comprehensive moral evaluation of fund raising must include an examination of fund raisers' values and motives, as well as of their attitudes toward prospective donors, toward themselves and their peers, and toward the activity of fund raising itself.

The comprehensive moral evaluation of social practices should not be limited to determining whether the individual actions that constitute those practices violate particular moral rules. Moral evaluation should also attend to what might be called the deeper moral significance of social practices, the extent to which they succeed in realizing important moral ideals of human interaction and character. Thus to focus only on whether particular actions violate moral rules is to operate with an unduly narrow conception of the scope of moral evaluation. Put most simply, an investigation of the ethics of fund raising should focus not just upon actions and whether they conform to moral rules but upon the character of the agents as well.

To evaluate the character of agents we must be able to discern their motives and values. But how may we best do this? I shall show that an analysis of the discourse of fund raising reveals much about the motives and values of fund raisers. Attention to the discourse of fund raising is the key to a more comprehensive moral evaluation of fund raising.

Analyzing the discourse of fund raisers is not the most familiar way of exploring the ethics of fund raising. Much more common is the use of case studies in which the activities of fund raisers at least appear to violate widely held moral rules. This approach might be called the method of negative example. For instance, recently much attention has been devoted to cases in which fund raisers practice deception (by failing to divulge accurate information to donors about the financial condition of the institution or the actual uses to which the donation will be put) or violate the privacy of the prospective donor (by secretly gathering information about his or her tastes and interests).[1]

What is essential to this orthodox conception of the moral evaluation of fund raising is the assumption that what matters, exclusively or at least primarily, is whether the fund raiser's conduct, including verbal conduct, complies with or violates moral rules ("Don't deceive," "Respect people's privacy," etc.). Such rules tell us which actions are morally permissible and which are morally impermissible. Since they focus only on the rightness or wrongness of actions, moral rules make no direct reference to the rightness or wrongness of the agent's motives or values. Once we see that morality is essentially concerned not just with right action but with character as well, it becomes clear that the orthodox approach to the ethics of fund raising is deficient.

Within the area of fund raising for higher education there are a number of morally distinguishable forms of interaction. Each deserves careful and patient examination. I shall not attempt here to provide an exhaustive ethical analysis of the discourse of fund raising for higher education. Instead, I shall attempt to show how certain forms of discourse implicate several different pictures of the self and of its relationship to other selves. My conjecture is that even if we cannot at present fully articulate and agree upon a comprehensive moral theory that explains precisely why certain pictures of the self and of human interaction are more appropriate than others, we may find a good deal of consensus on which pictures are more fitting. In the end, the most important moral question about fund raising—and about most other human activities—may not be "Does it violate any moral rules?" but rather "What sort of person does that sort of thing, and is that the sort of person I want to be?"

## The Study of Rhetoric versus the Analysis of Discourse

Rhetoric is "that art . . . by which discourse is adapted to its end."[2] Thus to examine the discourse of fund raising as rhetoric would be to determine how that discourse serves the end of raising funds. My analysis in this chapter recognizes the role of discourse as rhetoric— as an instrument employed to achieve an end. Unlike the study of rhetoric, however, our analysis is not limited to an evaluation of the effectiveness of discourse in achieving its end. Rather, our concern is with the analysis of discourse as a key to understanding the character of those who employ it and the nature of their interaction with others. As we shall see, different modes of discourse suggest different pictures of human interaction. Since these pictures of interaction are rather abstract, they can be referred to as models.

## A Model of Exchange and a Model of Obligation

When fund raisers say to a potential donor that they are pleased to offer an "opportunity" to have a building named after the donor, they make a statement that may suggest a particular model of the interaction between the fund raiser and the potential donor. The model of interaction implies a certain conception of the nature of the act of giving and of the act of asking. According to one view, the "opportunity" is an opportunity for self-interested gain. This is the model of *a mutually beneficial exchange between self-interested individuals.* According to this model, the fund raiser is literally an entrepreneur (a middleman, one who conveys something from one party to another, facilitating an exchange between them in the market). Fund raisers are agents of coordination: they bring together the two parties to an exchange, the prospective donor and the institution or organization to which the donation is to be made. According to the mutually beneficial exchange model, the act of giving is a self-interested act in which the donor gains something from the exchange; it is not an act of sacrifice. The act of asking is not an attempt to get someone to make a sacrifice; it is the offering of an opportunity for the donor to gain. According to this model, the activity of the fund raiser and of the donor is simply market activity.

In contrast, if the fund raiser tells the potential donor, "I know you'll want to do your fair share in our drive to fund more scholar-ships for minority students," another model of the relationship and another conception of the nature of the acts of asking and of giving is implied. This is the model of *discharging an obligation,* of doing one's duty. The fund raiser does not offer the donor an opportunity to gain by giving. Instead, the fund raiser reminds potential donors of what they ought to do. Here the fund raiser's role is not that of an entrepreneur addressing a self-interested individual in the market. Rather, the fund raiser is acting as the spokesperson for the donor's moral self, an external amplifier of the voice of the donor's con-science.

The relationship between a form of discourse, on the one hand, and a model of the activity of asking and the nature of the act of giving, on the other, is reciprocal: the discourse suggests the model, but the model makes sense of the discourse. Presenting an opportu-nity for self-promotion or self-gratification through having a build-ing named after one in exchange for a sum of money makes sense within the market exchange model, while an appeal to the donor's sense of fairness does not. Addressing a person's sense of duty by offering an opportunity for purchasing a mark of prestige would be just as inappropriate. Once we become sensitive to the different models of interaction that different modes of discourse suggest, we can learn much about the nature of fund raising and the character of fund raisers.

## Three Discourses of Fund Raising

There are in fact three discourses of fund raising. The first is *the discourse of asking,* the language the fund raiser directs toward the potential donor in attempting to secure funds. The discourse of ask-ing encompasses more than the actual request for funds: it also in-cludes the various uses of language that lead up to the request, as well as the fund raiser's responses to the potential donor's response to the request. (For example, if the initial response to the request is negative, fund raisers may change their strategy.)

The second discourse is that through which fund raisers talk with one another about their efforts to raise funds; this is *the peer group discourse* of fund raisers. It appears in conversations, journals, news-letters, and conferences for fund raisers. The peer group discourse has two main components: the language of technique, by which fund raisers inform each other about which methods of fund raising are effective and which are not, and the language of inspiration, by which fund raisers attempt to motivate their peers (and sometimes themselves) to devote their energies to the task of fund raising. The language of technique is employed to develop and communicate to other fund raisers the most effective discourse of asking. The language of inspiration is itself rhetoric in a straightforward sense: it is the use of language to serve the end of motivating fund raisers to raise funds.

The third type of discourse is *the discourse of theory.* It is the use of language to articulate explanatory models of donor behavior. Conceptual frameworks and techniques from empirical social psychology are employed to determine what motivates those who give and to specify what stimuli trigger or inhibit this motivation to produce an act of giving. In the discourse of theory the donor is an object of scientific study. We can learn much about fund-raising activities and the character of fund raisers by focusing not only upon the discourse of asking but especially upon both components of the peer group discourse, the language of technique and the language of inspiration.

## The Language of Exchange versus the Language of Obligation

A number of writers have noted that the theory of fund raising has changed as the practice of asking and giving has evolved from altruism to self-interested exchange.[3] But the impetus for change can operate in the other direction as well. The relationship between the language of theory and the language of asking is one of reciprocity: changes in practice stimulate changes in theory, but once a theory gains wide acceptance it can influence practice, at least by reinforcing and sustaining the momentum of changes already occurring. Fund raisers' choices of certain forms of the language of asking may be influenced by their acceptance of a particular theory of donors' behavior. If they believe that individuals are more effectively motivated by self-interest than by a sense of duty, they will offer "opportunities" rather than make appeals to conscience.

Given this possibility of reciprocal influence between the theory and practice of fund raising, it is especially important to characterize the exchange model accurately. An examination of the three discourses of fund raising reveals that there are in fact several different exchange models, each with its own picture of the nature of the interaction between fund raiser and potential donor, and each with different implications for the moral status of the activity and the character of the fund raiser. Not only is talk about *the* exchange model analytically unrefined but, even worse, it obscures the fundamental issues. And as we shall see, some uses of the language of exchange are themselves instances of rhetoric: they enable fund raisers to present what they are doing—to themselves and others—in a more favorable light by glossing over fundamental conflicts of interest between the fund raiser and the potential giver.

Much of the discourse of the theory of fund raising refers to *the* exchange model and contrasts it with the model of altruism. There are, in fact, at least two, and possibly three, different exchange models. First, there is what game theorists would call the *pure coordination model.* The fund raiser merely brings together two parties, each with his or her own preexisting preferences, so that both sets of preferences may be satisfied through an exchange based on accurate information. This model presents a morally unproblematic picture of the interaction between fund raiser and potential donor. So it is not very surprising that fund raisers themselves find the exchange model, understood in this way, an attractive way to view their activities and themselves. Instances of the language of asking that present potential donors with "opportunities" for receiving in exchange for their contribution of various goods (prestige, recognition, perquisites of various sorts) suggest this model. For example, fund raisers are instructed to "take the attitude that you are offering the prospect a chance to participate in [the] project." [4]

The second exchange model might be called the *stimulated demand model.* The idea here is that fund raisers do more than merely bring together parties with preexisting preferences: they strive to create a preference, even a need, for giving. In some cases the language of asking is designed to create a need for giving by forging a new connection between giving and a preexisting motivation or preference that hitherto was not directed toward giving. Consider, for example, the following appeal to Wellesley College alumnae: "Alumnae looking forward to reunion in June have an opportunity to make their gifts to Wellesley count twice. . . . Donations or pledges received by January 31 will be credited for reunion totals and for the Campaign for $150 Million."[5] The appeal here is a competitive motive—class rivalries. The presumption is that if alumnae view donation as a form of interclass competition, some will contribute who otherwise would not have (and some will contribute more than they otherwise would have). An article in the peer group literature that focuses on the donating behavior of women graduates notes that competition in giving has now extended from interclass rivalries to rivalries between individuals within a class. "Competition was always part of it, but it was usually one class trying to beat the previous 25th-reunion gift. . . . Now, individuals compete."[6]

There is a more extreme form of the stimulated demand model, a form so extreme that it should perhaps be classified as a third model under the label *addiction model*. It is suggested by the following example: "The more promising models of individuals' behavior as donors depart from the model of pure altruism in favor of exchange models, which attempt to explain donors' motives based on receipt of 'goods'—perquisites, tokens, or honors—in exchange for the gift, and a repeated disequilibrium that follows leaving the donor with a need to respond to recognition and acknowledgment with yet more gifts."[7] The proposal here is not merely to satisfy a preexisting preference, as in the pure coordination model, nor even merely to stimulate a preference or create a need, but rather to use the "exchange" as a means of reinforcement that will produce an insatiable need—in the market language of the exchange model, an unlimited demand.

Other instances of the language of asking and of the peer group language show sharp departures from the pure coordination model and its benign assumptions. While the pure coordination model assumes a fundamental harmony of interests, the rhetoric of competition presupposes a conflict of interests between the potential donor and the fund raiser, with the fund raiser interested in "closing the sale" and the potential donor resisting "being sold." For example, in a peer group technique article entitled "Winning Words," volunteer fund raisers are exhorted to "keep the ball in your court" by taking the initiative to determine when a second visit to the potential donor will be scheduled.[8] Language suggesting manipulation and even deceit, as when fund raisers refer to "our tricks and devices," strongly suggests that there is at least a potential conflict between the donor's interests and the fund raiser's interest in "making the sale."[9] "The most important trick is ages old, but it still works. Try to steer the conversation in ways that get the prospect in the habit of saying 'yes.' You can do this by making statements and asking questions that make agreement inescapable. If your prospect has said 'Yes' repeatedly throughout the interview it is difficult for him to revert to 'No' when the time comes to close the sale."[10]

The use of this technique, as well as the choice of particular colors for mailing envelopes in the belief that they predispose people to comply with a request—"yellow sticks in the mind like no other color"[11]—rests upon the assumption that merely providing information to the prospective donor as a rational agent is not enough. In other words, the deliberate use of techniques of nonrational persuasion presupposes that making a donation (or making a large donation) is not really in the potential donor's interest and that the interaction is not necessarily one of mutually beneficial exchange. Consider the following statements:

> Don't reveal information you don't want in the mainstream ("We're doing this [undertaking this fund-raising drive] to keep the school from going under . . .").[12]

> [In drafting a direct mail appeal one should write as if one were writing] "for one person." Establish a close link between the prospect's support and accomplishing the goals of the institution.[13]

Both statements show a clear recognition of a fundamental structural conflict of interest between fund raisers and potential donors in the case of large-scale, multiple-donor campaigns. This conflict exists whenever there are threshold effects in the process of meeting the campaign's goal. For example, if the real goal of the campaign is to reach a particular level of funds necessary to avoid the demise of the institution, as in the first instance, then it may not in fact be in the rational self-interest of the individual potential donor to contribute if the current level is not near the threshold of success. From the standpoint of the donor as a self-interested agent, the idea of making a contribution to a sinking ship will not be a rational gamble. If donors know that the ship is sinking, they will not contribute. Hence, the fund raiser withholds information about how dire the institution's financial circumstances are. Talking as if the interaction in such cases were a mutually beneficial exchange serves to hide this fundamental conflict of interest.

The advice on technique offered in the second statement is to convince potential donors that the well-being of the institution depends upon *their* donation. Except in the odd case of a donor who has enormous financial resources—certainly not the typical donor solicited by direct mail—this simply will be false. There will be *no link* between the individual's contribution and the fate of the institution. The problem here is the familiar barrier to successful collective action illustrated by the throw-away-vote phenomenon: why should I vote (since this involves costs to me) when the probability that my vote will make the difference is negligible? This sort of problem is endemic to large-scale, multiple-donor fund raising. It does not arise in the more traditional context of an individual act of charity toward a particular individual (giving bread to a starving person), because the success of the charitable act in this case does not depend upon the actions of others. Yet large-scale, multiple-donor fund raising, not individual, independent acts of charity, is the dominant technique for generating private resources for higher education. The point these examples illustrate is then quite general: Whenever fund raising involves collective action, there is the possibility of a conflict between the interest of the individual potential donor and the interests of the fund raisers. And whenever there is a conflict, the use of the mutually beneficial exchange model to describe the interaction is seriously misleading.

The assumption of conflicts of interest between potential donors and fund raisers is also suggested by the pervasive use of war metaphors. Efforts to raise funds are called "campaigns." Prospective donors are "targeted" so that fund raisers can "put the hit on them." The importance of getting the development office's message out to the volunteers "in the trenches" is stressed.[14] And the technique of segmenting telephone solicitation lists with different types of appeals for different categories of prospective donors is called the "divide and conquer" strategy.[15]

So far, I have concentrated on ambiguities in the model of the interaction between fund raiser and potential donor as an exchange, noting that there are different interpretations of the nature of the exchange, with quite different moral implications. I have also noted that the dominant theory of donation has shifted from characterizing giving as an altruistic act to characterizing it as a self-interested bargain. It would be a mistake, however, to convey the impression that the language of asking has been adapted completely to the assumptions of the exchange models. Especially in the case of appeals to alumnae, the model of obligation is still at work. The following passage from a letter to "The University Community" suggests that those who have benefited from the institution have a special obligation of reciprocity. "When I think of my own personal reasons for 'giving something back' to the UA [University of Arizona], I see that it has contributed to, and been a great blessing to, members of my family and me. . . . We all benefited from the teaching and the many great and dedicated faculty that had an impact on our lives." [16]

It is perhaps worth noting that appeals to an individual's sense of obligation can sometimes succeed where appeals to rational self-interest may not. If potential donors believe that they are obligated to reciprocate for the benefits the institution has provided, they may decide to contribute regardless of whether they believe their contribution will be decisive for reaching the threshold of funding needed to reach a particular goal. They may give if they conceive of themselves as paying back a debt even though they would not give if they viewed the matter simply as an investment decision designed to maximize self-interest. Where appeals to the sense of obligation can be relied upon, the familiar collective-action problems that plague appeals to rational self-interest may simply be avoided. This means that sometimes the appeal to duty will be a more effective strategy than an appeal to self-interest. This simple fact should give pause to those who uncritically assume that the transition from altruism to self-interested exchange is an unmixed blessing in the evolution of fund raising.

## Offering Opportunities for Virtuous Behavior and Moral Growth

We have seen that the currently popular idea that fund raisers offer opportunities for potential donors to pursue their self-interest both obscures certain conflicts of interest that can be present in the interaction and may in some cases be less effective than appeals to duty or moral ideals. There is, however, a third, more profound limitation on the self-interested-exchange model: it overlooks a quite different sense in which the fund raiser can be said to be offering an opportunity to the potential donor. Some fund raisers report that they view themselves as offering potential donors opportunities not only for an individual act that is virtuous but for initiating a pattern of giving that will persist over time and can contribute to the moral growth of the donor.[17] Thus the fund raiser may help initiate the building of a commitment to helping an institution. In time donors may come to see this commitment as an important expression of the values they wish their lives to embody and hence a path toward becoming the kind of people they wish to be.

If donors believe that the cause is a worthy one, and if the initial act of giving grows into a pattern of concerned support for that cause, then eventually a point may be reached at which donors perceive this ongoing interaction as an important element of their identity—as a part of who they are, an expression of what they stand for. Simply to assume that the relationship between fund raiser and donor is or ought to be a self-interested exchange, like any bargain in the market, is to overlook this important moral dimension of fund raising entirely. So here again we see that the discourse of fund raising, in this case the currently popular slogan that it offers the potential donor an "opportunity," is highly ambiguous.

## The Language of Inverted Values

In some cases the language of asking and the peer group language suggest a set of attitudes in the fund raiser that can only be characterized as an inversion, if not a perversion, of values. Perhaps the most obvious examples of this phenomenon of inversion are those in which fund raisers are instructed to make friends with prospective donors in order to get them to contribute. This is an inversion of the values associated with friendship, since friendship is first and foremost something to be pursued for its own sake, not as mere instrument for the achievement of other, quite independent ends.

A more subtle but perhaps equally troubling type of inversion occurs in those instances of the language of technique that encourage fund raisers to engage in self-manipulation, that is, deliberately cultivating in themselves attitudes or motivations for purely strategic reasons. For example, fund raisers are instructed to avoid thinking of themselves as asking donors to bear a cost and instead to cultivate the habit of thinking of themselves as offering an opportunity.[18] This amounts to distorting one's perception of the situation in order better to achieve one's goals. The term *inversion* seems appropriate here, since we generally think that goals should be adapted to accurate perceptions of the facts of the situation, not that perceptions should be distorted to fit goals. A related inversion occurs when fund raisers are exhorted to "believe in your institution" in order to be a more effective fund raiser, as opposed to becoming an effective fund raiser because they believe in their institution.[19]

Finally, a distortion of priorities, if not an inversion of values, occurs when fund raisers cynically play upon potential donors' own moral values in order to "make a sale" even though the values are ones the fund raisers themselves do not endorse or even respect. "No matter how smart we are, we can't assume that direct mail donors will react to any of our tricks and devices. [One trick that didn't work was] an effort to pander to the environmental sensitivity of direct mail donors specially selected for their likely interest in environmental issues [by printing 'Recycled Paper' on the mail appeal]."[20]

The problem here is not deception in any obvious sense—the paper used really was recycled. The problem is that fund raisers themselves are pandering to the convictions of the potential donors. The use of the word *pander* here makes it clear that the fund raisers neither share nor even respect these convictions. Instead, the convictions of others are treated as levers to be manipulated. In that sense, fund raisers are doing the right thing, or what they believe the prospective donor thinks is the right thing, but for the wrong reason. This technique also indicates a fundamental distortion, if not a literal inversion, of values.

## Discourse and Character

Many commentators on the evolution of fund raising in the United States have noted a shift from appeals to altruism and obligation to the presentation of opportunities for self-interested exchange. In some respects fund raisers may welcome this transformation. Now fund raisers need not admonish prospective donors to do their duty or attempt to stimulate generosity by provoking feelings of guilt among the more fortunate. By embracing the exchange model, fund raisers and potential donors can face each other as equals in the morally neutral arena of the market. They can simply appeal to the potential donor's own good as the donor conceives it rather than asking the donor to sacrifice a part of his or her good for the sake of duty or for the good of others.

The analysis of the discourses of fund raising reveals that things are not so simple. Of the several exchange models, only the pure coordination model involves a genuine harmony of interests, a positive-sum game between fund raiser and potential donor. Yet much of the actual discourse of asking reveals a clear awareness of conflicts of interests, as well as an effort to conceal their existence from the potential donor.

By attending to the models of interaction implicated by the discourses of fund raising, we can achieve a richer moral evaluation of fund raising than we could solely by measuring the particular actions of fund raisers against familiar moral rules. Such rules focus on particular actions rather than on the nature of the interactions and the character of the agent who initiates them. It is important to see that particular techniques of fund raising are wrong because they involve actions that violate familiar moral prohibitions against deceiving or breaching confidentiality or privacy. Sometimes certain practices of interaction also require the fund raiser to manipulate his or her own beliefs and motives as well as those of the potential donor.

Focusing exclusively upon whether particular actions violate moral rule (e.g., "Don't deceive") may tempt those who defend such practices to make a familiar and facile reply: We are pursuing worthy ends, and to attain them in a world in which resources are scarce and there is much competition for them, we must sometimes bend or even break certain moral rules. Such recourse to the idea that the end justifies the means obscures something very important: that part of what is at stake here is not simply a relaxing of moral rules concerning which actions we may or may not perform but also the more fundamental issue of what sort of persons we should be and what ways of conceiving of ourselves, of others, and of our interactions with them are fitting.

There are morally troubling aspects of the practice of fund raising whose nature and seriousness are not adequately captured by the usual method of evaluating particular actions in terms of whether they comply with or violate moral rules. By decoding the discourses

## Social and Moral Foundations

of fund raising, we get a richer and deeper understanding of the moral issues, one that directs our gaze more squarely toward the kind of person one becomes through engaging in the practices.

My conjecture is that an appeal to the contrast between rival pictures of the person and of personal interaction may be more motivationally potent for the practice of fund raising than attempts to stimulate the sense of duty to conform one's actions to moral rules. If this is so, our examination of the discourse of fund raising may have led us to a valuable truth about the discourse of moral evaluation.

# 4

# Fund Raising
# as a Profession
## James A. Donahue

The last ten years have demonstrated a considerable shift in how
fund raisers are perceived as an occupational group. This shift is attributable to the enormous growth of professional associations such
as the Council for the Advancement and Support of Education
(CASE) and the National Society of Fund Raising Executives
(NSFRE); to the proliferation of conferences and publications on
fund-raising activities; to the increase in the number of fund raisers
who staff nonprofit organizations; and to the emerging self-
awareness among fund raisers that their work is guided by standards
and purposes similar to those of other established professions. A
consensus is emerging that fund raising is a profession, not simply
an occupation.

## The Significance of Being a Professional

There is a difference between being a member of a profession and
being a "professional." Being part of a professional group generally
means that one's work life is defined by certain kinds of generally
accepted practices and that one identifies with the general rules of
conduct that define a professional group. Each profession has accepted practices that describe what counts as being a member of an
occupational class, as well as public expectations that are particular
to that occupation. To describe someone as being a member of a
profession is to refer to that person's occupational status.

To describe someone as "professional" is to refer to that person
more in terms of the way he or she conducts him- or herself on the
job. The term usually refers to the quality with which one performs
a basic skill and the high level of excellence with which one under-

takes and completes a task. It has a generally praiseworthy quality. Referring to someone as professional is both a technical and a moral reference. It is a technical reference in that it assumes a basic level of competence in the performance of an activity. It is a moral reference in that it implies that there are certain exemplary ways of performing the tasks of an occupation. The person who embodies the qualities and traits (the virtues) that define the successful performance of a profession's tasks is considered to be a "good" professional (i.e., in a moral sense).

For fund raisers, there is an integral connection between being a member of a profession in a descriptive or functional sense and being judged professional in a positive sense. To be a fund raiser is to be part of an occupational group that has standards of excellence for the performance of the profession's practices. Being a "professional" fund raiser also suggests that a fund raiser follows those moral imperatives and standards of excellence that are intrinsic to being a member of the profession and bases his or her actions on the values, norms, ideals, expectations, and commitments inherent in the professional status.

The foundations for the norms and values that are appropriate and necessary for fund raising are found in the very definition of what it means to be a professional. I begin this chapter by exploring the qualities that constitute identity in a professional group. I will demonstrate the ways in which fund raising is a profession. I will then indicate those norms and imperatives that are generated by the claim that fund raising is a profession. My purpose here is to show that there are legitimate moral demands entailed in being a fund raiser and that these demands are largely grounded in the very fact of being a member of a profession. In other words, fund raisers are obliged and expected to be professional by virtue of being in a professional group.

As an example of the ethical distinction involved in being a professional, consider the difference between plumbers and lawyers. While plumbers can surely be professional in terms of the performance of their work, plumbing is typically not considered a profession; rather, plumbers are an occupational group. A plumber has no formal moral obligations outside of basic requirements to honor contracts and other similar business arrangements. When we speak of a plumber as being a "real professional," we generally mean that he performs his task with a high degree of competence and skill.

Being a lawyer can entail being a professional in two ways. On the one hand, lawyers are descriptively part of an occupational group that is termed a profession. On the other hand, for lawyers to "be professional" means that they perform their duties not merely in a functional or technical way but in a manner that is consistent with the highest standards set forth by the legal profession itself. These standards demonstrate a commitment to values that transcend the functional. For example, a lawyer who shows a sense of respect and caring for the client that goes beyond minimal professional requirements, who can distinguish issues of procedural and substantive justice, or is able to see and uphold the integrity of the legal system as a whole will be considered a real professional.

Like lawyers, fund raisers have commitments that derive from their identity as members of a profession. The point of my analysis is to explore the ways that fund raisers can be seen as a professional group and to indicate the significance of this categorization for an ethics of fund raising.

## Defining a Profession

The literature on professions provides an avenue for developing a professional ethic of fund raising.[1] There is considerable debate concerning what qualities define a profession. This debate is significant in that an understanding of the qualities that distinguish members of a profession from other occupational groups provides a basis for determining which norms, values, and expectations are appropriate to the professional's role.

The literature on professions suggests many qualities that constitute a professional, but some features are mentioned more often than others. A comprehensive definition of a professional would describe a person who:

- is engaged in a social service that is essential and unique;
- possesses a high degree of specialized knowledge;
- possesses the ability to apply a special body of knowledge;
- is part of a group that is autonomous and claims the right to regulate itself;

- recognizes and affirms a code of ethics;
- exhibits strong self discipline and accepts personal responsibility for actions and decisions;
- is committed to and has a concern for the communal interest rather than the self;
- is more concerned with services rendered than with financial rewards.[2]

This list of qualities represents an ideal type. That is, no one professional actually possesses all of these qualities; indeed it would be difficult to do so. Rather, this list represents those qualities that historically have come to be identified with professionals in American society. My contention is that, taken together, these qualities constitute an ideal for the conduct of professional practice. An investigation of each of these qualities as they relate to the activities of fund raising will help to clarify how these qualities create professionalism.[3]

*Being Engaged in an Essential and Unique Social Service.* To say that fund raising in and of itself is an essential service for the advancement of society is to overstate the case. Fund raisers do many of the same things that those in other occupational groups do: they market a product; they solicit support for their product; they constitute an external affairs arm of an institution; and at times they manage institutions.

The unique nature of their work is better understood in light of the institutions and causes they represent. The products that nonprofit fund raisers market are the causes and services their institutions engage in. These causes range from health care services to educational services, to the arts, to community service projects. The uniqueness of the fund raiser resides not in the particular skills and functions that he or she performs but in the fact that the not-for-profit, or independent, sector represents a unique set of purposes and functions in the larger societal context.

The essential nature of the social service rendered by fund raisers is a little less clear. An essential service is one without which it is virtually impossible for some good to be delivered or some service to be carried out. The literature on the role of the independent sector in the economic and social system indicates that without philanthropy and voluntary giving the nature of many voluntary associations would be dramatically altered.[4] Fund raising stimulates and directs that philanthropy. In a free-market economy there is, many assert, a vital need for a sector that is not driven by pure market or economic forces and yet needs economic resources to flourish. In this sense, then, it is possible to speak of fund raising in not-for-profit organizations as serving an essential social need.

*Possessing a High Degree of Specialized Knowledge.* The professional is one who has spent some time mastering a body of knowledge that is not generally familiar to the layperson, a knowledge that is acquired through intensive study or apprenticeship and whose acquisition "sets one apart." The skilled knowledge that the professional possesses is necessary for the successful exercise of the essential service that is rendered.

The fund raiser's specialized knowledge is the knowledge of what is necessary to create funding possibilities. The "special" or "dangerous" knowledge of the fund raiser—dangerous in the sense that it enables the holder to harm someone—is developed through many means. For most, training is received through a period of either apprenticeship with someone familiar with the particularities of a given institution or some kind of intensive involvement with a particular institution. Increasingly, many fund raisers receive their training in the increasing number of degree and certificate programs throughout the country. At this time there are no formal licensing or certification programs in fund raising comparable to the bar in the legal profession or licensing for medical practice. Training in fund raising has not yet become formalized or required; nevertheless, it has become virtually essential for success in fund raising.

*Possessing the Ability to Apply a Special Body of Knowledge.* The practical skills of the fund raiser entail bringing insights to bear on how to develop funding possibilities for the institutions or causes they represent. The fund raiser must learn to apply these skills well and creatively in a particular institution.

*Being Part of a Group That Is Autonomous and Claims the Right to Regulate Itself.* Being part of a group that is autonomous and claims the right to regulate itself presents an interesting set of issues for fund raisers, issues very much in flux. As described in chapter 1, there are laws that provide minimal standards for governing charitable solicitation, just as there are laws that provide minimal standards for medical practice. Civil and criminal laws pertain to affairs of fund raisers, and offenses are publicly punishable. General fund-raising organizations have formalized codes of ethics. The codes name ideals to be attained and practices to be avoided but appeal to moral persuasion and voluntary compliance. But fund raisers as a group have only recently developed codes and standards of behavior that go beyond legal minimums. There is a consensus among fund raisers that ethical codes ought to have some force,[5] but since there are no formalized licensing and certification programs that act as necessary steps for admission to the profession, there is little way of effectively regulating these practices.

The desire for self-regulation in the fund-raising profession is driven by the belief that the activities of the profession can be fully understood and realized only by those internal to a profession. Moreover, it is generally held that is necessary to protect people and institutions against abuses of the power that this special knowledge brings and that this can be done most effectively when those in the profession make decisions for themselves. These are compelling arguments that support a strong differentiation of the norms of the professional fund raiser from "general" moral norms applicable to everyone.[6] The virtue of self-regulation is that it better provides fund raisers means of developing and cultivating ideals for, and holding practitioners accountable within, the profession. Self-regulation creates a mean of identifying, developing, and providing professionalism for the community of fund raisers.

The ability to enforce ethical standards in the profession requires the existence of some type of regulatory power. If licensing and certification for professional fund raisers existed, then some penalties for infractions of ethical standards could be exercised. Otherwise enforcement of ethical standards either falls to civil authorities or depends on the moral persuasion and voluntary compliance among members of the profession. To date there seems to be little fund raisers can do about the unethical practices of other fund raisers except through the informal means of publicizing infractions and garnering public and/or professional disapproval of them.

## Fund Raising as a Profession

*Recognizing and Affirming a Code of Ethics.* The purpose of a code of ethics is to articulate some fundamental moral principles or ideals upon which to base professional activities. Codes generally attempt to (1) name the ideals and values of the profession and (2) indicate in a negative sense those activities that are judged to be unacceptable professional practices. While codes are limited in their ability to capture all the complexities, do explicate those values and behaviors that define moral excellence in the profession. A process of integration and application is necessary to ensure that the values are institutionalized in some programmatic way.

The existence of codes (see Appendix A for some examples) is evidence that fund raisers believe that it is important to articulate and uphold the values undergirding the profession. It is an indication of self-consciousness about the activities of the profession. A concern to encourage some practices and inhibit others suggests a form of self-identity that represents a the coming of age, or the establishment of the identity, of the fund-raising profession.

*Exhibiting Strong Self-Discipline and Accepting Personal Responsibility for Actions and Decisions.* Since one function of the fund raiser is to mobilize and organize the activities of others (administrators, directors, alumni, volunteers, etc.), actual fund-raising activities are often in the hands of others. Fund raisers are frequently handmaids to others in the asking process. Professional fund raisers have a responsibility for their own actions, as well as a responsibility to attempt to ensure that the actions of those whose activities they guide manifest the highest ethical standards. While limits of responsibility are an issue, fund raisers themselves are conscious of the need to act ethically. As previously indicated, however, they lack the power to effectively monitor and police their own professional activities.

*Having a Commitment to and a Concern for the Communal Interest.* Of all the identifying features of the professions, the most distinctive historically is that members of the professions (e.g., law, medicine, the ministry) were seen as committed to the well-being of the common good as opposed to their own gain. Moreover, the community would frequently provide structures that allowed for both the delivery of and payment for the services rendered. The congregation would provide for the living and family needs of the minister; a town or community would secure a local doctor by "paying" in bartered goods and services; the lawyer would be provided the necessary tools and structures for delivering services.

This feature has undergone a radical transformation in contemporary society. The economic, social, and cultural changes that have taken place over the last century have fundamentally altered the way the professional is perceived and the contexts in which professional services are rendered. "Fee for services" was not the primary structuring principle of the relationships between professional and client. Many would argue that the modern lawyer or doctor is no longer motivated by the desire to provide service for the common good. Furthermore, the structural arrangements in which professionals now operate are not oriented to providing services for the general well-being without regard to cost.

We can say that the modern professional has lost some aspects of this crucial historical identifying feature. The shifting standard makes it difficult to use altruism as a basis for analyzing or judging the motivation of the modern fund raiser.

*Being More Concerned with Services Rendered Than with Financial Rewards.* A concern with services rendered is similar to a commitment to and a concern for the communal interest in that it suggests that the professional is motivated by the desire to deliver essential services regardless of the personal cost. Again, it is difficult to generalize about individual professionals, but the structural orientations have changed to the degree that professionals, as we now understand them, are far more oriented toward financial reward than they were historically.

## Professionalization of Fund Raising

One immediately faces several problems in attempting to characterize fund raising as a profession. The first is how to make some conceptual sense of the qualities just described. Some lack precision, while others are defined so exactly that they can be construed to be too narrow. Each needs to be explained in greater detail.

One must also decide how these qualities function in determining the professional. Some of the defining characteristics are historically

## Fund Raising as a Profession

descriptive, while some are current characteristics of professional status. As a group, they indicate the qualities that have come to be associated with professional groups over time.

Occupations become professions over time, and the profession's maturation can be plotted as points on a continuum. To the degree that a professional group possesses the qualities named above, it can be seen as a profession in a stronger or weaker sense as follows:

| (Weak) | | | | (Strong) |
|---|---|---|---|---|
| 1 | 2 | 3 | 4 | 5 |

An analysis of the qualities enumerated in the fund-raising profession will help us gain a sense of the strength of the professional identity of fund raisers.

- Being engaged in an essential and unique social service: 2.0
  The uniqueness of the fund-raising profession lies in the institutions and causes represented. These causes are important to a society and in that sense are "essential," but in a weak sense of that term. The skills and functions that are performed are particular to these institutions, but in themselves they are not unique: they are duplicated in many other occupational contexts.
- Possessing a high degree of specialized knowledge and the ability to apply that knowledge: 1.5
  The fund raiser possesses a set of important and particular skills but does not possess highly specialized knowledge. The knowledge is available to others and is generally acquired through experience or perhaps an "apprenticeship" with others who are senior in the field and have accumulated practical experience. This knowledge does not require extensive training for certification and licensing.
- Being part of a group that claims the right to regulate itself: 2.5
  The practical norms, rules, and laws that fund raisers use to conduct their practice are not particular to the fund-raising profession; nor are the moral norms of conduct unique to fund raisers. The codes of ethics, while providing a start to self-regulation, are not enforceable.
- Recognizing and affirming a code of ethics: 4.0

## Social and Moral Foundations

The proliferation of codes of ethics at individual institutions and within national professional societies is a healthy sign of the particularization of the fund-raising profession. It represents a desire to scrutinize one's own colleagues as well as to be able to be relied upon by the public to carry out the practices of the profession in a responsible manner. The codes that exist have primarily exhortative and persuasive power but little coercive power.

- Exhibiting strong self-discipline and accepting personal responsibility: 3.0
  Professional fund raisers and their professional associations exhibit a strong interest in their responsibilities. They are conscious that only by acting in a responsible manner and in being perceived as acting that way will fund raisers be successful in generating support for their causes. They are also aware that a degree of social approval can be gained from being known as ethical practitioners.

- Having a commitment to and a concern for communal interest: 3.5
  This quality stands out significantly in the assessment of professionals in fund raising. Fund raisers exhibit strong concern for their causes, which could be viewed cynically as narrow self-interest. However, the independent sector has structural commitments to the general welfare that are not tied to self-gain, so the commitments of fund raisers are primarily oriented to the public welfare. The causes to which nonprofits are committed can generally be construed as serving the public welfare, albeit in a very specific way.

- Being more concerned with services rendered than with financial rewards: 3.5
  Since most fund raisers are capable of earning far more in the private sector, they generally are not motivated by financial rewards. While the financial remuneration of fund raisers varies from organization to organization and within an organization, the pay scales of nonprofits are almost universally lower than those of the private sector.

The average of these marks is 2.85. Fund raising shows both strong and weak signs of being a profession but is becoming stronger. As the focus on training and articulation of standards by professional groups intensifies, fund raising is rapidly becoming a profession and is increasingly exhibiting stronger rather than weaker indicators of professionalization.

## The Ethical Significance of Professionalization: What Ought Fund Raisers to Do?

What is at stake in the definition of fund raising as a profession? When we describe fund raising as a profession, we make assumptions about what values we expect fund raisers to hold, we name the commitments and ideals that are to be encouraged, and we identify a particular group that contains a distinctive ethos. The ethos of fund raisers is one that supports certain kinds of activities and expects the realization of their "excellence," while it discourages practices that are deemed nonconstructive to the fund raisers' professional commitments.

From the previous analysis several norms or values emerge as central to the professional ethic of fund raising: a basic commitment of competency; the priority of communal over self-interest; the idea of service as the context for fund raising; the articulation of formalized codes of ethics; the importance of caring for the rights of others; trustworthiness as the basis for professional relationships; and concern for the larger social order.

*Competence.* At minimum, fund raisers must be proficient in what they do. They must know their institutions, their clients, and their various audiences well and be able to perform well the functions internal to fund raising. Competence is the very foundation for a fund-raising ethic.

*Communal over Self-Interest.* A professional ethic for fund raisers requires an understanding that the interests being served are not solely one's own but those of the institution for which one works, the client (typically the donor), or the profession itself. The historical tension between altruism and self-interest as the basis for professional identity, while it is clearly in transition in our modern economic times, must still be skewed toward performing services for the other.

## Social and Moral Foundations

*Service.* Service is a variation on the idea of communal over self-interest. When service becomes the dominant theme in a profession's identity, it provides the basis for cultivating activities that will enhance the general welfare of all parties concerned. For fund raisers in higher education, a consciousness of goals surfaces toward acting in the service of the advancement of education as manifested in a particular institution.

*Codes.* Some of the professional norms of the fund raiser are spelled out in the existing codes of professional ethics. While these codes certainly are not without some ambiguity, they represent a fair articulation of the values that fund raisers ought to uphold.

*Caring for the Rights of Others.* For fund raisers to care for others means that they must show a basic respect and regard for the rights and dignity of the many people with whom they relate. In general, they must always treat people (their multiple audiences) as ends in themselves rather than as means to an end.

*Trustworthiness.* Fund raising can flourish only when there is candor, openness, and truthfulness between the parties involved. Trustworthiness is a quality that is essential if fund-raising relationships are to be constructive. When fund raisers can be relied upon to be honest in communication and true to their word, an atmosphere of trust develops that enables the successful actualization of fund raising in higher education.

*Concern for the Larger Social Order.* Professionals should develop awareness of and concern for the advancement of the larger purposes of society, not just their own self-interests. In higher education this is achieved by advancing the "higher-order interests" of the educational institution. Fund raisers must develop a broad scope of concern for the advancement of higher education in general and understand the interests of their own institutions in light of these "larger" concerns. The values, expectations, and assumptions that constitute the fund raiser's professional ethic need to be made clear in order to determine whether they in fact represent qualities that are desirable, worthwhile, and constructive.

As fund raisers increasingly see themselves as members of a profession, they in turn establish a set of common values for those in the profession and distinguish the profession from other occupational groups. An adequate professional ethic will require an assessment of the norms of the particular professional ethos in relation to the norms of the larger social, economic, and political structure. This cross-analysis provides a way of correcting potential deceptions and distorted tendencies in any professional subcommunity.

Professional identity is valuable as a basis for understanding fund raising because the actual practices of the profession form the foundation for its ethic. This identity provides fund-raising practitioners with a means of understanding the source of norms and professional ideals and establishes a basis for their defense and justification. Comprehending the nature of being a professional is the first step to understanding fund-raising ethics.

# Areas of Concern

# 5

# Handling Prospect Research

## Mary Lou Siebert, Deni Elliott, and Marilyn Batt Dunn

Few topics have caused as much debate and discussion among fund raising professionals in higher education in the last few years as the activity called prospect research. The majority of development officers who must use or produce prospect research information are comfortable with the process and content, but occasionally they encounter situations in which they recognize a conflict between advancing their institution's goals and being sensitive to the privacy of individuals who support the institution financially. The overall goal of philanthropy is to foster a mutually beneficial relationship between worthy institutions and interested benefactors for the purpose of advancing the institutions' missions. Development officers are the professionals who serve as intermediaries in this relationship, garnering financial support for their institutions and overseeing stewardship and recognition activities directed toward donors.

This chapter is intended to increase awareness of ethical issues inherent in prospect research, which we identify as issues of privacy, confidentiality, and secrecy, and to recommend guidelines for making responsible decisions about research activities. We use hypothetical examples of ethical problems throughout the chapter. Some reflect the kinds of problems that come up routinely; others are meant to be exaggerated. The purpose of the latter examples is to illustrate what development officers as a professional group probably would agree is unethical behavior. Sometimes the point of ethics is to clarify what makes certain actions wrong rather than to present a single "right" answer.

Morality, at its core, is a system of rules and ideals for how people should treat one another. When an individual is being harmed, we have the makings of a moral problem. Privacy, confidentiality, and secrecy are moral considerations in prospect research because harm can be caused to prospects by

- the methods of collection;
- the information contained in files;
- the sharing of the collected information;
- the secrecy involved in the process.

Prospect research, sometimes known as donor or advancement research, generally is defined as the ongoing investigative and synthesizing process by which an institution identifies prospective contributors (individuals, corporations, foundations, or governmental agencies), assesses gift capacity and inclination, and explores a prospect's interests in order to motivate the prospect to contribute.[1] That information then is woven into an ever-changing tapestry that development officers use to create a philanthropic relationship between the institution and the potential contributor.

## The New Environment of Prospect Research

It is difficult, if not impossible, to pinpoint exactly where or when sophisticated prospect research activity began in the United States. Prospect research was initially done informally at private educational institutions. It may have been no more than a quick review of a file maintained by the chief development officer to recall the name of a prospect's spouse, basic information about family and business, and the prospect's gift and degree history. Sophisticated recordkeeping was more difficult before computer technology. Interactions between prospect and institution tended to have a highly personalized nature. Prospects were fewer in number, and they were generally known to development officers, who tended to be alumni themselves and, frequently, longtime university or college employees.

The fund-raising environment in which prospect research activities take place today is very different. Information technology is complex. More staff members, many of whom are not alumni, are involved with fund raising. Financial goals are larger, and the volume of prospects being cultivated for support also has increased. The institutional status and importance of prospect researchers have grown with pressures on development organizations to meet ambitious campaign goals and to compete with other nonprofit organizations, sometimes for the same prospects.

Increasingly, technological advances within institutional advancement are changing the nature of prospect research. A trend exists toward putting a scientific veneer on decision making about gift capacity. Development officers now have access to such large-scale resources as electronic geodemographic screening of prospect pools that try to predict giving behavior of individuals; profiles-on-demand from private firms that search centralized public records in order to produce profiles; on-line commercial databases that contain business information; and sophisticated prospect-tracking programs. These technological tools form a pyramid in which the bottom represents large-scale, impersonal information and the top represents the most specific information that can be found regarding an individual.

At the bottom of the pyramid are what are known as geodemographic screening systems, which are marketed by several fundraising consulting firms in the United States. Geodemographic are statistical analyses of where people live and what demographic characteristics they display, for example, their age, education, income, and spending habits. These systems enable institutions to compare their donor databases with geodemographic information supplied by consulting firms. From these broad "lifestyle" ratings an institution may discover its most affluent potential donors and then match them with institutional needs. The institution thus manipulates its own information about existing alumni and donors, but within a new structure.

Next up the pyramid are commercial electronic databases, such as DIALOG Information Services, containing prospect research information that is accessible by anyone with the appropriate computer tools. Information potentially found includes addresses, phone numbers, occupations, salaries, and stock holdings of officers of publicly held corporations, as well as records of real estate property ownership.

At the top of the pyramid are prospect research profiles-on-demand, based on public records and produced for a flat fee by some consulting firms. The third-party aspects of such services set them apart from the usual prospect research activities, conducted internally by institutions. In addition, an institution can now purchase computer software to track progress in soliciting prospects. Such software enables the internal tracking of practically thousands of prospects, including dates of events and meetings, staff and volunteer assignments, wealth ratings, and anecdotal comments about relationship-building, or "cultivation," activities. This software is different from the pyramid in that it does not provide new information. However, by comparison and compilation, new understandings can be derived from existing material.

Prospect research is intended to help an institution focus its efforts on contributors who may be inclined to give an appropriate amount of money at the best time for both contributor and institution. Decisions constantly must be made regarding what information to acquire and what to retain. Once the information has been acquired and retained, the moral question concerns how access to it can be controlled to preserve confidentiality. The question is not new; the new technology only makes potential problems more obvious.

## The Collection of Information: A Problem of Privacy

The first group of ethical issues inherent in prospect research relate to how material is collected and what material is retained in research files. Philosopher Sissela Bok defines the concept of privacy as the "condition of being protected from unwanted access by others—either physical access, personal information or attention."[2] How prospects define unwanted attention or access to personal information will vary. This is what makes prospect research work so sensitive. Some prospects may even expect the institution to "do its homework" before cultivating them. Other prospects may be quite offended if the information retained about them comprises more than degree, gift, and address.[3] Realizing that prospects exist at both extremes does not change the need for the research office to set its own limitations.

For example, everyone would agree that it would be immoral for a development officer to bribe a prospect's psychiatrist for information that might help influence the prospect to make a donation. On the other hand, everyone also would agree that no ethical problem is presented by a development officer's asking, "Who else in your class do you think we ought to contact?" The latter instance presents no ethical problem because the donor decides whether and upon what basis to respond.

What makes the first instance immoral is that if the development officer is successful, he or she deprives the prospect of the privacy expected in confidential relationships and causes harm by using the prospect's psychiatric status in a way that the prospect did not authorize. Even if the development officer is not successful, he or she has violated social expectations in the act of trying. We certainly do not want doctors, lawyers, or others with whom we have confidential relationships to disclose our secrets. Nor do we want other groups in society to even attempt to persuade, let alone pressure, our fiduciaries to reveal those secrets.

This exercise of deciding what clearly is in the scope of acceptable behavior and what is not also can help clarify what justifies unusual actions. If we trace our outrage at the hypothetical development officer who thinks it appropriate to bribe psychiatrists, we find that two tests for justification emerge. Usually the tests give the same result. First, what is the societal consequence of allowing this kind of action? If damage to societal trust is likely to result from the action, it is very difficult to justify. Second, would the development officer be willing to publicly disclose his or her actions? Since morality is a public system, basically a system of rules for how people ought to act in regard to one another, exceptions to the rules need to be public as well.

We allow physicians an exception to the rule "Don't cause pain," magicians an exception to the rule "Don't deceive," and judges an exception to the rule "Don't deprive of freedom." Although these exceptions have different justifications, they are publicly known and accepted. A final test for any questionable action is, "Would you be willing for your process to be known publicly?"

Let us take a look at a dilemma that is closer to the situations that development officers usually face. No development officer is going to bribe a psychiatrist to further prospect research, but how about asking psychiatrists, lawyers, accountants, bankers, and other fiduciaries to serve on screening committees? In many cases clients will not be among those screened, but sometimes they will. Does the development officer have a moral obligation to avoid those conflicts or to include a clear statement that the professional *ought not* to comment on any person with whom he or she has a confidential relationship?

Let us apply the tests: Is the development officer engaged in conduct that has the potential for damaging societal trust? Probably not, as long as the inclusion of fiduciaries on a screening committee is accidental. What about the test of public disclosure? How would the community of prospects be likely to respond if they knew that their fiduciaries were among those on the screening committee? They would probably feel best about it if it were clear that the development officer had done everything in his or her power to protect against the disclosure of confidential information. A clear request for nondisclosure in such instances is not likely to cost the development officer anything and will make the institutions' intentions clear. The researcher wants information but does not want anyone to do anything unethical in disclosing it.

## The Content of Research Files: Another Problem of Privacy

What are the limitations on what can ethically be included in a research file? Informal information acquired and retained from volunteer and staff contact with prospects is most problematic. The challenge is to retain relevant information without including information that might harm or embarrass the prospect.

Let us assume, for example, that a volunteer mentions to a development officer that a prospect (a peer of the volunteer) has "deep pockets and short arms" when it comes to contributing money. That comment is then recorded verbatim in a contact report by the development officer and sent to the prospect research office. Let us apply the test: First, retaining such information would damage trust in that the prospect would feel that his relationship with his classmate has been misused. Second, the inclusion of such offensive statements could not withstand public scrutiny. The development office would not want to publicly explain retaining such information. The prospect research manager should ask the development officer to rewrite the comment. The revised text, "volunteer feels prospect may not be philanthropically inclined at this time," can relate the relevant information while maintaining respect for the prospect. The same decision path could be followed in other instances in which the content of nonpublic information is questionable but potentially relevant to the philanthropic relationship between prospect and institution.

In a somewhat different but related example of sensitive information from a nonfiduciary source about a prospect, a development officer has dinner with an elderly prospect who has put the institution in his will. The resulting file memo about the dinner discusses at length the prospect's rambling conversation and confused state of mind. The author's tone is patronizing. The development officer ends the memo by diagnosing the prospect as suffering from Alzheimer's disease and recommending no further personal cultivation, because it is "frustrating and unproductive."

Once again the research manager must decide whether such information is factual and, if so, relevant. Without a direct call to the prospect's physician or family, it would be hard to verify a medical condition. Yet the recommendation not to spend the institution's time and money on further cultivation possibly is well-founded. The ethical approach is to include what is relevant in a way that both maintains public trust and withstands public scrutiny. The research manager could ask the development officer to delete the subjective information about the prospect's mental state and tone down the recommendation to a statement such as "further personal contact with prospect probably would not be productive."

Another key to achieving acceptable ethical standards regarding the content and relevancy of prospect research information is to avoid documenting or verbally spreading information that could be merely gossip. This is more easily said than done, since almost everyone engages in some form of gossip occasionally. Sissela Bok defines gossip as having four elements: "It is 1.) informal 2.) personal communication 3.) about persons who 4.) are absent or excluded." She also differentiates between harmless or supportive gossip and speculative, degrading, or invasive talk that harms the privacy of a person.[4]

If two development officers are chatting about a prospect and one says, "I hear Barbara is a fantastic tennis player," that is an example of harmless, unimportant gossip. However, if the comment is, "I hear Barbara doesn't give a darn about her kids, and my friend, who is her neighbor, says she has huge credit card debts," that obviously is invasive, speculative gossip and should not be recorded in the file.

Even information that is part of the public record can be problematic. For example, having in one's research files a copy of a prospect's messy divorce settlement found in court records is defensible, since it already is public information, but it may have little cultivation worth. In addition, serious disruption of development relationships may result if prospects know such information is included in their files.

Again, it is helpful to separate some actions that clearly are acceptable from some that are not. Everyone would agree that it is appropriate to include in the research file a newspaper clipping about a prospect's business venture. Everyone would also agree that it is not appropriate to include sensitive nonpublic information about a prospect's family. Sensitive family information, such as being married to a philandering spouse, represents an intimate part of the prospect's life that ought not to be used without permission, even if it is helpful in figuring out how to present a funding opportunity. Use of such information violates the privacy of both prospect and spouse.

Some forms of communication need to be protected except in extraordinary circumstances. A societal need to understand the mind and life of some great thinker or notorious criminal may override protection of intimate information, but the desire to encourage philanthropic behavior is not compelling in the same way. Again, the idea of public disclosure applies in situations like this. The public approves of the collection and dissemination of morally obtained intimate information in the cases of published biography; however, there would likely be a public outcry if it became known that everyone's college development office housed such personal information. Retaining intimate information about individuals without their knowledge and consent, with the intention of using it without their direct knowledge, deprives them of freedom.

Now, we assume that people generally can gain certain information about us, such as our physical appearance, address, phone number, car, and so on. It takes little sophistication to realize that in some ways other people know more about us than we know ourselves, for example, our unconscious mannerisms. Personal knowledge is different from information that is collected, printed, and disseminated to others. The prospect who shares information willingly with the development officer who he thinks is a trusted friend might well feel differently about the information residing in his research file. The knowledge that he has been the subject of a systematic collection of information, whether from the public record or personal recollection, may well be troubling to the prospect. He may feel violated, harmed and deprived of freedom.

Applying the tests for justification can help development officers decide which information it is acceptable to retain in the file: Does the development office damage societal trust by holding the information? Probably not, so long as the information has been collected from public sources. If, however, observations by purported friends have been included, damage to the friendship might result. What about public disclosure? The more secretive the process, the more vulnerable the target of investigation. What the development office is willing to retain should be identical to what the development office is willing to publicly admit to holding.

## Confidentiality: The Control of Information

According to Bok, confidentiality means guarding access to the information on a prospect that is already known and deemed acceptable to keep.[5] The effort to keep information confidential often is complicated by the scattering and fragmenting of information beyond centralized prospect research files among different offices within the institution. Information also is stored and transmitted in many different formats, such as written, electronic, microfiche, and fax.

Let us assume, for example, that a major prospect's son or daughter is severely ill with AIDS and that the family does not want this information to be publicly known. The information is shared orally with the prospect research manager, but in order to protect the family's privacy, it is not written down or stored electronically. Later, a copy of the obituary mentioning the cause of death is placed in the prospect's hard-copy file, so that a public record is available for future reference when cultivating the prospect. In this way, the confidentiality of private information is maintained until it becomes part of the public record.

A second point of confidentiality is the distribution of information held by the development office. Most development officers would agree that a prospect's file may be shared among senior development officers. Most development officers would also agree that it should not be sold to a commercial enterprise. There are many possibilities in between. What can development officers do with the information? What would they be willing to disclose publicly? The answer to this second question can be found in the intent behind the collection of information. Information about prospects is collected to further the relationship between the institution and the individual. Any other use of the information without explicit permission of the prospect is misuse.

## Secrecy: Who Knows What about Prospect Research

The major stumbling block in ethical considerations relating to prospect research often seems to be public disclosure. There are no examples in the literature of institutions that have communicated openly the presence of research activities and offered to reveal to prospective donors the contents of their files; however, some academic and media representatives have suggested that institutions should do just that.

All systems of morality are dependent upon the players' knowing the rules. Secrecy can be tolerated in some cases in even the most open society, but the scope of agreeable secrecy must at least be acknowledged to all concerned. Secrecy in government provides a good example. Some information collected by the government is open; some is not. Individuals may not be able to access that information, whether it be a defense strategy or notes concerning the individual's own security check—but they know the arena of secrecy and can check into the safeguards that protect that information.

It is important to public trust that university development officers offer the public no less than the government in this regard. The existence of prospect researchers and research files should not be concealed. For example, an institution's prospect research director should be introduced to volunteers as exactly that, rather than vaguely as a "development staff member." It is in the institution's best interest to be open about the existence of researchers and files; however, the institution can still exercise professional discretion in revealing the exact content of the files. For instance, a prospect's lecherous behavior with development officers can be noted neutrally in a file for future reference as follows: "Development officers or volunteers are encouraged to speak to the Director of Prospect Research or the Vice President for Development before contacting this prospect."

Ethical collection and use of information concerning donor prospects correlates with the hypothetical test of what the development office would be willing to disclose publicly. Many of the ethical difficulties relating to prospect research could be solved with a true test of public disclosure. Colleges and universities could take the initiative to inform donors about the prospect research process.

## Suggested Guidelines for Prospect Research

Guidelines for acceptable handling of prospect research will vary among development offices. Reasonable individuals at different institutions can disagree. We offer the following guidelines for development offices concerned with holding high ethical standards for information collection and use:

- Establish written prospect research guidelines that are supported by top management and communicated to all staff and volunteers. Such guidelines encourage responsible decision making and set content and access boundaries. Ideally, guidelines would be communicated to new development staff as part of their training and reviewed with all development staff annually.
- Periodically review prospect files to make sure information is both current and relevant. In line with the institution's overall policy for records management, old or irrelevant file information should be shredded or deleted.
- With the institution's public relations office, develop a plan for responding to inquiries from prospects, volunteers, and the press about files or research activity. The purpose of such a plan is to inform and reassure the public that only relevant information from public records and carefully chosen internal sources will be gathered, retained, and disseminated on a prospect. The institution's president, chief development officer, chief public relations officer, and prospect research director all should be involved in developing the plan and should be supportive of the final product. The three main components of the plan would be:
  a. *A written prospect research ethics policy statement* signed by the

chief development officer. For example: "[Institution's name] strongly believes in protecting the privacy of our philanthropic supporters and the confidentiality of information concerning them. It is our policy to abide by specific written guidelines for handling prospect research activities in an ethical way. These guidelines are available upon request from the chief development officer. Individuals who wish to review the contents of their own paper or electronic development files may do so following a request to the chief development officer."

b. *Written guidelines* appropriate to the institution.

c. *Specific steps to handle inquiries from prospects.* For example: "After reviewing written policy and guidelines, if the prospect wants to see his or her own file, the chief development officer notifies the prospect research staff; the prospect reviews materials in the presence of a senior development officer who can explain material as appropriate or comply with requests to delete information."

- Prohibit deceptive techniques regarding prospect research.

It would be unethical, for example, to keep a "viewable" set of prospect records in one place and second, secret set somewhere else. It also would be unacceptable for researchers to attempt to obtain public records information without revealing the institution's identity. Being honest about prospect research activities ensures accountability and responsibility.[6]

The Council For Advancement and Support of Education (CASE) and the American Prospect Research Association (APRA) have also produced guidelines for ethical prospect research. The extant guidelines—the prospect's right to privacy, the principle of information relevancy, maintaining the confidentiality of prospect information, restricted sharing of information with another institution, and not revealing prospect information learned at one institution when changing jobs—reinforce what we have discussed above.[7]

Above and beyond institutional and professional association guidelines, individual moral judgment inevitably will be required to protect prospect privacy and further worthwhile institutional advancement goals. Even with guidelines, prospect research still comprises more art than science. However, by planning ahead rather than waiting until a crisis occurs, the institution may minimize potential distrust. If institutions responsibly administer prospect research programs, regulation by other agencies may be avoided. It is in the fund-raising profession's enlightened self-interest to regulate itself and maintain control over the legitimate processes by which higher education institutions raise private money.

Finally, as Michael J. Worth noted in a June 1991 article in the journal *Fund Raising Management,* ethical prospect research activities and guidelines can enhance greatly the relationship between an institution and a prospective donor by providing realistic, relevant information and by building trust between the two parties.[8] Trust is the foundation for all good relationships.

# 6

# Fund Raising and Friend Raising: Institution-Donor Relationships

### Judith M. Gooch

This chapter deals with the ethical issues that surface in regard to relationships between the institution, personified by the development officer and other institutional representatives, and its current or potential philanthropic supporters. It focuses on the potential or actual "major donor" because this person is most likely to be engaged in an ongoing face-to-face relationship with representatives from the college or university. However, elements of these same issues are present in any attempt by institutional representatives to seek philanthropic support, whether by form or personal letter, phonathon, or any other means.

I discuss the inherent conflict between representing an organization dedicated to the service of humanity to those who are acting out of concern for others' welfare (philanthropically) and the fact that by doing so development officers are acting in their own self-interest (earning money for doing so). And I clarify the institutional representative's responsibilities to the individual who may support the institution, including the difference in the relationship between donors and volunteers and between donors and development officers.

Tight budgets, megacampaigns, and increasing financial demands place considerable pressure on those raising funds to get the largest possible commitments. But in the long run, getting the money, or taking the money through dubious or unethical behavior, will exact penalties. Unethical behavior may adversely affect individual fund raisers, corrupting their judgment and destroying their sense of self-respect; it will certainly affect the institutions they serve. By destroying people's trust in an institution's integrity, it will destroy the institution's long-term ability to attract the philanthropic dollars it must have in order to prosper.

## Fund Raising and Friend Raising

All sorts of people associated with the college or university—the president, members of the board and other volunteers, members of the faculty and staff—become involved in obtaining gifts from individuals and organizations. "Prospects" may be alumni or alumnae or members of their families, parents of current students, neighbors or others with reason to feel some sense of connection to the institution, or organizations with an interest in the college or university's programs and purposes. Each person or group will have a slightly different relationship with the institution, but all relationships are based on interactions between individuals. When fund raisers say, "People give to people," they are saying, on the one hand, that one person asking another person directly for a gift is a successful fund-raising technique. They are also alluding to the fact that although the gift may be designated for the English department, for example, its donor has been strongly influenced by a person or persons connected with the department or the subject. The influence is not necessarily that of the individual who asks for the gift, but may be that of those who taught or befriended or inspired admiration in or otherwise affected the donor.

The task of the development officers is to facilitate the relationships between actual or potential donors and the institution. Their goal is to motivate the prospects to make gifts to the institution. But only some means to the end are ethical; for example, it is morally prohibited for fund raisers to deceive prospective donors.

It is morally required that fund raisers do their job, that is, that they raise money for the college or university without causing harm to themselves, their institution, or their prospects. This implies that fund raisers become knowledgeable about their institution as well as skillful in their approach. The process may include arranging meetings between the prospect and faculty, students, volunteers, or other staff members; arranging tours; writing letters and supplying written materials and other forms of prepared information; and generally educating the prospect about the institution's strengths and needs. This presents the first ethical challenge: how does one put forward information that will cause prospects' sense of connection with the institution to grow without allowing them to develop a false or distorted picture of the institution?

Imagine a situation in which the prospect is a man who majored in economics and started his own highly successful biotechnology company. He is grateful for the fine education he received and appears to be a good prospect to fund an endowed junior chair in economics. He is also an ardent "protectionist," especially vocal about America's need to legislate against Asian competition. The economics department is about to announce the appointment of a new faculty member who is well known for his views on the necessity of avoiding protectionist measures and reforming American industry to compete better with international companies. Does the development officer have a duty to tell the prospective donor that the department is about to hire a professor whose views directly contradict his own? The question is clearly one of deception. This information is relevant to the donor's decision to make, or not to make, the gift. Pragmatically speaking, this kind of information is probably impossible to hide, but that is not the point. Fund raisers have an obligation to give donors information that the fund raisers have reason to believe they would consider relevant. Otherwise, the donation is a product of trickery rather than of a trusting relationship.

For the development officer, one of the easiest ways to make sure that the information he or she conveys to prospects and donors is honest is to participate on a regular basis in campus activities. Spending time with faculty and students, attending campus events, and reading everything from the newest faculty book to the student newspaper will help members of the development staff remember what their jobs are all about. Through such contacts the development officer can also identify faculty and students who might be asked to meet with the donor. Such meetings should be arranged whenever possible, and the importance of contacts between the donor and faculty and students should be emphasized in an institution's fund-raising policy. Not only are such contacts the best possible means of educating donors and making them feel close to the institution but a focus on facilitating this sort of contact helps development officers maintain the appropriate understanding of their own roles.

The development officer often serves as gatekeeper and interpreter to the prospect, and this can pose some ethical issues as well. It is natural for someone to need "a place to start" in making inquiries about a puzzling situation, or trying to get certain information. Suppose an alumna, a major donor, is approached by a friend whose child has applied for admission to the university. The friend asks

## Fund Raising and Friend Raising

whether the alumna can find out how the child is doing in the admissions process. The donor is likely to call her closest contact, the development officer. The development officer may be faced with a tricky situation. If the institution has a policy forbidding release of any admissions information prior to the official notification date, it would be clearly unethical for the development officer to obtain and pass along information about the candidate. So the development officer is ethically bound to refuse the request, citing the policy. Competent development officers will also help donors understand the necessity for the policy and will be able to convey this information to donors without embarrassing or annoying either party.

The development officer's job (and that of the volunteer or any other institutional representative) is infinitely easier if the institution has established and enforces policies about matters such as this and makes no exceptions for VIPs, alumnae, or others it is trying to court or to avoid annoying. Those policies should be clear, comprehensive, openly discussed, and consistently applied. Neither the development officer nor any other individual involved in fund raising should promise or imply, or be able to promise or imply, that a particular donor will receive special favors; all million-dollar donors, for example, should be treated in similar fashion. The word always gets out; if exceptions are made for some, others will expect special treatment too.

Policies should also be sensible. Several years ago a wealthy couple asked a major university what benefits they would get for a gift of five hundred thousand dollars. They were informed that they would be given the title of officers of the university, library privileges, and positions on two advisory committees. When this information became public, people were outraged. These benefits contradict the basic premise of philanthropy, namely, that it is for the benefit of others, not oneself. A gift is not a purchase.

Everyone representing the institution needs to be familiar with all such policies and the reasons for them, whether they concern admissions, graduation requirements, financial aid, tenure decisions, the acceptance of gifts, tickets to football game, or parking privileges. In addition, staff and volunteers need to know where to turn when the prospect or donor becomes unbearably insistent. Those at the top should be ready and willing to take a firm stand and to back their staff.

Is any compromise possible? Of course. A good fund raiser should have the capacity to listen creatively—to try to find some sort of institutional match for the donor's interest. It is often possible to accomplish this, though it can be extremely time-consuming. One liberal arts college now has a chair in entrepreneurship; in lengthy discussions with the president and the dean, the definition of *entrepreneur* evolved from the donor's original business management orientation to a multidisciplinary concept that has supported a physicist who pioneered in the field of holography and others with no profit-making affiliations whatsoever.

But donors' wishes should never be the tail wagging the dog. Some years ago a major research institution was approached by an extremely wealthy individual who offered to supply the funds to establish a medical school. However, the institution declined the gift after careful deliberation, since its board did not think that a medical school would meld with the basic mission of the institution.

Telling the truth about the institution is not often difficult. But what about the development officer's relationship with the donor or prospect? What is the truth of that, and what sorts of disclosure rules should be in force? The development officer usually spends a substantial amount of time getting to know the prospect and in turn becoming known by the prospect. They may have meals together or take trips together. The development officer may escort the donor to "social" functions arranged by the university, and the prospect may provide hospitality to the development officer. They may do many of the kinds of things that friends do together. They may enjoy each other's company. They are often friendly; but as long as the development officer is being paid to "cultivate" the prospect, they are not friends.

Friends are people who are bound together by affection or esteem. While development officers and prospects or donors may indeed feel both emotions toward each other, the fact remains that as long as development officers are working for the university they are under obligation to *use* the relationship with their prospect for the benefit of the institution. The primary loyalty of development officers in the relationship is thus not to prospects but to their employers. Development officers must not abuse their connections with prospects by lying or by failing to disclose pertinent information, but even more than that, they have an obligation to make sure that the donor understands the relationship in the same way that the institution and the development officer understand it. To allow the prospect to think anything else would be deceptive and therefore unethical.

If development officers have made it clear from the beginning that they represent the institution, the prospect is much less likely to expect the development officer to become the his or her advocate. Development officers act as facilitators, as go-betweens; if and when they advocate, they plead the case of their employer, the college or university. This is not friendship but a professional relationship. Although there may be mutual liking and there should always be mutual respect, the development officer is paying attention to the prospect so that the prospect will respond favorably to a request for money. The development officer must therefore behave as a professional, not as a friend. This might require the tactful refusal of symphony tickets (though the development officer could suggest that music faculty or students would enjoy using them) or the use of a vacation home, a gift, or a personal favor.

Under no circumstances should the development officer allow relationships to develop in such a way as to lead the prospect to leave money to the development officer in his or her will or to name the development officer executor of the prospect's estate, to cite two recent occurrences. Should the donor make some such a designation, it is incumbent on the development officer to refuse to accept it. Even if the development made no attempt whatsoever to seek such a connection, the development officer and the institution must be aware of how others could regard such actions. The appearance of ethical behavior is as important as the behavior itself, since the reputations of the institution and the individual can be easily tarnished. Regardless of the facts, a development officer will appears to have abused the institution by using an employer-mandated relationship for personal gain. In addition, it could be inferred that the development officer deflected the deceased's interest from the institution, abusing the prospect's trust.

It can be extremely difficult for the development officer to maintain a clear sense of what constitutes a professional, ethical relationship. Over a number of years development officers may come to know some donors extremely well. But they should not allow donors to treat them as confidantes or advisers. With tact, but with firmness, they must remind donors that their primary loyalty is to their employers. They must be forthright if the donor begins to share personal information that they suspect the donor would not like to have repeated: "You must realize, Emily, that I'm always acting as the college's ears. I wish you wouldn't share this with me unless you mean for me to relay it to the president," or something similar, would be appropriate. It is up to the development officer to disallow the possibility of deception.

It is easy to see that development officers should not become sexually involved with prospects or donors. But where does pleasant conversation become flirtation, the beginning of seduction—or sexual harassment? Neither the development officer nor the prospect should use sex as a tool; it is not an appropriate part of the relationship. While development officers can and should monitor their own conduct, they cannot control the feelings or, usually, the actions of the prospect. But they can make sure that contacts with the donor take place over lunch in a public restaurant rather than drinks at the prospect's home, that when a discussion turns intimate the subject is rapidly changed. Others can be included in all meetings and gatherings. If necessary, the development officer can ask that someone else assume primary responsibility for dealing with the prospect, and the institutional climate should be such that such a request is taken seriously, is handled responsibly, and does not penalize the development officer.

Maintaining an unambiguously professional distance and avoiding the unethical abuse of a relationship is easier if the development officer is able to minimize 'friendlike' interactions with the prospect while still drawing the prospect closer to the institution. The development officer can do this by setting up meetings or gatherings for prospects with faculty, students, and staff connected with the ongoing work of the institution rather than by undertaking all cultivation activities herself. But today more than ever development officers are expected to 'be a friend' to the prospect, not just to develop the strategy that engages the prospect's interest but to pursue the personal contacts deemed necessary to bring the prospect to the point of making a contribution. Additionally, a number of institutions are moving from a volunteer-based gift solicitation program to staff solicitation programs, making a close relationship between prospect and development officer apparently more desirable than ever.

## Fund Raising and Friend Raising

When the development officer is expected to ask for the gift in addition to building the relationship to a point where a request is appropriate, there are some additional ethical concerns. Prospects should be able to respond to requests in a professional manner, saying yes or no based on their own circumstances and inclinations, the latter determined by how they feel about the institution and its needs. However, the right solicitor is often defined as the person the prospect cannot turn down. The prospect is perceived as responding to the request because of the influence of the person who makes it, not because of the prospect's interest in a particular aspect of the cause. This argues against identifying the solicitor as an openly professional instrument of the organization; anyone can certainly turn down a request or an opportunity offered by someone whose job it is to offer such opportunities without taking the personal relationship with that individual into account. If the development officer has been honest about the relationship, then he or she is unlikely to have the personal influence with the prospect to ensure a major gift.

Through the years the most successful solicitors have generally been the prospects' "peers," individuals with a good deal in common with those they solicit. The commonalities include those of propinquity (classmates, neighbors, parents of children who were undergraduates at the same time, fellow board members) as well as those of similar giving capacity. Someone who can give ten thousand dollars is better suited to ask someone else for that amount than someone who can only give one hundred dollars. In addition, there are various factors of clout: the solicitor should be perceived as knowledgeable about the cause, able to make things happen (to make sure that the donor's gift makes a difference, a key motivation for giving), committed (measured by the solicitor's own financial contribution plus the voluntary commitment of time), sincere, trustworthy, and respected by the prospect. An effective solicitor is also perceived as a philanthropist, someone who acts selflessly, supporting the cause for reasons other than personal material reward.

The development officer simply cannot be as effective a solicitor as a volunteer. Few development officers share the financial capacity of major gift prospects, and their commitment to the institution is measured at least in part, and usually in large part, by a paycheck rather than volunteered time. Thus, they are acting out of self-interest, not humanitarianism. They would not be doing what they are doing if they were not getting paid. They care about it because of what the cause is worth to them, not because of the worth of the cause. Yet they are asking the prospect to respond as a humanitarian. Thus the prospect and the development officer are inherently dissimilar. If the development officer tries to act as a peer in articulating the argument for the prospect's support, he or she can be readily perceived as deceptive. It is not that friends cannot solicit friends: they can and do. But the basis of the relationship between the development officer and the prospect is not friendship; nor do they share a perspective of concern. This weakens the force of any appeal from the development officer.

In addition, development officers may be able to describe the way in which someone's contribution will make a difference to the college or university, but they cannot guarantee that it will do so. The fundraising function does not set policy in regard to academic and related activities; it finds the money to make these things possible after the bodies responsible for governance have determined what the needs are. Few development officers are in a position to commit the institution to a particular course of action or even to accept a gift officially. They may be staff for the board of trustees, and the chief development officer may be a trusted member of the president's top advisory group, but they are rarely officers of the college. The development officer is staff, not management.

Colleges and universities are increasingly trying to get around the inherent weakness of the paid professional solicitor by turning to a more businesslike approach—comparing development to marketing is a current trend—and by urging development staff to do a better job of taking on what has traditionally been the job of the solicitor. The first method is not unethical, though it is possibly unproductive; the latter is both unethical and probably unproductive in the long run. The largest gifts come from people who are convinced of the rightness of the cause *and* care very deeply about it—a combination of intellectual and emotional commitment. The development officer can stimulate the former but not the latter.

Attempting to find a solicitor to whom the prospect cannot say no brings up another set of ethical concerns. Where is the line between encouraging potential donors to make contributions and trying to force them to do so? We would all agree that it would be wrong to blackmail someone into becoming a donor. But how far should solicitors go in using what they know of their prospects to push the right buttons? Just as it is unethical for development officers to gather certain sorts of information about people because doing so violates their privacy, it is also unethical for them to use confidential information to persuade people to give. It is a clear signal to prospects that their privacy has been violated and, further, that the institution is responsible for the violation. By using the confidential information, institutional representatives demonstrate that they are not to be trusted, which throws the possibility of a good relationship with the prospect into doubt.

Even though the institution has policies about collecting and storing information about prospects, the development officer who prepares, or oversees preparation of, briefing material for solicitors should double-check to be certain that there are no references to information that would embarrass prospects or lead them to conclude that the institution knows about things they would prefer to keep confidential. Development officers are sometimes instructed to convey verbal warnings to solicitors; indeed, many times confidential information is sought and kept on the grounds that it will help those involved in cultivation and solicitation deal tactfully with sensitive issues. Staff are also often concerned about fully preparing the solicitor, especially if it is the president or a member of the board. For the most part this concern is unnecessary and may in fact lead to unethical abuse of privacy. The solicitor who brings up a sore subject may see some fireworks, but at least the institution is cleared of any appearance of improper knowledge. If the topic is sad—an impending divorce, a child with AIDS—the solicitor's sincere apology, "Oh, I had no idea! I'm so sorry," should reassure the prospect about the college's handling of confidential matters and may provide an opportunity for the prospect to share a heavy burden with a compassionate listener.

Volunteers also face a separate issue: how to use, or avoid using, other aspects of their relationships with their prospects. It is one thing to refer to shared college experiences. Is it ethical to refer to social, religious, political, or other ties? What if the solicitor is on the admissions board of the country club that the prospect wants to join? There are also professional connections to consider. Is it ethical for a trust officer to solicit a client, even if they were in the same college class? What about a lawyer, or a doctor, soliciting current or former clients or patients? What about having the boss solicit his or her employees, or the board chairman solicit the faculty?

The principle here is that making a gift should not be able to be perceived as something on which the continued relationship of the people involved depends. This is easier in a relationship of equals than in a relationship in which one party clearly depends on the good will, the services, or the continued patronage of the other. Classmates and other alumni can certainly solicit each other based on their shared college experiences. That relationship is clean; that is, it is not complicated by additional personal or professional ties or hierarchical relationships. And personal or professional ties between solicitor and prospect are not automatically wrong. Such mutual knowledge may well have led to mutual trust and respect, and the solicitation will proceed as it should. But when the solicitor is one who can affect other aspects of the prospect's life (e.g., as an employer, counselor, doctor, religious leader), the solicitor clearly has the power to exert unfair—and unethical—pressure on the prospect. One of the responsibilities of the development officer is to be alert to such possibilities and to arrange for a solicitor without ties that the prospect might perceive as threatening.

There are other types of pressure. Sometimes solicitors refer to this directly: "Joe owes me one, so let me talk to him about the annual fund." It is not unethical for a solicitor to ask someone who approached him for a donation to another cause to support his cause in return. However, in the long run this form of leverage is likely to be less productive from the institution's point of view than an effort to get Joe more involved with the institution. Joe should not give just because Fred asks him to do so; he should give because he cares about the institution *and* he is asked.

Appealing to the prospect's sense of obligation, old school ties, guilt, or other emotional rather than rational motivations is ethically doubtful for a development officer. The prospect can easily perceive it as an attempt to manipulate. It is also deceptive. An emotional appeal works when the prospect feels that the solicitor is sincere, and part of the reason the prospect believes that the solicitor is sincere is that the solicitor appears to share the emotion. A fellow alumnus, the parents of a current student, board members, and other key volunteers, even the president, can use the emotional appeal in addition to or instead of the intellectual approach and be believed because they share with the prospect other connections to the institution. They speak with the authority of experience—often experience shared with the prospect—about those ties and how a gift could enhance the institution they both care about.

There is an inherent falsehood in the emotional appeal when it comes from someone paid to make it. Even if both solicitor and prospect are classmates, the fact that the solicitor stands to benefit from the prospect's gift, even though not directly, sours this form of approach. In using the language of business—speaking of the gift as an investment, for example—the solicitor is being open and honest. But because it is indeed a business for development officers, they must be careful not to assume to share, or necessarily to understand, the prospect's emotional bonds to the institution. Development officers may surely assume that there are emotional aspects to making a gift, and may speak of others' joy in giving or sense of obligation met. They may also be pleased for the donor, but they should take care in expressing this. Such statements as "Mr. and Mrs. Smith have been very pleased with the way their chair has helped attract such capable young faculty" or "I'm delighted you've decided to support the scholarship fund; it will help so many future students" are fine. "Your gift gives me such personal pleasure," may lead the donor to think that the development officer's raise was contingent on the success of this solicitation.

Good development officers have an inherent respect for others that frames every relationship in which they are involved. In the course of exercising their profession, development officers demonstrate this respect inside as well as outside the institution. In the development office, integrity shows in staff attitudes toward prospects. All too many development people share a tendency to ridicule prospects—to laugh at names, to joke about personal matters, to react with scorn to a gift that is smaller than hoped for. Such attitudes are usually defensive. Prospects have the power to make the development effort succeed or fail, so development staff members try to redress the imbalance by cutting them down to size. But defensive attitudes can produce a climate in which unethical behavior is sanctioned, because staff members feel as though the prospect deserves it.

*Areas of Concern*

A crucial task of the chief development officer is to build and maintain an atmosphere in which such attitudes are unthinkable and unethical conduct, if it takes place, is quickly recognized and corrected. One of the key methods is to establish regular and frequent contact between development staff at all levels and people who are or may become supporters of the college or university. Such contact helps staff members (and supporters) see each other as human beings with a mutual interest in the college or university. It is easy to depersonalize someone you have never met or have viewed at a distance during some major gathering. Give everyone the opportunity to hand out nametags, host tables, serve as escorts, hear the alumni panel discuss careers in computing, and so forth. Like mingling with faculty and students, mingling with donors will give development staff a greater understanding of the purpose of their tasks, greater sensitivity to their part in the whole of the university, and an awareness that these wealthy individuals are people too.

Sometimes a bad attitude toward prospects is rooted in an individual's negative feelings about wealthy people. Few members of any development staff have the financial resources of most of their prospects. To spend one's working hours examining the lives of the rich, perhaps visiting them on location and seeing how they live, as many development officers do, can evoke feelings of envy. In addition, the development officer is quite likely to encounter some wealthy folk whose attitudes say "We're great because we have money (and those who don't have money aren't great)." Coupled with exposure to lifestyles of the wealthy is often exposure to the opposite, academic attitude that wealth is unimportant or even A Bad Thing. (This belief does not hinder most on campus, however, from wanting what the gifts of the wealthy can buy.) At worst, the development officer is caught between on-campus hypocrisy and off-campus elitism, and it takes a deep-seated maturity to maintain an emotional balance and sense of perspective. One of the responsibilities of chief development officers is to be alert to comments that signal emotional difficulties regarding wealthy donors among their staff members and to address the issue of haves and have-nots directly.

Ethical relationships with donors cannot be built by the development officer alone. They require an institutionwide awareness of why fund raising is necessary and general agreement on the need for support. They require, as well, the willing participation of many people on campus, all of whom should be aware to some degree of the ethical issues. There should be a clear policy in regard to fund-raising interactions and regular discussion of its implications as they affect the activities of the group discussing them. In addition, throughout the campus and the volunteer organizations there should be continued alertness to the implications of individuals' actions. It is the responsibility of the president to make sure that all division and department heads are not only familiar with but subscribe wholeheartedly to the premise on which the institution bases its not-for-profit educational status. The department and division heads in turn are responsible for making certain that all members of their staff understand the principles and how those principles affect what they do for the institution.

Coupled with the institution's principles should be a brief, coherent statement of its mission. Again, the mission must be understood by all who serve the institution, from the chairman of the board to the food service worker, though each may apply the meaning of the mission in different ways. Those involved in fund raising, because they so often need to articulate or interpret the mission to current and potential supporters, must be especially knowledgeable about the institutional mission. The messages they convey must make it clear to potential donors that the funds they seek must serve to advance, rather than to shape, the mission. Further, they must be clear in their own minds that their task is not simply to raise money: it is to raise money to advance the institution's mission.

No organization can mandate integrity, only actions consistent with integrity. For development officers the basis of ethical behavior is remembering that their role is to connect the institution to its current and future supporters. The best way to do that is to seek every opportunity to bring the supporters into contact with those who make the institution what it is. Development officers may represent the college, but they are not the college. Support for the institution should not depend on the relationship between the development officer and the prospect; it should depend on the relationships between prospects and others at the institution. The development officer's task is to build those relationships, not to insert themselves between the institution and the donor.

In the long run, adopting this principle will provide great benefits to the institution. Development officers come and go, as do presidents and volunteers. A donor who feels a sense of connection with what the institution is all about—the faculty and the students—is likely to continue to support it, and to make gifts to meet real needs.

# 7

# Gifts and Donors' Expectations

## Holly Smith and Marilyn Batt Dunn

Why do individuals contribute gifts that support institutions of higher education? According to Barbara Brittingham and Thomas Pezzullo, early philanthropic support for American higher education institutions came from donors who were apparently motivated by an altruistic desire to help disadvantaged individuals. Most institutions receiving philanthropic support were private, church-related institutions, and donors saw themselves as serving the poor or the church.[1]

More recently, donors have perceived themselves—and have been perceived by others—as being motivated more by philanthropy than by the desire to help particular individuals. Philanthropy, in the words of Maurice G. Gurin and Jon Van Til, "takes a more impersonal and dispassionate approach to bettering the human condition by institutionalizing giving, focusing beyond the immediate condition of people on root causes of human problems and systematic reform, recognizing a responsibility to the public interest, and helping to effect social change."[2]

Through their gifts, donors may wish to improve the social potential of certain classes of individuals (e.g., women or minorities) or contribute to advances in knowledge in a field that concerns them (e.g., medicine). Donors may wish to support general social betterment by supporting institutions of higher education rather than improve the welfare of needy individuals directly.

Still more recently, students of philanthropy have recognized that some giving is not purely selfless: the donor's motives may be a mixture of altruism and egoism. Such a donor is moved not only by altruistic desires to help others or to improve society but also by the impact of the action on the donor's own interests. A donor who contributes to the support of an institution of higher education benefits the institution, its students, and the causes it promotes but also receives return benefits, such as public recognition, the sense of personal association with a worthy cause, pride in participating in a successful class campaign, the chance to repay benefits received as a student at the institution, or the indirect financial benefits produced by investing in research activities of the institution that may assist the individual's business or industry. Donors may even receive return benefits that exceed the value—for them, although not for the university—of the gifts. For example, a donation of one thousand dollars may provide a donor with access to university skybox seating and the attendant chance to make business contacts worth hundreds of thousands of dollars.

Because the prospect of personal benefits can form an important part of certain donors' reasons for giving, institutions have increasingly provided such benefits. Thus institutions offer various forms of explicit recognition, such as prominent publication in lists of donors, and other, even more tangible returns for gifts, such as enhanced seating at athletic or cultural events. Although such return gifts can be costly to the institution, they are often believed to be worthwhile on the ground that they may increase the frequency and amount of giving.

It is worth noting that some donors are reluctant to accept recognition. But even when donors seek recognition, there is nothing inherently wrong in bestowing recognition that is appropriate to the size and nature of the contribution, consistently offered to other donors of similar gifts, consistent with an institution's policies, and freely provided by the recipient institution.

Such interactions can be understood from the perspective of *gift exchange theory*.[3] Gift exchange theory suggests that a gift upsets the initial equilibrium between two parties by making the beneficiary beholden to the benefactor. This equilibrium can be restored by a return gift, which may restore the original equilibrium but creates a new disequilibrium that must be removed by a new gift from the original benefactor. According to this view, the college can be seen as the original benefactor, which gives the alumni substantial gifts— their advantage in life, their education, their first jobs. The alumni are then offered the opportunity to restore the balance by giving time, energy, and financial support to annual campaigns. The college responds to these donations with gifts of recognition such as membership in giving clubs and invitations to recognition luncheons. In response to these returns on earlier gifts, the donors are then encouraged once again to restore equilibrium by moving to even higher levels of giving, for which they receive higher levels of gifts in return, such as an honorary degree or having one's name put on a building or scholarship. Institutions make use of donors' desire to give something back, as well as to their desire to contribute to the public good, in order to elicit major support for the institution.

How important self-interested motives are in leading to philanthropic donations is a matter of debate. Jerald Panas, author of *Mega Gifts: Who Gives Them, Who Gets Them,* asserts, on the basis of his interviews with thirty-two donors of $1 million or more in this country, that donors quite often insist that they do not seek "personal aggrandizement for making a mega gift." This accords with the personal experience of one of the authors (Dunn). Nonetheless, Panas maintains that appropriate expressions of appreciation from the beneficiary institution are important.[4]

These acknowledgments tend to increase in number and cost in direct proportion to the size of the gift received. At some point, given the number, permanence, visibility, cost, or frequency of the acknowledgments, it could be argued that the recipient institution is returning benefits to the donors that in some cases may influence their interest in providing the acknowledged gifts or in considering future gifts.

In an era of educational philanthropy in which donors may be led to expect a variety of returns for their gifts—returns without which some gifts might not be forthcoming—ethical problems can arise. Both donors and institutions can be placed in a difficult position if expectations encompass returns that would be unethical for the institution to offer. But how can the line be drawn between legitimate and questionable returns for donors' gifts? To answer this question, let us start by looking at some of the ways in which institutions express appreciation to donors for their financial support.

All gifts, regardless of size, are acknowledged by the institutional beneficiary, normally in the form of a letter signed by an appropriate institutional representative. A receipt for tax purposes usually accompanies the letter. Letters serve not only as a prompt return expression of thanks but also, among the more attentive organizations, as stewardship opportunities, that is, regular reports that assure donors that their gifts are making a difference and continue to be appreciated.

"Honor rolls," publications in which institutions list the names of donors—individuals, corporations, foundations, and organizations—from whom they have received financial support in the last period (usually the fiscal year or term of campaign) are regularly published and broadly distributed. Producers of such publications increasingly categorize listings, making more prominent the sections that recognize donors at the highest levels. Acknowledgments of major donors also occur in alumni and university publications. Donors and their gifts are the subjects of feature articles. Some institutions now recognize major donors by presenting them with awards, often at the same occasions at which other institutional awards for teaching and public service are presented.

Most institutions have giving clubs in which they recognize donors whose total gifts (usually on an annual basis) fall within certain levels; for example, individuals who contribute one hundred dollars a year may belong to a "Century Club," and individuals who contribute at least one thousand dollars a year may belong to a "President's Club." Generally, the rewards attached to a "President's Club" will be greater than those enjoyed by members of a "Century Club." For example, "Century Club" members' names may be listed in an annual report that is distributed to all donors. "President's Club" members may enjoy campus parking privileges, seating enhancements (football, theater, etc.), library privileges, other benefits, or a combination of the above, plus a listing in the annual report.

An institution also may host a special lunch, dinner, or reception to honor the donor of a large gift. Involvement in an institution through service on boards and committees often is cited by donors and development professionals as a key factor in the decision to make a gift. An institution occasionally will honor a donor by inviting him or her to serve on a board or advisory committee. For example, an institution may "cultivate" a relationship with a successful business person by inviting her to serve on a School of Business advisory committee. Through involvement in the school's activities and invitations to meet with students and faculty, the business person may become persuaded that the school deserves her financial support. Such invitations should correspond not only to the prospective donor's interests but also to the institution's need for and willingness to accept his or her expertise. The invitation for involvement should be genuine.

Naming opportunities abound, particularly in connection with campaigns. Endowed chairs, professorships, graduate fellowships, and scholarships at most institutions have names of donors attached to them. These generally are obligations on the part of the institutions that agree in perpetuity to invest the principal and award the income in the name of and for the purpose(s) indicated by the donor. Naming opportunities are not limited to endowments. Private institutions traditionally have enhanced their physical plants by agreeing to name all or parts of buildings for those whose gifts made the construction possible. Recently, public institutions also have initiated building projects funded entirely or partially from private sources and for whom such projects are named. Some institutions present gifts of tangible objects to donors. These may take the form of reduced-scale versions of statuary or towers unique to an institution. Decorative glass or metal objects may be inscribed with the donor's name and a message of appreciation.

Acknowledgments provided to donors at the same gift level should be consistent and should be appropriate for the size of a gift. And the acknowledgments should not exceed in value the limits set by the Internal Revenue Service.[5] Acknowledgments such as those described earlier, separately or in combination, are used in some form in most higher education fund raising, almost always appropriately. However, in return for an actual or prospective gift, donors may occasionally expect other or additional benefits occasionally, the appropriateness of which presents a greater challenge to the fund raiser and the institution.

Clearly, there are many types of benefits that should not be provided to donors because they are illegal, unethical, or contrary to institutional policies. In addition, such benefits undermine the institution's reputation for integrity. Some examples follow:

- In return for a large donation, an institution renames a facility to honor the current donor. Twenty years before, the institution named the facility after the person who donated the largest portion of construction costs.

  Renaming the facility breaks an institutional promise, perhaps even a contractual obligation, to the first donor. It also could discourage potential donors whose gifts require trust that the administration will carry out its obligation and keep its word.

- A condition attached to a major gift to create an endowed chair is the donor's ability to influence hiring, promotion, or curricular decisions.
  Decisions to hire, promote, or determine curriculums reside with the faculty and the administration. Compliance with this condition would be inappropriate. Not only is it contrary to traditional institutional policies but it violates legal requirements that a donor not retain rights of ownership.
- In consideration of a cash donation, an institution contracts with an outside business enterprise for certain services, even though the enterprise cannot provide the best value in this type of service.
  This practice likely would violate institutional policies requiring that contracts be awarded on the basis of competitive bids. It would be equally wrong to award the contract to the enterprise for other reasons, such as the fact that it is owned by the brother of a trustee. If an institution awards contracts to firms less likely to provide good value, it fails to uphold its duty to follow responsible business practices.
- In return for a substantial gift to a current campaign, an institution credits the donor for a total gift to this campaign that includes donations received prior to the start of the campaign.
  Crediting prior gifts misleads the institution's public about the nature and success of the campaign. Because it deceives, it is an objectionable practice even when it is not done in response to an additional gift.
- In order to elicit a gift of real estate for which institutional representatives believe the donor has secured a highly inflated appraisal, an institution agrees not to sell the property for at least three years. This enables the donor to claim, without challenge, the full appraised value of the real estate. It is suspected that if the property were sold within two years of the donation and reported to the Internal Revenue Service, the sale value would be found to be significantly lower than the appraised value.
  Because the institution takes no position regarding the value of the property for which an independent appraisal has been secured by the donor, it may not be wrong for the institution to retain the property for three years or longer in order to meet its own needs

## Gifts and Donors' Expectations

(e.g., property on which to establish a new college, timberland that can be used as a field classroom for a forestry college, etc.). However, it would not be appropriate for the institution to be a willing participant in a transaction that arguably is intended to defraud the government.

- In appreciation for a history of gifts from a wealthy alumna, an institution admits her child in the freshman class, contrary to announced admissions policies stipulating that admissions decisions are made on the basis of scholarly standards alone, standards not met by the alumna's child.

  Admitting the student on the basis of the parent's gifts rather than on the basis of her own qualifications violates institutional policy. Note, however, that there are legitimate alternative institutional admissions policies. Many private institutions explicitly give preference to children of alumni in order to strengthen family ties to the institution and to encourage traditions of financial support among generations. What is important here is that the institution comply with its publicly announced policy.

- In return for a substantial donation, an institution awards the donor an honorary degree. The institution's written policy stipulates that honorary degrees are given in recognition of "significant contributions to knowledge, human welfare, or high attainments in the recipient's career," none of which can be claimed for the donor.

  Here again, awarding the degree on the basis of financial support rather than on the basis of qualifications specified in the institution's policy violates that policy and undermines public trust in the value of previously awarded honorary degrees. Had the institution adopted an alternative policy that permitted awarding of honorary degrees for support of the institution, the problem would not arise.

This chapter is not intended to focus on issues confronting the development professional that would involve illegal activities. For example, an individual's offer to make a major gift to an institution with the condition that it will backdate the receipt does not present a troubling ethical dilemma: the backdating can be rejected as illegal. Nor is an ethical issue involved in accepting the offer of a gift by a donor who requires that it fund a scholarship for the student the donor selects or who requires that minority students be excluded from consideration as recipients. Both offers require the institution to violate the law; neither can be accepted as a gift.

Rather, we have attempted to (1) describe situations in which representatives of institutions comfortably could recognize contributors and express appropriate levels of appreciation (e.g., return benefits) to donors; and (2) heighten awareness of the potential for ethical problems when meeting donors' expectations, explicitly or implicitly communicated, would be unethical and contrary to institutional values. In connection with the latter, we are confident that we have not described all or even most of the situations in which development colleagues may be challenged to react responsibly and ethically. In the remaining paragraphs, we suggest ways the development professional might plan to avoid being confronted with an ethical issue and, if he or she is so confronted, how best and with whom to develop a response on behalf of the institution.

Ideally there is clarity of communication between the prospective donor(s) and the institutional representative(s) negotiating the gift. The expectations of both should be clear to both parties at all times. In addition, institutional development programs should have in place policies and procedures, and these should be widely distributed—to volunteers and other administrative leaders—and periodically updated. Such practice reduces the likelihood that a representative of the institution will place him- or herself or the institution in an uncomfortable position by unintentionally assuring a prospective donor, explicitly or implicitly, that unacceptable conditions attached to a gift are acceptable. Further, broad distribution of policies and procedures helps to assure the campus community and donors that the development program is being administered professionally, consistently, and ethically.

Included in the policies and procedures manual, in addition to organization charts and policies that describe requests for prospect assignments, processing and reporting of gifts, and other administrative matters, would be a gift recognition section in which questions such as the following are answered:

- Who has authority to accept gifts, and under what guidelines? What value is assigned, and by whom?
- What naming opportunities exist? Who approves naming re-

quests? Are there any circumstances under which an already named facility, in whole or in part, could be renamed? If so, what is the process?

- Are there overhead charges on gifts of which the donor should be made aware?
- What are the selection policies—for scholarships, fellowships, professorships, and chairs—that govern administration of gift funds?
- What in-house recognition opportunities for recognition exist, and at what gift level(s) does each apply?
- What are the policies for crediting gifts? Who can make an exception to these policies?

Policy and procedure manuals should be provided to and reviewed with all new staff and volunteers as part of an orientation process. In addition, these materials should be reviewed and referred to regularly and "tested" for usefulness and relevance by incorporating into staff meetings and retreats case-study discussions on ethics. Continuing conversations about such cases and their nuances and complexities will help alert development officers to potential but covert problems, to the strategies that may assist them in helping potential donors to understand why certain kinds of expectations cannot be met, and to opportunities for designing alternative gifts and expectations that more effectively meet the concerns of both the donor and the institution.

The written policies and procedures help to define a culture that encourages clarity of communication so that there are no surprises, either to the donor or to those representing the institution. Managers responsible for policies and procedures also would be expected to encourage professional staff to follow up on any of the prospective donor's comments or implications about which there is any degree of discomfort and to understand clearly the expectations of the donor.

If a donor's expectations do not appear to fall clearly into legitimate categories of "benefits returned," development professionals must act. If they are concerned that the offer may be inappropriate, they should consult with institutional leadership, often at the highest levels. What is being sought by both parties (i.e., who wins) at what cost to each (i.e., who pays) and what effect this has on any other party(ies) (i.e., who else wins or loses) must be clearly understood and carefully considered. Among the questions that must be answered are: Are the conditions within the law? Is anyone being deceived or cheated? Are we keeping all past promises made—and implied—by this institution? Are we doing our duty to those directly and indirectly involved?

Finally, ethical managers, as well as the development professionals who report to them, understand that some offers of gifts are best declined. If that becomes necessary, these development officers, because their volunteer and administrative leaders are aware of and subscribe to the institution's policies and procedures, are confident of the support of their leadership. There are some things, indeed many things, more important than the bottom line.

# 8

# *Planned Giving*

## Frank A. Logan

*There is a strange charm in the thoughts of a good legacy, or the hopes of an estate, which wondrously alleviates the sorrow that we would otherwise feel for the death of friends.*

—Don Quixote

Planned giving is different, slightly but significantly removed from the mainstream of institutional advancement. The dominating elements are service, not salesmanship; problem solving, not promotion. For an educational institution, planned giving often allows alumni and alumnae, in particular older ones, to give back to a school or college in tangible form what was intangibly received, to help ensure the future worthiness of its educational mission. The central core of planned giving is the life income plan. Because of the retention of a lifetime income stream by the donor, with its *irrevocableness* and *irreversibility* for both the donor and the donee institution, the economic risks can be great, as can be the rewards.

Played out against an intricate background of federal tax statutes, estate and financial planning principles, investment policies, close long-term personal relationships, and marketing strategies and techniques, planned giving serves as the chief endowment builder for most educational institutions. The skills and knowledge of a planned giving officer must therefore be multidimensional, ranging from a mastery of a specialized body of tax law, to a knowledge of personal and public communications, to an understanding of the needs and expectations of older people. Moral decisions abound on an everyday basis, since the officer represents the interests of the employing charity and, at the same time, helps to conserve and enhance the economic and financial well-being of the donor and, often, members of the donor's family.

This chapter addresses the role planned giving plays in advancement—the special gift vehicles, the legislative backdrop, the relationships between donor and gift practitioner, capital campaigns, the binding legal contracts—all of which converge to place planned giving at the center of a number of ethical issues.

## Definitions

A planned gift is a charitable gift of capital for any purpose in any form requiring the assistance of a professional adviser, retained either by the donor or by the donee institution. The gift can be outright or deferred. It can be a lifetime gift or a gift made at the time of death. A planned gift is usually donor-driven, rather than institution-driven, which means that the gift process focuses largely on the donor's needs rather than on the needs of the institution.

Planned giving can also be defined as a method of motivating people to transfer discretionary capital property to a charity in return for some economic benefit for them now and perhaps for the rest of their lives, and possibly for the lives of others. Planned giving was originally referred to as *deferred giving;* in some quarters the preferred name is now *gift planning.* For many donors, planned giving makes charitable giving *affordable.* And for most donors, a planned gift is their "ultimate" gift; that is, it will be the largest and most significant charitable gift they will ever make.

The planned giving officer is usually responsible for the acceptance of noncash gifts other than marketable securities, regardless of the form or method of the gift transfer. Examples are privately held stock, real estate, tangible personal property (works of art, antiques, collections, etc.), life insurance contracts, mining interests, copyrights and patents, partnership interests, and warrants.

## In The Beginning

In a sense, planned giving in the United States extends as far back as the founding of the colonial colleges. John Harvard's bequest established the distinguished college bearing his name in 1636. Bequests and testamentary trusts founded or nurtured many educational institutions. It is assumed that these donors always planned their gifts according to their personal circumstances and objectives. However, actual charitable estate planning in this country was largely limited to philanthropic individuals of wealth, acting in conjunction with their advisers and responding to early appeals from charitable organizations for bequests.

Charitable gift annuities first appeared in the mid-nineteenth century, sponsored by the American Bible Society. Still, planned giving as a formal branch of the practice of philanthropy and as a component of a comprehensive system of advancement are relatively recent developments. Planned giving as it is known today was created by the Tax Act of 1969. Prompted by growing abuses and inequities with respect to private foundations and charitable trusts, the statutes added to the Tax Code by Congress at that time provided for the vehicles of planned giving—remainder trusts (unitrusts and annuity trusts), pooled income funds, charitable gift annuities, charitable lead trusts, and gifts with retained life tenancies—arrangements that combined a donor's personal financial objectives with his or her charitable objectives in ways that would enhance both. (These plans are also called "split-interest" plans for this reason.)

Subsequent tax acts embellished the legislative framework on which planned giving operates today. The 1976 Tax Reform Act revised the sections of the code referring to gift and estate tax; 1984 legislation tightened the appraisal requirements for noncash charitable gifts (a possible overreaction to a scattering of well-publicized abuses); the 1986 act included the onerous provision that made gifts of long-term appreciated property subject to the individual alternative minimum tax; and beginning in 1989, "floating" monthly discount rates were required for certain life income plans.

More than any other area or subspecialty within the field of advancement, planned giving is practiced against an ever-changing background of both federal and state statutes, U.S. Treasury regulations, IRS rulings, and appellate opinions. This alone places the planned giving officer in a position of considerable responsibility when representing his or her institution to prospective donors and their advisers. With the rise, since 1969, of the major and mega–capital campaign, some with nine- or ten-figure dollar goals, planned giving has been thrust into a highly competitive climate. It is not uncommon for these ambitious campaigns to include a significant component of planned gifts, one third or more of the dollar goal for gifts from individuals, bringing additional internal pressure upon the planned giving office and further challenging sound ethical practices.

## The Contractual Agreements and the Donors

Planned gifts include both charitable bequests (transfers made at the time of death) and charitable remainder trusts and gift annuities (gifts usually made during the donor's lifetime). Remainder trusts and gift annuities generally involve a gift of cash or property in exchange for income payments (a retained life income interest), usually for the life of the donor and sometimes for the lives of others as well. Some plans are for a specified number of years only, not to exceed 20. When the plan ends, the remaining assets are released outright to the named charity. These income reservation plans are complex and *irrevocable* legal arrangements.

Moreover, the plans are primarily directed toward, and are appropriate for, people who are at or approaching their retirement years, some of whom because of age or attitude are vulnerable to misrepresentations, misinformation, or misjudgment. They are frequently dependent, in part, upon the expected lifetime income streams from such plans. When the income payments fail to meet those expectations, the consequences can be most severe, lowering the quality of their retirement years.

It is precisely because of this unusual set of donor-donee conditions that a very heavy burden is placed upon the planned giving officer, a burden of both technical expertise and moral responsibility when working with donors. In this regard, veteran advancement officer and consultant Norman S. Fink has observed:

> Unlike the annual giving program or even the capital campaign, planned giving involves an extended personal relationship between a charity and a donor or his designated beneficiaries, much like a marriage, only there are no ways to divorce. Indeed, the commitment on both sides is replete with such a high degree of trust and confidence that no charitable institution should undertake such a program without due consideration of the implicit risks as weighed against the potential benefits.[1]

## Ethical Issues, Large and Small

Among planned giving officers, the issue of professional ethics peaked as an area of primary concern in 1990, according to the publication *Planned Giving Today*.[2] In its annual survey of subscribers in 1991, ethical behavior was the third most pressing issue in planned giving, ranked behind "negative legislation" and the "role of financial professionals." However, when asked to rank criteria according to their importance for determining the level of planned giving professionalism, the respondents listed ethical behavior first, followed by technical expertise and then marketing skills.

Planned giving officers must make decisions on a wide-ranging set of questions and circumstances, such as:

- Whether to decline a life income gift that may be too large, given the donor's financial circumstances.
- Whether to accept a personal gift offered by a grateful donor with whom the officer has had a long-term professional relationship.
- How to avoid potential conflicts with board members and influential alumni who sell financial products and services (insurance, securities, trust management, etc.) relating to life income plans.
- How to deal with the donor who resists the payment of any legal and appraisal fees, insisting that the donee institution should pay the fees in return for the gift, that is, discharge the donor's legal obligation.
- How to determine the legal capacity of a donor and avoiding undue influence.
- Whether to accept designated gifts that may be impracticable or improper for the institution to administer.
- Whether to negotiate a payout rate with a donor that could be unrealistically high in the light of current economic indexes, thus reducing significantly the charity's eventual gift.
- Whether the institution has the managerial resources to administer certain planned gifts over a long period of time.
- Whether to credit planned gifts in a major campaign and jeopardize the campaign's credibility by including an unjustified amount of "soft money."
- When to call in specialized advisers.
- Whether to respect a donor's desire for anonymity and confiden-

tiality, including a disregarding of children or others in the gift discussions.

The most alarming abuses and excesses in planned giving were spawned by the Tax Reform Act of 1986. With the virtual removal of the artificial tax shelter industry in this country, a few of the entrepreneurs and financial advisers who profited from such schemes turned to the charitable remainder unitrust and began to promote it aggressively as the "last remaining tax shelter," with little or no regard for its charitable purposes. Emphasizing the unitrust's tax-exempt status and the avoidance of capital-gains-tax liability on gifts of long-term appreciated property, these hucksters quickly devised an array of slick promotional strategies and techniques that were often characterized by (1) the near absence of donative intent, (2) unreasonable and unwarranted fees and charges, (3) minimum disclosure, and (4) a disregard for realistic investment returns. Such allied professionals as life insurance agents (especially), financial planners, accountants, real estate agents, investment managers, and attorneys have, sadly, all appeared in this sordid scenario. The abuses and excesses of those in the allied financial services are understandable, however. They have a different goal, namely, profit, and they are far less concerned with donative intent on the part of the donor than is the planned giving officer representing a charitable institution. In short, they have not been socialized in the philanthropic tradition. Therein lies the conflict.

In the early days following the 1986 Tax Act, the emerging tax shelter merchant (operating mostly out of California and Arizona) blatantly demanded a "finder's fee" from the charity for his or her "services" in return for the gift, often a significant percentage (7 or 8 percent) of the gift itself. More sophisticated but equally questionable compensation techniques have now largely replaced or supplemented the finder's fee, including an exit fee, a percentage of the trust assets at termination. However, the pattern of exploiting the capital-gains-tax bypass at the expense of the true charitable nature of the charitable remainder unitrust continues.

Besides the individual for-profit abuser, the planned giving profession has been concerned with the more recent appearance of two equally disturbing trends. First, regional and national networks of franchises have been established for the sole purpose of retailing charitable remainder unitrusts, often by means of misleading seminars. Second, the decision by some of the major stock brokerage houses to promote unitrusts as alternate retirement plans, with advertising programs that inflate payout rates, target young professionals and avoid or deemphasize any reference to charitable purposes. These are flagrant abuses that, while technically within the law, clearly are not within the spirit of the provisions of the Tax Act of 1969 and the historic goals of philanthropy.

These dubious activities have not been hindered by occasional articles in popular magazines and other print media. The most notorious of these was the ill-conceived and unbalanced November 1990 piece in *Forbes* magazine entitled "Tax Dodges Begin At Home."[3] Describing the legitimate tax benefits as "tax loopholes," the author painted a distorted picture of "donors" reaping a veritable harvest of tax advantages and income benefits with little regard for the interests of charitable organizations. The article concluded by stating that "it's only a matter of time before Congress gets wise to this loophole."

The time may soon be at hand. In a September 12, 1991, letter to an officer of the American Bar Association, Florida Congressman Sam M. Gibbons of Florida, the ranking Democrat on the House Ways and Means Committee, wrote: "The Joint Committee Staff is now collecting data on how these trusts are becoming 'the' tax avoidance devices of the 1990s, even to the point of becoming used as substitute retirement plans." There is increasing concern that some form of Draconian congressional response to these abuses is a real possibility, particularly as Capitol Hill looked for new revenues. Among the changes that could be brought forward for this purpose are (1) an arbitrary minimum charitable remainder value for trusts, say, 20 percent; (2) a maximum on permissible payout rates for standard unitrusts; (3) a prohibition on the sale of appreciated property funding a trust of two years; (4) a capital gains tax on appreciated property funding a trust.

Fortunately, the Tax Bill of 1993 did not incorporate any of these changes. On the contrary, the bill favored planned giving by repealing retroactively the onerous alternative minimum tax on charitable gifts of appreciated property and by reducing the estate tax rates. However, congressional concerns are still very much in evidence. In mid-1993 the House Ways and Means Subcommittee on Oversight held a hearing looking into the possible abuse by some charities of their tax exemption by permitting donations to be used for the benefits of executives and other insiders.

## The Response

By 1989 the level of concern over these issues and abuses within the planned giving community had risen significantly, but without political leadership at the national level there was no effective means of responding. However, in June of that year a seminal initiative was taken by a small group of planned giving officers meeting at Saranac Lake in upstate New York. This was the annual meeting of the CANARAS group, fifteen officers representing mostly independent colleges and universities in the northeastern United States. The group drafted a statement (purposefully polemic in nature) that was designed to draw attention to the abusers, to reaffirm the primacy of the charitable contribution with respect to life income plans, and to denounce the use of the finder's fee and other unreasonable fees and commissions. The statement was unanimously adopted and was named *The CANARAS Convention*.[4] It closed with the following warning:

> Unless these issues are addressed by the charitable community in a prompt and constructive fashion, the misguided efforts of those for-profit promoters who seek to subvert the charitable tax deduction as a tax shelter could cause a congressional and public opinion backlash which will seriously undermine the future of philanthropy.

During the remainder of the summer and early fall of 1989, *The CANARAS Convention* was distributed widely throughout the planned giving community, and additional subscribers were recruited. A critical next step was the introduction and discussion of the *Convention* in the fall by the three hundred participants at the Second National Conference of the National Committee on Planned Giving (NCPG) in Indianapolis. Formed in 1987 in response to the exploding interest in planned giving, NCPG is a federation of local planned giving councils whose purpose is to encourage the education and training of the planned giving community and allied financial professionals. Today, with more than sixty affiliated regional and local councils and a membership of some five thousand professionals, NCPG is the leading national professional association for gift planners.

*Planned Giving*

Following the 1989 NCPG conference, there was further dissemination of *The CANARAS Convention* within the local councils, in the public media, and in the trade journals. Eventually the IRS took notice of the profession's efforts to expose and confront the abusers. Writing to the original signatories in the spring of 1990, then Assistant Commissioner Robert I. Brauer said: "I recently received a copy of *The CANARAS Convention*, the manifesto that you and your fellow fund raisers have developed as a response to promotions 'selling' federal tax deductibility. As you know, my office has been involved in a campaign aimed at curtailing abuses of the charitable contribution deduction and I am greatly heartened that you have developed this statement of principles. I firmly believe the success of our campaign depends, for the most part, upon the willingness of the charitable community to police its own ranks."[5]

Buoyed by the positive reactions from practically all quarters of the planned giving community, the CANARAS group drafted a second document at its June 1990 annual meeting, with the objective of providing a needed professional guide of practices and principles for all gift planners, including those in the for-profit allied professions. The result was *The CANARAS Code*, which was, in its own words, "intended to assure that the [gift planning] process is conducted in a professional and ethical manner that achieves a fair and proper balance between the personal interests of the donor and the purposes of the charitable institution."[6]

Like its predecessor, *The CANARAS Code* received widespread distribution following its initial adoption. It was also the principal topic at the 1990 NCPG conference. Speaking at the conference, a representative of the CANARAS group urged the adoption of the *Code* and summed up the "sacred trust" of the work of the planned giving officer by stating:

> Should we not therefore strive to elevate the public perception of planned giving by these means? Should we not extend a helping hand to fellow professionals who find themselves in cloudy ethical situations from time to time? And should we, as professional gift planners, not move towards the formal adoption of a set of standards that will enhance not only the *appearance* of propriety in the eyes of those clients and donors we serve, but more importantly will enhance the *reality* of our deeds and services?[7]

Following considerable discussion and a favorable polling of those in attendance, the NCPG board of directors formed a task force on ethics that was charged with developing a formal guide of ethical behavior for gift planners, building upon both the *Convention* and the *Code.*

## Model Standards

The task force was chaired by Tal Roberts, the chairman of the Committee on Gift Annuities, a sister institution of NCPG that represents more than twelve hundred public charities around the country. Working through the fall and winter of 1990–91, the task force drafted *Model Standards of Practice for the Charitable Gift Planner.*[8] It is a statement that not only clarifies the primary purpose of planned giving (to benefit worthy charities) but also expresses a level of professional behavior to which gift planners are encouraged to aspire, with special emphasis on areas such as disclosure, compensation, and competence. To no one's surprise, the debate over compensation practices, specifically the finder's fee, was a key factor. Although some NCPG members preferred more restrictive language, the final version stated that such fees and commissions as a condition for the delivery of a gift "are never appropriate."

*Model Standards* was adopted unanimously by the NCPG board of directors (April 30, 1991) and the Committee of Gift Annuities (May 2, 1991). As of mid-1992 it had been ratified by over 450 sponsoring institutions, most of the NCPG councils, and countless other independent professionals involved in the gift planning process. As a sign of the landmark importance of *Model Standards,* the NCPG board of directors decided in June 1992 to require its adoption by all current and new member councils. A standing committee on ethics has also been established by NCPG to serve as a combination watchdog, clearinghouse, and adjudicator for matters pertaining to ethical behavior.[9] (Interestingly, another national association of fund raisers, the National Society of Fund Raising Executives, or NSFRE, hesitated to take a stand against the finder's fee out of concern that such a policy would run afoul of antitrust law. However, as of mid-1992, NSFRE's Ethics Committee had recommended the adoption of a clause in its *Code of Ethical Principles* that would prohibit percentage compensation and finder's fees.[10] Also, the American Association of

Fund Raising Counsel now bars its members from accepting payment based on how much money they raise for client charities.)

With *Model Standards* in place, the planned giving community was provided with a centralized conscience, a reference point, a body of guidelines and principles. And it is working

- as a comforting lighthouse for the inexperienced or part-time practitioner caught up in a difficult and confusing gift situation;
- as an everyday reminder and code of conduct for the veteran planned giving officer;
- as a warning to the tax shelter merchant and licensee who risk becoming outcasts by flouting *Model Standards;*
- as a reaffirmation of the primacy of charitable intent in planned giving for the major brokerage houses and insurance companies;
- as a source of support for the planned giving officer dealing with an unenlightened board of directors or supervisory administrators;
- as a professional statement of reassurance to both the concerned individual donor and the public at large; and
- as an overdue message of integrity and commitment for the common good to the public servants and oversight committees in Washington.

## Enforcement

There is no licensing agency for planned giving officers, no certification program, no grievance commissions, no formal program of sanctions. In short, there is no enforcement mechanism whereby those who are guilty of misconduct can be censured and removed from further practice. The NCPG has decided to delegate responsibility for whatever action needs to be taken to the local councils. In the final analysis, it will be peer and social pressure more than anything else that will bring about needed behavioral change on the part of those who ignore or misinterpret *Model Standards.* This self-policing policy, as advanced in 1990 by Commissioner Brauer, holds the most promise for maintaining not only the appearance of propriety in the eyes of the public but also the integrity of the day-to-day actions by individual gift planners.

Should such a self-policing policy fail, there would most likely be external enforcement and change through congressional or Securities and Exchange Commission (SEC) action. Possible congressional responses have already been mentioned (a minimum remainder value, etc.). In the case of the SEC, the decision could be made to treat planned giving vehicles as full-fledged commercial investments, rather than charitable arrangements exempt from regulations, because of the payment of finder's fees and other special compensation. This would be a reversal of a history of preferential no-action rulings and would bring these gift vehicles under federal and state securities regulations, requiring their registration and other onerous and expensive administrative procedures.[11]

## Summary

From a fledgling group of qualified gift officers at the time of the 1969 Tax Act to a greatly expanded national association of competent gift planners in the early 1990s, the profession of planned giving has grown to become a major component of institutional advancement. Armed with a specialized body of technical knowledge and working with older donors who place considerable trust and confidence in them, planned giving officers occupy a unique position in the marketplace of philanthropy. They have to weigh the interests of their employing institutions against the interests of prospective donors—everyday gift transactions that are pregnant with ethical considerations both large and small—compounded greatly by the increasing level of competition for the philanthropic dollar.

Although planned giving in the United States came of age during the late 1970s and 1980s, a time of unusually strong economic performance, providing both life income donors and institutional endowments with attractive returns, there is growing evidence that the "golden age" of planned giving may lie just ahead. Two principal demographic and economic trends since World War II could account for this: (1) the aging of the American society and (2) the buildup of wealth within the graying population as a result of family incomes, real estate values, Social Security payments, and stock prices, all of which outpaced inflation during most of this period. Attorney and fund-raising consultant Robert F. Sharpe, Jr., supports the view of the beginning of a golden age of planned giving and observes that "members of an aging population seeking ways to continue to support their philanthropic interests in later years are finding more and more creative opportunities to do so." [12]

A 1990 study at Cornell University projected an unprecedented and imminent aggregate transfer of wealth at death. The study was the subject of an article in *Fortune* magazine that year, which stated that "$7 trillion of privately-held wealth will pass from the post-war generation to the next generation during the period 1990–2010 . . . the biggest intergenerational transfer of wealth in U.S. history." [13] This accumulated wealth will pass to family, to the government (in taxes), and to charity. Since planned giving usually provides the philanthropic interface with the older donor, this should be the major arena of heightened gift activity during this period.

It therefore behooves every college and university to make certain that its planned giving program is up and running to take full advantage of these fruitful years. And it is vitally important that the planned giving officers responsible for those program make certain now that their ethical house is in order, through adoption of *Model Standards,* through a personal set of operating guidelines, and through the existence of an institutional code of understanding that will be unequivocally supportive at all times.

# 9

# Corporations and Foundations

## Judith M. Gooch

The relationship between an institution of higher education and a foundation or corporation is more complex than the institution's relationship with an individual. It depends on interactions of both organization's people over a protracted period of time, and yet it exists apart from the relationships of any of those individuals with any others. It is more formal and intellectual and less amenable to control than the relationship between individuals. It brings with it some unique ethical concerns.

This chapter identifies areas in the relationship between higher education institutions and corporations and foundations in which ethical dilemmas are most likely to occur. It discusses types of situations likely to arise in the course of obtaining corporate and foundation support, attempts to clarify the issues, and suggests some corrective and preventive measures. In addition, it examines the role of grant officers in regard to the grants process and discusses their special responsibilities to their employers, to the fund-raising profession, and to philanthropy. For the purposes of this discussion, *corporate support* includes all dollars from a corporation, whether or not they are routed through a corporate foundation. *Foundation* refers to independent, operating, or community foundations as defined by *The Foundation Directory*.

In 1989–90, according to *Giving USA,* corporate and foundation support of higher education amounted to $4.09 billion, some 42 percent of all donations to colleges and universities. Although only a few institutions, primarily large research universities, actually received 42 percent or more of their support from foundations and corporations, the sheer amount is certainly one reason why institutions are pursuing corporate and foundation dollars with great vigor. A foundation or corporate grant has impact well beyond its dollar value. Many current and potential donors see foundation and corporate support as an independent, objective measure of institutional quality. Individuals may be swayed by sentiment. Foundation and corporate decisions are made, at least in theory, after a careful evaluation of the applicant institution's strengths and weaknesses, its ability to carry out the actions it has described, and its value to society as a whole. A strong record of receiving grants is thus a positive factor in attracting support from other foundations and corporations and from individuals.

Competition for foundation and corporate dollars has risen dramatically over the last decade. Although higher education has gained slightly in its share of overall total support from corporations and foundations and the dollars contributed have increased substantially, many more not-for-profit organizations now want a share of the pie. Growing financial needs, the sense of increased competition, and the perceived value of corporate and foundation support combine to produce considerable pressure on those responsible for obtaining grants and gifts. They include faculty, senior administrators, and key volunteers, as well as staff members with responsibility for corporate and foundation relations programs.

Where there is intense pressure to succeed, there is always also the potential for unethical behavior. Sometimes such behavior is deliberate, but most often it is inadvertent and stems from ignorance or incomplete understanding of a situation or relationship.

The following examples demonstrate some of the ethically problematic situations that might arise for the foundation and corporate relations officer:

- A faculty member, under pressure to demonstrate grant-getting ability as a requirement for favorable tenure review, appears in the Development Office. "Just tell me what they're giving money for," he says. "I'm sure I can come up with a good project."
- A corporation annually gives the institution a full scholarship for a student whom the institution selects. The scholarship comes with a summer job at the corporation. This year's scholarship recipient does not want to take the summer job but wants to work at a rival company instead.
- Joe Smith, '88, is fund chairman for his fifth reunion. His com-

pany has a generous, three-for-one matching-gift program. Joe wants to offer his classmates the opportunity to give him their gifts. He will then write the college a check for the total and claim the corporate match.

- At a social occasion the grants officer hears a faculty member say something that indicates that she may have misused a grant. The grants officer knows that the foundation has already received a report saying that the grant was used as described in the funded proposal.
- A colleague from another institution calls to talk with the grants officer about a recent foundation grant to this institution. The other institution is planning to apply to the same foundation. He asks for a copy of the grant proposal.
- A foundation executive is quite friendly with a faculty member at an institution that has recently applied for a grant. The faculty member has not been involved in preparing the proposal. The foundation executive plans to do a "reality check" by talking with her friend about the institution and the people involved in the project described in the proposal.
- A member of the university's board of trustees is on the contributions committee of a company that has just given fifty thousand dollars to the university's capital campaign. The board member has made only a small personal contribution to the campaign but wants to be named to the Keystone Club, which recognizes gifts at the fifty-thousand-dollar level.
- The college's proposal to a foundation has been turned down. A member of the board of trustees plans to call the chairman of the foundation's board, who is a friend of his, and ask that the foundation reconsider its decision.

The mission of a corporate and foundation relation program is to promote relationships with foundations and corporations that are beneficial to the college or university. A productive relationship depends on three elements: mutual concerns; a perception that each organization can help the other; and most important, the trust that comes from understanding and respecting each other's integrity, culture, and goals. Trust such as this is based on honesty, openness, and a shared history of well-met expectations and appropriate behavior.

The primary job of the grants officer (or the staff member responsible for the corporate and foundation relations program) is to help bring the institution and the corporation or foundation together to discover mutual concerns and to develop the trust that will allow them to explore areas of common interest. People throughout the foundation or corporation must believe that those at the college or university make good-faith efforts to present honest information and to propose realistic courses of action and will work hard to carry them out. Those at the college or university need to feel confident that the foundation or corporate representatives present honest information about what their organizations will support, understand what can and cannot be accomplished, and judge applicants' proposals fairly.

A trusting relationship between a corporation or foundation and a college or university develops over a period of time and is not static; it is always "in process." Both organizations continually share information about themselves. What is this particular college all about? What are its strengths, its needs, and what sets it apart from its peers? What has happened recently to change or reinforce its capacities? What does the foundation or corporation support, and how does it make decisions? Where do its interests and those of the institution overlap? What can the college or university do about a particular problem if the foundation or corporation provides some money? Is it capable of doing what it claims? Is this likely to be the most effective use of corporate or foundation dollars? Will support advance the interests of both entities in desirable ways?

To complicate the picture, many people in addition to those who "officially" represent each organization may be involved in the relationship between a corporation or foundation and a college or university. A university and a major pharmaceutical company may have an enormous number of connections. The company might employ fifty-two alumni, appoint several of its faculty to advisory committees each year, sponsor research in one or more faculty laboratories, and give annual scholarship grants to three undergraduates. The chairman of the board may be a member of the university's board of trustees, and parents of five current undergraduates may work for the company. Even a small college and a small company may share two or three people.

Foundation contacts are likely to exist as well, though they will be fewer in number. A key college volunteer may be a close friend of a foundation board member, or the dean may also know the executive director of a foundation because they served on the same panel years before. A "past parent" may be the lawyer for another foundation, or an alumnus may be a program officer. Wittingly or not, these people help each organization develop an understanding of the other; in addition, they represent each to the other, and their conduct provides a basis for judgment, if not action. Notably, too, what many of them say or do is not usually under the control of either organization with which they have ties. All too often, in fact, the official representatives are unaware of these connections.

## Getting Acquainted

Fear—"If we don't say the right thing, we won't even get in the door"—sets the stage for the development officer's first ethics test. Clearly, unless the institution can get an initial hearing, there is no hope of a grant. It is certainly unethical for the grants officer to lie about the average board scores of his institution's students in the hope that the foundation or corporate executive will be so impressed with the quality of the student body that she will agree to an appointment. It is also foolish, because the chances of being caught are very great, given the likely number of contacts between the institution and the organization and the independent sources available to verify such claims.

A basic fact sheet about the institution is very helpful. It should summarize information about the institution's enrollment, mission, student-faculty ratio, library holdings, budget, endowment—all the important general facts about the college or university. This tool, updated at least once a year, should be approved by the senior administration and should be used by every person officially representing the institution when they present information about it to any interested parties. It is useful as a crib sheet; and it keeps everyone consistent as well as honest.

But there are cloudier issues, and these are often issues of context. Is it ethical to talk about the increased number of science majors this year without mentioning the precipitous drop during the last three years? How about faculty-student ratios, often seen as an indicator of quality: should the institution use the most favorable ratio (counting all individuals with faculty status even if they do not teach) without explanation? Financial information can be especially tricky. Deficits are commonly regarded as bad things. Suppose the institution is running a deficit. When, if ever, does this get mentioned? only if the institutional representative is asked? What about using "old school ties"? Is it ethical to drop names ("Mr. Smith, vice president for sales at your company, is one of our trustees and he suggested that we contact you . . .") or to use professional contacts developed by the grants officer while working for another institution?

The key to ethical behavior at this stage is to understand what is deceptive and not deceptive in a particular context. Each organization needs to find out whether a joint venture is in the interests of both. The goal of the grants officer is to help each organization get to know and begin to trust the other. The grants officer, therefore, has to represent each organization to the other as honestly and appropriately as possible. The university is not just looking for money (though the grants officer may be under considerable pressure to find money); it is looking for support for some facet of its educational mission. The corporation or foundation will respond based on its own mission. The grants officer needs to provide information about the institution focusing on the aspect of its mission that is most likely to interest the corporation (science education for a pharmaceutical company, for example) and a context ("We have had to develop some ways to attract more students to science because our science programs suffered a drop in enrollment"). Initially, general background and some information that bears on the area of mutual interest is relevant. The deficit need not be mentioned in a request for an appointment, though it is certainly part of what the potential donor needs to know later, in the context of a discussion of institutional strengths and problems.

Using Mr. Smith's name to open the door (with his permission, of course) is perfectly acceptable, though using it as a threat ("Mr. Smith said he was sure you'd be able to do something for us") is unwise. Mr. Smith is part of the ongoing relationship between the institution and the company. It is also perfectly acceptable for the grants officer to use contacts made in previous jobs to seek appointments with corporate or foundation personnel. The relationship between the corporation or foundation and a college or university is unique and neither transferable nor subject to plagiarism. Staff contacts may open doors, but a relationship will result only if it turns out to be in the interests of both organizations.

During initial discussions of programs or projects the grants officer must be especially careful not to promise or even to imply more than the institution is willing to deliver. Deception is self-defeating as well as unethical; the grants officer who promises and cannot deliver will not remain a grants officer for long. It can be difficult to avoid inadvertent exaggeration, though. Many of us have discussed project ideas with faculty, then with potential grantors, and returned to campus to find that plans had changed or that the faculty member had decided that a particular idea was not practical. In that case, the ethical act is for the grants officer to inform the potential grantor that the situation has changed since their conversation, describe the new situation, and ask whether interest still exists. Grants officers will find this whole situation easier if they realize from the beginning—and can make it clear to potential grantors—that they are facilitators, not authorities. They can describe but cannot commit. And their credibility is established in part by the honesty and consistency of the general institutional information they present.

In addition to making the college or university known to the corporation or foundation, the grants officer needs to learn about the mission and goals of the potential grantors. Corporate and foundation giving is not monolithic, though at many institutions the two types of organizations are regarded as one category of prospects. They have motives in common, to be sure; both foundations and corporate giving programs certainly respond to a desire to help society. But there is one major difference between them, and it profoundly influences their decision making.

Philanthropy is a foundation's sole function, and solving certain problems is its goal. A corporation exists to make a profit for its owners. While the desire to do good may be reflected in the fact that it gives, generally a company's philanthropy is incidental, a small part of its operation. A corporation will practice philanthropy to strengthen its profit-making ability. It might support a college that trains its employees or a university that produces research results that lead to new products it will manufacture. It might imitate other corporations' philanthropy so as to be in good company. It might be a "good neighbor" and support the local schools to improve the quality of life for its employees and to help future employees get a good education. It might support the arts to improve its image. Although it certainly wants to help solve problems, the problems it wants to solve are usually chosen out of self-interest centered on its profit-making function.

Understanding the differences, as well as the similarities, among organizations' missions and goals will enable the grants officer to understand each organization's expectations in regard to a relationship with the college or university. A major part of the grants officer's role, therefore, is to learn how a particular corporation or foundation interprets its mission and then to share the information with interested parties on campus. Anything less than "full disclosure" by the grants officer, including failing to report his interpretation of less than direct signals from the potential grantor, is unethical. For example, after discussing the president's dream project with a program officer at a foundation, the grants officer should not hold out false hope if the program officer has said, in effect, Yes, we support that field, but it doesn't sound as if this project is particularly unusual. The implication is that the foundation is unlikely to fund something that others are doing, and the grants officer must assess the chances for a successful proposal. This is a situation in which knowing what to do is easy but doing it may be difficult; delivering bad news to the president often makes the messenger unpopular, though in the long run a truthful messenger will be respected and trusted.

Now let us consider an example cited at the beginning of this chapter:

> A faculty member, under pressure to demonstrate grant-getting ability as a requirement for favorable tenure review, appears in the Development Office. "Just tell me what they're giving money for," he says. "I'm sure I can come up with a good project."

This example suggests at least two possible areas of ethical concern. First, it is in the best interest of the institution and the potential funding source to make the best possible use of donor funds. The institution should send out proposals based on real strengths, not just needs. This candidate clearly has needs, but whether there are strengths is open to question. The grants officer should explore the faculty member's areas of interest and try to match them with known sources of funds. But he or she should also check with the department head to get a reading on the situation. A weak proposal will not help the institution's relationship with the potential grantor; a deceptive one will damage it. The grants officer's goal is a trusting relationship, and behavior that would weaken trust is likely to be unethical.

The second concern is broader. Grant-getting ability is often viewed as an indicator of faculty quality and weighs in tenure decisions. This puts considerable pressure on young faculty to focus their work on what will be funded, and this may not always be the best use of their talents. Nor is it clear that funding sources are capable of judging the "best" areas of research. The obvious question is, Best for whom? Forcing faculty research to depend on external funding in anything more than a trivial way lets outside interests have a strong say in determining the individual's, the institution's, and the nation's research priorities.

This is true in other areas of institutional need as well. Colleges and universities will try first to get funds for what they define as their most pressing needs, but if funding sources will not support those requests, the institutions are likely to ask for things that will be supported. Foundations and corporations thus have a potentially enormous impact on institutions' priorities. All concerned should be aware of the forces driving applications for support and alert to the potential for imbalance.

## The Proposal

As the relationship between institution and foundation develops, the institution is likely to submit a written request for support. Proposal preparation brings some new areas of ethical concern, chief among them money. How much should an institution request? Should it be the honest cost (whatever *that* is) of the project or purpose, or should the amount requested (and the budget supporting the request) be exaggerated to leave bargaining room? If the foundation or corporation says it will not pay overhead, is it ethical to add a little bit to each cost it will cover in order to cut some of the burden imposed on the institution? Is it ethical to describe the request as seeking "new" money rather than replacement funds if the proposal asks for support for a slightly changed existing program? Is it ethical to send out proposals for nine different needs and describe each as the college's priority? Is it ethical to send out nine proposals for the same project, each asking for the full amount? What is the institution's responsibility if more than one is funded?

Here the first key to ethical behavior is a clear understanding on both sides of what the grantor will and will not fund. If the corporation or foundation expects to bargain about costs, the applicant should be aware of it. The grantor should describe the basis on which costs should be calculated, and the applicant should abide by it. If there are questions, the grants officer should discuss them with a representative of the corporation or foundation. The grants officer should not permit anyone to suggest that everybody inflates costs (they do not) and should question each item included in the budget. An institutional practice requiring each grant recipient to "repay" certain administrative costs is no justification for hiding that repayment in the budget. The potential grantor must agree that the repayment may be included. Most foundations and corporations do not cover these costs.

The key moral concept is to refrain from cheating. There are rules and expectations that everyone is expected to follow. If a grantee knowingly violates a rule (implicit or explicit) concerning how costs should be calculated, that grantee has "cheated." It has not played by the rules. The creative and unethical proposal writer has many opportunities to cheat. For example, *startup grants* and *seed money* are terms commonly used by funding sources to describe kinds of projects they prefer to support: new endeavors, things that have not been tried before, experiments. Good communication will prevent unethical behavior here. It should be clear to all concerned that the grantor is not interested in helping support an already established program or project (though there may be an offshoot that qualifies). An attempt to disguise an ongoing project as new is both unethical and doomed to failure; there are too many ways for the grantor to check on the project.

It is deceptive to cry wolf, for example, to threaten that the institution will close if a particular grant does not materialize unless the institution will truly have to close its doors if it does not receive the grant. But there is a certain license in describing institutional priorities for the specific funder. Funding sources have different priorities themselves. The institution's top priority in admissions (increasing the number of minority men, for instance) may be of interest to one particular corporation, while another may be interested in curriculum development.

Sending out several proposals for the same project is acceptable provided that each potential grantor is aware that the institution is approaching other sources of support. What is not acceptable—and may hurt the institution's case—is implying that each approach is the only one. If more than one proposal is funded, the institution has several options: to accept only one; to see whether all the grantors will agree to fund a share of the project; to discuss multiyear funding. Accepting several grants, each purporting to cover the full cost of the project, is unethical. The grants officer may encounter situations in which it appears that this has happened: it is not unheard-of for faculty to have simultaneous grants for research, and the grants officer has an obligation to clarify the amount of faculty time being assigned to each.

> At a social occasion the grants officer hears a faculty member say something that indicates that she may have misused a grant. The grants officer knows that the foundation has already received a report saying that the grant was used as described in the funded proposal.

The faculty member who was "indiscreet" at a party has done something wrong, and the situation must be put right. Regardless of the source of the information or the circumstances in which it was gained, the grants officer must look into the matter and make sure that corrective actions are taken both on campus and with the grantor. To fail to act would be unethical for on the part of both the grants officer and the faculty member. Establishing and maintaining trust takes time and requires a lot of work from many people. Damaging it is unfortunately all too easy. If the grants officer does not do something about the misused grant—talk with the department head, file an amended report, or even see that the college gives back the grant money—and the foundation's program director finds out about it, the college has lost its credibility. It may take years before that foundation will support another proposal from that institution. In addition, foundation people talk to each other, and word will spread. The grants officer's highest loyalty here is not to her employer but to the trust between the employer and the grantor.

> Joe Smith, '88, is fund chairman for his fifth reunion. His company has a generous, three-for-one matching-gift program. Joe wants to

offer his classmates the opportunity to give him their gifts. He will then write the college a check for the total and claim the corporate match.

The loyal alumnus who wants to maximize support for his reunion gift program is also damaging trust. The company's matching-gift program is intended to encourage its own employees to support their schools. Whether or not there is language explicitly prohibiting the action proposed by Mr. Smith, it is definitely contrary to the company's intent, and the college must honor that intent. If it does not, the college has cheated. It has violated a convention that the grantee had a right to expect was being observed. If the plan has been put in motion, development staff must act to correct the situation (explaining the problem to the volunteer and his classmates, returning the matching-gift check, apologizing to the company). To prevent this sort of occurrence, during volunteer training staff should make sure that all members of the gift committee are aware of how matching-gift programs work.

## Decision Making

Corporate contributions committees and foundation boards depend on many sources for information to help them decide which proposals to fund. Some information comes from objective sources: lists of grant recipients or National Academy of Science appointments or lists of the institutions attended by National Merit Scholars. Other purveyors of information may include the president of the university, the sophomore who tells her dad, who works for the corporation, that "the math department stinks," university publications, the faculty member who was denied tenure, the chairman of the board, the graduate of 1928, and the parent of the rejected applicant. One of the greatest safeguards against fraudulent claims by the institution is, in fact, the web of relationships likely to connect people at the institution with the organization from which it is seeking funds. Almost every claim can be checked.

A foundation executive is quite friendly with a faculty member at an institution that has recently applied for a grant. The faculty member has not been involved in preparing the proposal. The foundation executive plans to do a "reality check" by talking with her friend about the institution and the people involved in the project described in the proposal.

The foundation executive would be remiss if she did not try to learn enough about the college to allow her make an appropriate recommendation, and so she is certainly justified in using her friend as a resource. (If the institution was attempting to define an old project as new, the matter might then come to light.) Weighing her friend's judgment more heavily than other factors, however, is probably unethical, since the friend is both uninformed about the project and unlikely to be completely unbiased about the individuals involved. In addition, it would be highly desirable for the foundation executive to mention in the course of discussions with institutional representatives that she is well acquainted with this faculty member. The faculty member too ought to feel some obligation to notify the grants officer that his opinion is being sought. This gives the grants officer an opportunity to share the proposal with the faculty member, enabling him to base any comments on knowledge rather than speculation.

Good communication within the "community" of the applicant will go far to reinforce the institution's external and internal reputation for honesty and fair dealing and to prevent ethical abuse. To the extent possible, people who participate in a relationship between the applicant and a potential grantor, officially or not, should know what is going on. In the course of developing the relationship to a point where a proposal is appropriate, the grants officer should be able to identify, and may want to consult with, many of these connections. Although it may be impossible to identify them all and clearly impractical to consult or inform them (for example, if a university has many alumni working at a company to which the school intends to send a request, the grants officer will not speak with every one), the key people should know what is happening. The institution cannot possibly control the flow of information; its only hope is to make the official version widely available.

Sometimes the president of an institution, or the head of a division or department, claims that only very discreet negotiations will lead to a particular grant. In such cases, the person pressing for closed-door negotiations is often trying to make something happen that will not be acceptable to others who feel they have some right to participate in decisions about the subject. While this strategy may get the grant, in the long run it harms the individual who used it, and probably the institution as well. One college president who was determined to bring a "business" orientation to a liberal arts college raised several million dollars from foundations and corporations and then informed the faculty that they were committed to establishing a business-related program. Although the program was established, and indeed flourished for a time, it destroyed faculty trust in the president and quite probably prevented adoption of a number of other needed and desirable changes. Taking the time to garner faculty agreement would have maintained trust within the institution and enabled it to present a united and stable appearance to those it sought to engage.

Foundations and corporations will make exceptional grants under exceptional circumstances, usually centering around a special relationship with a particular institution. The CEO's alma mater may get a chair from the company the year the CEO retires; the foundation board may acknowledge its founder's school with a bricks-and-mortar grant, though it makes no other such gifts. It would be hard to find an exceptional grant for which a justification of this nature does not exist. However, this justification is often not clear to potential applicants, who interpret the action as playing favorites. If the justification for exceptional grants is not made public, potential applicants may begin to feel that the game is rigged. They tend to view grant getting as dependent on the "old boy network" or think that if the grants officer is just smart enough to identify the magic words, the purse strings will open. Unsuccessful applicants become bitter and distrustful of the whole grants process.

Whether exceptional grants are ethical problems for foundations and corporations is a matter for debate; generally the discussion among recipients and disappointed applicants ranges along expected lines. Most program officers dislike exceptions; grants officers dislike them too. They are often widely (and inaccurately) reported, and sooner or later the institution president, a board member, or a professor wants to know why his college or university cannot get one. Because they appear to contradict the giving guidelines that the funder gives to prospective applicants, the exceptional grants lead to many questions and many "exceptional" proposals that will never be funded. Exceptional grants create a problem of appearance, if not of substance.

In all likelihood, colleges and universities will continue to ask for exceptional grants, and companies and foundations will continue to make them. More publicity about the circumstances of the grants, rather than efforts to conceal them, is the only way to combat the appearance of unethical behavior. If a foundation or corporation is one that makes special grants, the information it supplies to the public should indicate that program officers have certain discretionary funds or that the organization occasionally recognizes a particular circumstance with an extraordinary contribution. The principle of providing appropriate information applies as much to the grantors as to the applicants.

> The college's proposal to a foundation has been turned down. A member of the board of trustees plans to call the chairman of the foundation's board, who is a friend of his, and ask that the foundation reconsider its decision.

There are still people who believe that "it's all in who you know." This is what motivates the member of the board of trustees to call his buddy on the foundation board and ask him to reconsider the proposal just declined by the foundation. But he may be asking his buddy to behave unethically. This is potentially embarrassing for him and may hurt the school. A more effective use of his relationship with the foundation should be in checking out possibilities for future grants. At present, a staff member should call the foundation for feedback on why the proposal was declined.

One way to prevent ethical problems is for the grants officer to keep a broad perspective. Those concerned with corporate and foundation support must try to see actions in a larger and more objective context than the need of one particular institution at any given moment. By talking with grantors and other grants officers, reading trade papers and annual reports, and attending conferences and workshops, the grants officer can develop a sense for the field of corporate and foundation giving and see where the particular institution fits into a much larger picture. The grants officer should share this perspective with other fund-raising staff, administrators, faculty, and volunteers whenever possible.

## Using the Funds

Once the foundation or corporation has agreed to fund a particular program or project at the college or university, a contract has been established. This is legally binding; in addition, honoring the intent of the contract is clearly an ethical imperative. Fortunately, there are few instances of deliberate misuse of grantor funds, though inadvertent misuse may be fairly common.

To avoid problems, everyone involved in using the grant must be aware of the terms according to which it was given and understand how funds may be spent. If no grant money can be spent on overseas travel, the traveler needs to bill his plane ticket to a different account. If one-third of the money is earmarked for computers to be installed in residence halls, this expenditure should be documented so that an auditor would be able to track it. If there is any question about an expenditure, the grants officer or the person responsible for overseeing the implementation of the grant must check with an appropriate person at the granting organization and seek approval. It is better to make a telephone call that turns out to be unnecessary than to assume that it is all right to juggle grant money from one pocket to another.

Dealing with the dollars is fairly straightforward, assuming that the proposal was well thought out. Dealing with the actual work being funded can raise its own set of ethical concerns. Suppose that several weeks into a newly funded summer research project an exciting new possibility emerges that is quite different from the work described in the proposal. Is it ethical for the faculty member to use funds awarded for the original project to pursue the new avenue? The key, once again, is communication. The ethical action is to share the information with the grantor and make sure that any changes are acceptable. Concealing changes is certainly wrong; assuming that they can be explained "later," when the institution reports on its use of the grant, is dangerous. If the institution was wrong to assume that a particular change would be approved, it will have to do some fancy footwork to correct the use of the funds, and the trust between the two organizations will be tarnished.

Any number of colleges and universities across the country have experienced the following situation. After considerable debate, often heated and usually public, the institution has divested itself of stock in a company doing business in South Africa or otherwise acting in ways judged undesirable by those in a position to make their opinions felt. Is it ethical, in that case, for the institution to request a grant from the company? It is necessary to look at the situation in a broad rather than a narrow context. Sending a proposal is not betraying trust; the institution has been open about its beliefs and has taken a public stand. It is not attempting to conceal anything about itself or mislead the company. Presumably the request for funds describes something of interest to the company as well as the institution, and a grant could serve both organizations well. But by asking an organization whose business practices it deplores to give it money earned by those same business practices, the institution certainly appears hypocritical, inconsistent in its moral stand. Although strictly speaking it is not unethical to send a proposal, it certainly does not add luster to the institution's reputation. It would be far better to wait until those who decide are comfortable buying stock in the company again, make a public announcement, and then apply for a grant.

> A corporation annually gives the institution a full scholarship for a student whom the institution selects. The scholarship comes with a summer job at the corporation. This year's scholarship recipient does not want to take the summer job but wants to work at a rival company instead.

The immediate reaction on campus to the student's announcement that she prefers to spend the summer working for a competitor is likely to be concern about the relationship between the donor company and the university. But an objective examination of the situation will minimize the possibility of an unethical response. The company's expectations in granting a scholarship that includes a summer job should be clarified. It probably has several goals: to help society by enabling a talented but needy student to get a good education; to build its relationship with this particular institution; to give itself some good visibility among future employees and faculty who may influence students' choices of an employer; and to "try out" the scholarship recipient as a potential permanent employee. It expects the university to choose a scholarship recipient who meets agreed-on criteria (state of origin or major, for instance) and to exercise some care in the choice (to select a student with a respectable academic record). The company may also expect regular reports on the use of the scholarship and the opportunity to come into contact with the recipient. When there is a summer job component, such contact is clearly a company goal. The university expects the student to work hard at her studies and interact appropriately with the donor of the scholarship, whether this consists in writing occasional thank-you letters or having lunch periodically with the company recruiter. While university personnel may expect the student to take advantage of the summer job, they are no more likely to command that she do so than they are to insist that she take a permanent position with the company after graduation.

Before making a final determination about the situation, it would be important to discover the student's reasons for wanting to take a different summer job. If she is taking a political or moral stand against the company, the institution is probably justified in assigning her a different source of financial aid and choosing another recipient, and this should not be concealed from the company. But in any other circumstance—the scholar has decided to go to medical school and feels that a summer spent doing research will be more valuable to her than a summer at the company; the competitor is offering more money or more interesting work; there is a location problem— the grants officer or another university representative should talk with the company representative. Perhaps the company has another plant closer to the student's home or will offer to increase the summer stipend to cover rent. There may be other areas inside the company that would be of greater interest to the student. The grants officer's obligation to all concerned is to get all the facts and possibilities on the table and to make sure that everyone has some input into whatever decisions are made.

## Recognition and Reward

Thanking the donor of a gift to the college or university is a critical part of the philanthropic relationship. The key to ethical behavior here is understanding what is appropriate. This is determined by examining both parties' expectations, measuring them against the policies of both, and giving careful thought to the method of saying thank you. In the case of the company scholarship discussed above, visibility on campus is both recognition and a form of reward. Generally, scholarship donors are listed in the college or university annual report and other widely circulated publications. This gives the grantor public recognition and also demonstrates the institution's ability to attract corporate and foundation support.

More complex is the issue of grants to support research. Naming the company or foundation that supported research in published reports is a very common and noncontroversial way to recognize support. The reward for the company may range from prepublication copies of articles to easy entree to the lab in which the work is being carried out. It may include access to graduate students and postdoctoral fellows the company is eager to hire or the opportunity to engage eminent faculty as consultants or advisers. These days there is considerable debate about the ethics of allowing corporate access to the campus. There is no easy resolution to this debate, and there are many issues to explore. Once again, however, all decisions should be based on open and honest examination of facts, implications, and perceptions; all parties should be encouraged to view the situation from the broadest possible perspective.

> A member of the university's board of trustees is on the contributions committee of a company that has just given fifty thousand dollars to the university's capital campaign. The board member has made only a small personal contribution to the campaign but wants to be named to the Keystone Club, which recognizes gifts at the fifty-thousand-dollar level.

The volunteer on the corporate contributions committee who wants to receive personal recognition for the company gift presents a problem more of tact than of ethics. Recognition "clubs" are established to honor donors, not those who have simply arranged for the gift to be made, and this man is not the donor. Having a written policy describing the criteria for club membership will prevent problems of this nature or at least give the staff justification for denying his request.

There are some instances when a corporate or foundation check results in the naming of individuals to recognition clubs, for example, when the company is solely owned by its head or when the foundation is the personal charitable tool of its (still living) founder or founders. A pragmatic test, though it should not be the only one, is whether the request for funds is handled as a personal solicitation or the institution has gone through the whole procedure of learning about foundation or corporate guidelines, developing a relationship with the organization (not just with the president or founder), and preparing and submitting a written proposal.

Reporting to the foundation or corporation on the use of its funds is another function in which there is room for ethical abuse. In addition to the problem of the faculty member who misuses her grant, where the fault is obvious even if action is difficult, there is the more subtle temptation to exaggerate success. The grants officer should make strenuous efforts to resist this temptation, since it is both un-ethical and, in the long run, unproductive. Inflation sooner or later catches up with the institution; its reputation for honest dealing is tarnished, and future requests will be received with skepticism.

A good safeguard against exaggeration is to find some independent validation of the gift's impact: copies of publications written by the holder of the named chair or a list of graduate schools that have accepted scholarship recipients. Above all, the institution should encourage contact between those involved in using the funds and representatives of the donor organization. (This is also a superb means of cultivating the organization for future support.) Even if the project did not achieve what was intended, it is important to report fully and honestly to the grantor. Not all experiments succeed; not all changes are for the better. Whatever the results, people at the institution have learned things that will make the institution stronger in the long run, and that is no small benefit.

## Special Responsibilities of the Grants Officer

Although many people at a college or university participate in the corporate and foundation relations program, the grants officer bears the primary responsibility for developing strategy (or seeing that it is developed), implementing or overseeing implementation of plans, and monitoring the institution's relationships with past, current, and potential organizational donors. A large institution may have close to a hundred staff members engaged in technology transfer plus a significant number of others directly involved in fund raising from the corporate sector. It may have a separate foundation relations function with additional staff. A mid-sized institution may have a combined office with five or six staff, and a small college or one just getting into foundation and corporate fund raising may have only one person, or even a half-time position.

Regardless of the size of the staff, the individual in charge (or the heads of the foundation relations and corporate relations programs, if they are separate) must be sure that every staff member is aware of what constitutes ethical behavior. A written policy is a great help in educating staff, and every institution should have one, but it does not substitute for regular discussion of issues. The grants officer is responsible for maintaining a climate in which ethical behavior is unquestionably the norm and where every staff member feels free to raise a question if he or she is in the least bit uncomfortable or un- sure about how to handle a particular situation.

The grants officer is responsible for seeing that people at the insti- tution and those connected with it know what they need to about the institution's relations with corporations and foundations. This includes timely and accurate news of new giving programs, grants to the institution, and other forms of connection such as a list of this year's foundation scholars, appointments to funded chairs, the re- cently awarded challenge grant for library construction, and pending proposals. But where does the importance of spreading the news conflict with issues of confidentiality?

It is only reasonable to supply all those who helped develop a pro- posal with a copy of the final version, as they may get calls from someone at the foundation or corporation requesting more informa- tion or clarification. Obviously, once the proposal has left the institu- tion, no one at the institution has control over how it is circulated. The safeguard here is making certain that the proposal is truthful and factual and contains nothing that would embarrass the institu- tion if it were made public.

The question of general access to proposals (and to any informa- tion about the institution's relationships with specific foundations and corporations) is thorny upon first examination. Development offices are customarily quite reluctant to open their files even to members of the college community, and most have strict (and ap- propriate) policies of keeping individuals' records confidential. In addition, "development" has traditionally been viewed with mixed feelings by faculty and some administrators, often regarded as a nec- essary evil but not credited for any particular integrity or profes- sionalism. Development staff respond defensively to this perception.

But staff need to realize that the privacy they protect by declaring files confidential is that of the individuals described in those files, not their own or that of the institution.

It is inappropriate to apply such a policy to foundation and corporate relations. If a faculty member or administrator appears in the office and asks for a copy of a proposal, the grants officer's first reaction is likely to be, "Why do you want it?" This is a legitimate question, but whatever the answer, denying access to any proposal or any other information about the institution's corporate and foundation relations program may well be unethical. Foundations and corporations are organizations, not individuals; their finances are matters of public record (in most cases), and information about their support for this or any other institution is available to the general public. There is no reason, therefore, for the development office to guard grant information.

As to details of the relationship, including successful, unsuccessful, and pending proposals, there appears to be no justification for keeping them from members of the college community. Anything proposed by the institution to a funding source surely is subject to institutional governance, in which faculty play a crucial role. Since the principle of individual confidentiality does not apply to foundations and corporations, there is no need to guard the documents as one would guard correspondence between the institution and an individual or information collected about an individual. In the private sector, at least, the ideal of the university is an open community. There should be nothing in the relationship between the institution and a funding source that could not stand scrutiny, nor should the files contain any material that would be embarrassing or harmful.

In fact there is much to be gained in the long run by maintaining a policy of openness on campus about the school's corporate and foundation relations. If members of the academic community are aware of what is happening, they are much more likely to volunteer their own connections with funding sources and to share news of new programs, and so forth, with the grants officer. The foundation director's "reality check" will not catch the institution by surprise, or if it does, the faculty member is well positioned to respond knowledgeably. A greater understanding of the process of developing good relationships with funding sources will also help build confidence in the development program and the fund-raising staff.

Discussing a grant already received by the institution with a colleague from another institution is certainly ethical and often useful. It allows the grants officer to develop a broader perspective and sets the stage for reciprocity. Each institution's relationship with each funding source is unique and cannot be duplicated; even very specific details of what was contained in the funded proposal would not give the second institution additional leverage.

## Conclusion

The grant-making function is part of the power of the corporation or foundation, not of any single individual in the granting organization. Grant getting too is a function of the college or university, even when the grant appears to benefit only a certain individual. By demonstrating personal integrity and by guarding the integrity of the organizations and institutions involved in the relationship, grants officers achieve their goal of promoting a healthy, mutually beneficial relationship between one institution and its grantors, and between higher education and the corporations and foundations that support aspects of its mission.

# 10

# Comprehensive Fund-Raising Campaigns

## Richard F. Seaman and Eric B. Wentworth

By mid-1994 seven major American universities were engaged in unprecedented megacampaigns with fund-raising goals of at least $1 billion apiece. An eighth had already completed a $1.1 billion campaign. Meanwhile, scores of smaller institutions were undertaking or engaged in campaigns that, relative to the size and resources of the institutions, were just as large. This proliferation of huge institutional campaigns has become one of the most dramatic developments in educational fund raising over the past decade. These campaigns render especially important the ethical issues that are always inherent in fund raising. They also raise issues peculiar to campaigns.

This chapter discusses the principal ethical issues that arise in planning and conducting megacampaigns. They fall into several general areas:

- Campaign size and scope
- Campaign structuring and marketing
- Keeping score: gift counting and reporting
- Campaign cost-effectiveness
- Relations with donors

One result of the recent trend is that immense campaign goals have begun to draw more attention than the purposes for which the funds are to be raised. With public attention already focused on relentless tuition increases, some worry that megacampaigns may give the wrong impression. "Many professionals share a deep concern that to the public, today's billion-dollar campaigns spell greed rather than need—and that this perception hurts all our educational institutions," wrote Peter McE. Buchanan, the president of the Council for

Advancement and Support of Education (CASE) and formerly the chief fund raiser at Columbia University, in the October 1991 issue of *CASE Currents*.[1]

As the dollar goals rise—whether to $1 billion for a major research university or $40 million for a small private college—other stakes become higher as well. In presenting a case to donors, campaign leaders spell out the institution's identity, strengths, potential, and aspirations. They put the institution's prestige, as well as their own reputations, judgment, and commitment, squarely on the line.

"A major campaign can put an institution on the map by increasing its visibility locally and nationally," wrote Rita Bornstein, president of Rollins College and former vice president for development at the University of Miami, in the January 1989 issue of *CASE Currents*. "An ambitious goal, successfully achieved in less than the stated time frame, strengthens an institution's credibility by signaling that donors have great confidence in the quality of its research and teaching."[2]

While success can pay rich dividends above and beyond the dollars raised, failure threatens a different outcome. Pressures to avoid perceptions that a campaign is proving less than hugely successful, perceptions that could be self-fulfilling, can become intense. With such high stakes, comprehensive campaigns command total commitment from all concerned. For presidents, trustees, other volunteer leaders, and their associates, campaigns offer status and prestige—as well as risk. For the institutions' chief fund-raising professionals, the opportunity to direct a campaign culminates years of grooming and experience and involves mastering and applying a full arsenal of advancement principles and practices. For donors, the campaign tests the depth of their commitment to philanthropy and their bonding to the institution, as measured by their generosity.

The planning and conduct of high-stakes, high-visibility campaigns test both the ethical integrity of the institution and the ethical behavior of everyone engaged in fund raising—the president, trustees, other campaign volunteers, fund-raising professionals, faculty and other campus constituents, alumni, and the donors themselves. Fundamental issues of truth telling, openness, fairness, trust, and integrity are always present in fund raising. So are more particular issues: respect for privacy (in donor research), conflicts of interest, and a broad spectrum of issues involving relationships between fund raisers and donors.

In the glare of a major campaign, the compelling imperative of success can repeatedly challenge the ethical principles and sensitivities of those involved. Temptations to put expediency before principle—to cut corners, bend rules, embellish or disguise the truth—are always lurking. Questions what gifts to count or not count and how to count them become crucial, and subject to intense pressures. Fortunately, educational fund raisers who face temptations and pressures generally resist them effectively and help maintain a high ethical tone in their work. What makes ethics so important in fund-raising campaigns is that the behavior of individuals reflects the integrity of the institution as well as their own. An institution without integrity may not survive.

## Ethical Issues Associated with Campaign Size and Scope

By the summer of 1994, Cornell, Columbia, New York University, Pennsylvania, Yale, and Michigan were well into billion-dollar drives. Harvard had just announced its $2.1 billion campaign. Stanford had completed its $1.1 billion campaign. Other institutions had launched or were considering campaigns that for them were just as dramatic.

In the early days of fund raising, a college or university would usually identify one particular need—a new gymnasium, an endowed professorship—and determine an appropriate dollar goal to meet that need. It would launch a campaign to raise funds for that specific purpose and only count gifts for that purpose toward the campaign's goal. Today's major campaigns typically seek money for an array of purposes: professorships, facilities, general endowment, student aid, and current operations, among others. Because of the dramatic sums, as well as multiple purposes, overall dollar goals tend to attract more attention than these purposes.

Some of the largest multipurpose campaigns cover a limited list of top-priority needs. They seek funds only for these priorities and may not count gifts for other purposes. If they were to incorporate every item on every dean's wish list, they would have far higher goals.

But most campaigns today are defined broadly enough that almost any gifts for any purposes can be counted, whether or not they meet the institution's top-priority needs. "It's the path of least resistance," Buchanan commented in his *Currents* article.

Fixation on total dollars can arouse intense competition as institutions determine how high to set their campaign goals and then set out to achieve or surpass them. A rival institution has launched a $120 million campaign. Does your institution dare set a lesser goal? How much higher should yours be? Presidents, trustees, other volunteers, alumni, faculty, and fund-raising professionals can all get swept along in tides of institutional pride, spirit, and enthusiasm, as well as self-interest, in determining the goal. The underlying question in setting a campaign goal is whether the decision is driven primarily by competition or by the institution's strategic objectives and top-priority needs. Do the institution's leaders want to set a high campaign goal primarily as a collective "ego trip" or because everyone else is doing it? Or have they concluded that a large campaign is truly necessary and will serve the institution's long-term best interests?

A number of distinct issues are associated with setting campaign goals and duration. Should the institution's leaders be aggressive and set a lofty goal to leverage larger gifts from constituents? Generally, the larger the goal, the larger individual donors' likely gifts. Lofty goals, particularly if not clearly related to important needs, risk being seen as institutional greed. Moreover, the higher the goal, the higher the risk of failure, intensifying pressures and stresses for all concerned, and increasing temptations to bend the rules. To attain a high goal may also require a large proportion of deferred gifts that will not yield spendable support for years to come. If this is the case, then institutional strategists have a responsibility to make sure that all concerned, especially faculty, understand the time frames for actually realizing the benefits of a successful campaign.

Conversely, institutional decision-makers can play it safe and set a comfortably low goal that they can be sure to attain. They will not, however, be serving their institution well if it has serious needs that the campaign overlooks but might meet if it only addressed them.

Decision makers should ask whether the campaign will serve the institution's long-term best interests and protect its integrity. Have they resisted succumbing to competitive pressures? Do the campaign's purposes that they have selected reflect the institution's greatest needs and highest priorities? An institution can only go to the well with its major donors so often. It should do so only when the purposes for which it seeks their support are absolutely vital to the institution's welfare and future strength.

# Ethical Issues in Structuring and Marketing Campaigns

To plan and conduct a campaign that addresses important institutional needs and can attract the desired support requires sophisticated packaging and marketing decisions that present fund raisers with numerous ethical issues. For example, institutional leaders may recognize that a particular need—funding deferred maintenance, for example—is a top priority but not readily salable to donors. Should it be omitted from campaign objectives?

Ideally, institutional leaders should carefully determine the institution's top priorities and incorporate them into the campaign goal whether or not these priorities will be intrinsically popular with donors. They can recognize that raising funds for some priority needs will take a lot more work and persuasion than raising funds for others but conclude that if a need is truly crucial, the campaign should include it. In fact as they determine what to include or exclude from the campaign's purposes, institutional leaders may try to strike a balance between top needs and priorities as objectively determined, regardless of appeal, and those likely to attract donor support. The institution may desperately need a new heating system, but chances are slim that any wealthy alumni will make large gifts to fund it.

One strategy can be to solicit gifts in the campaign for popular purposes currently covered by general operating funds and then redirect those operating funds to the less-popular needs. It is crucial in such instances that the campaign make clear that donors' gifts will be used to provide budget relief rather than budget increases. At the other extreme, decision makers who want to set a high goal but make sure they attain it may be tempted to include in the campaign only those purposes that they know will have broad, sure-fire appeal, whether or not they represent top-priority needs.

Strategists can rigorously package a campaign in such a way that gifts for purposes that are not top priorities are excluded from the campaign total (though they may be gratefully accepted and recognized in other ways). They can also define purposes in broad enough terms to allow considerable leeway for counting gifts that bear some relation to the campaign's priority needs, or in such general or open-ended terms that almost *any* gift can be counted toward the total goal.

Another packaging issue involves whether to include in the campaign the volume of donations that the institution would be receiving through the normal flow of annual and capital gifts. To include these donations allows setting a larger goal and counting a larger flow of gifts. On the other hand, some may view this as overstating the size and success of the campaign. They would argue for defining the campaign as covering only the additional or incremental support that it generates. The issue here is a simple one: whichever approach is taken, campaign leaders should clearly disclose it and stick with it.

Some institutions enhance campaign totals by including federal or state government grants, particularly if they are *challenge grants,* which require the institution to raise private matching support. Fund raisers at other institutions firmly oppose including government grants in campaigns. As with any strategy questions, the ethical issue turns on playing by the rules and on disclosure. Were government grants to be counted under the original campaign plan, or are they to be added under a midcourse rules change? Do they satisfy clearly stated campaign goals? And are government grant funds clearly identified for what they are? Contracts, whether government or private, are another matter entirely, well outside even the most broadly defined campaign.

Whether an institution includes unrealized bequests (testamentary intentions) and deferred gifts in a campaign—and if so, how—can also raise questions. Some oppose including unrealized bequests at all, arguing that such commitments can change because of a donor's circumstances or decisions and that, in any event, the institution may not see gift proceeds for many years. There is another consideration: counting an unrealized bequest from a young donor today may increase the risk that the bequest will be counted again when it is at last realized. Opponents of counting unrealized bequests deem it a dubious way to inflate a campaign's goal and its subsequent results. If a campaign's success is disproportionately dependent on unrealized bequests, it may give a misleading picture of the near-term benefits to the institution.

It can be even more problematical if the campaign includes unrealized bequests from donors with long life expectancies. If the bequest commitment is expressed as a dollar sum (rather than a percentage of the estate), the buying power of those dollars may have shrunk significantly by the time the gift is realized. Many fund raisers contend that if unrealized bequests and other deferred gifts are counted, they should be assigned dollar values that allow for such shrinkage; this is usually referred to as "discounting to present value." Others, concerned that discounting dollar amounts of gifts would upset donors, firmly disagree. Fund raisers who favor including deferred gifts contend that if a campaign takes a truly long-term view of the institutions's needs, commitments that will yield important resources at some future date have a legitimate place.

Expanding the number of unrealized bequests can itself be a worthy fund-raising objective. Those who favor including them contend that bequests represent investments in the institution's future and often yield endowment funds when realized. A major campaign offers an ideal opportunity to swell the ranks of donors making bequest commitments. Counting these commitments toward a campaign goal, at no immediate cost to the donor, offers an incentive to make such commitments.

When institutions can identify testators (donors making unrealized bequests), they can set about showing those donors the advantages of converting such commitments to life income gifts: the donor makes an irrevocable commitment of principal in return for a tax deduction and assured income from that principal. Such gifts assure that the institution will receive that principal at some future date. The basic issue is whether the campaign includes unrealized bequests primarily to allow setting and attaining a larger goal or primarily to serve the institution's long-term best interests.

How campaigns treat deferred gifts other than bequests, such as charitable remainder trusts and other life income gifts, can also be ethically complex. Should they be counted at all? And if so, should they be discounted to reflect the value of the donor's actual charitable deduction?

Still another way to inflate a campaign's goal is to extend its duration, say, to a decade or more. Some would ask whether a campaign ceases to be a campaign over such an extended period. Others might say that institutions today must maintain a constant campaign mind-set anyway.

These in themselves may be strategy decisions. But it is important to recognize that almost all strategy decisions have ethical dimensions. Do the strategies put the institution's integrity and best interests first? Are their purposes justified? And are the strategies and the reasons behind them disclosed and openly discussed? As in other areas of fund-raising campaigns, the basic imperative is that campaign leaders establish firm rules, communicate those rules and their ramifications clearly and consistently to all concerned, and then abide by them as the campaign moves ahead.

Campaign marketing involves efforts to create and maintain a campaign's essential momentum. Communications strategies may involve a theme, a case statement, a logo or other visual identity, possibly a video, and an array of newsletters, press releases, and other written communications. Issues in campaign marketing arise in the inevitable tensions between enthusiastic hyperbole and low-key candor. At what point does putting the institution's best foot forward step over the line into misleading boosterism?

Tensions may occur from the very outset, in preparing basic communications materials. Do they describe the institution as it is—both its strengths and its weaknesses—fairly and accurately? Do they assess the institution's needs and potential with suitable objectivity? Do they define and describe the campaign's goal and purposes in a credible way?

Campaign marketing also raises critical issues involving disclosure. Once the campaign is underway, pressures to report only good news about fund-raising progress, lest momentum suffer, are inevitable. Such pressures can extend to reporting about the institution itself during the campaign. Should there be bad news, whether a faculty scandal or campus drug bust, an applications decline or budget deficit, some may be tempted to downplay it for fear it will make donors wary. After all, the stakes may be very high. But the institution risks losing credibility with donors and with the public at large if it skirts the truth about bad news. Ethical conduct dictates never misleading by omission except where some other value, such as protecting an individual's privacy, is more compelling.

## Comprehensive Fund-Raising Campaigns

Suppose that a campaign is well under way but results are lagging behind expectations. Can marketing strategists extend the campaign in hopes of eventual success? It will depend on how they announce and explain such a decision. Certainly, if they present their decision deceptively, they risk being seen as manipulating the truth; and if they are perceived that way, the institution can lose irreplaceable trust.

Donors' perceptions and degrees of trust in the institution and in those who lead and represent it affect their sense of bondedness with it and thus their generosity. The institution's leaders must act, and be seen as acting, in the institution's best interests, not just their own. This indeed should be the campaign's imperative in all its marketing activities.

## Ethics in Keeping Score

How an institution counts gifts it receives can raise ethical issues that reflect on its integrity. Questions arise involving what gifts to count, how and when to count them, and who to credit for them. This is especially true in large, comprehensive fund-raising campaigns. Counting and reporting gifts is how an institution keeps score in its efforts to raise private support. And scorekeeping inevitably reinforces the element of competition: Did we meet our goal? How do this year's results compare with last year's? How have we done compared with our sister colleges' performance?

For fund raising in general, institutions since 1982 have been able to follow rules spelled out in the "green book"—*Management Reporting Standards for Educational Institutions: Fund Raising and Related Activities*—developed by CASE and NACUBO (the National Association of College and University Business Officers). The Council for Aid to Education's annual "Voluntary Support of Education" survey contains institutional fund-raising data that permit some comparisons. Until very recently, however, no particular set of rules had been developed for keeping score in campaigns, which meant that trustees, presidents, volunteers, and fund-raising professionals at each institution were left to their own devices. In her *Currents* article, Dr. Bornstein describes a 1988 survey she conducted of campaign practices, reporting sometimes wide disparities in the many aspects of campaign gift reporting.[3]

*Areas of Concern*

In a high-stakes campaign the pressures for success can make scorekeeping rules and practices especially crucial. Campaigns intensify competitive factors. Institutions take a keen interest in comparing their own fund-raising results with those of other institutions, even though the fact that individual institutions set their own scorekeeping rules makes comparing results objectively difficult, if not impossible.

There is an inevitable temptation to establish rules for one's own campaign that will help ensure that it produces high gift totals. At the same time, individual institutions may reserve the right to establish rules they deem appropriate to their particular circumstances and histories, including liberal rules for counting gifts. The preferable course, in almost all cases, is to establish scorekeeping rules that are clear and explicit, leaving little room for self-serving interpretation later on. More important is whether the institution's fund raisers abide by these rules as the campaign progresses. It is true, of course, that circumstances may arise that invite special exceptions to the rules; and there may be gray areas that the rules simply do not cover.

To the extent that today's campaigns focus primary attention on large dollar goals, they provide fertile ground for ethical concerns in counting and reporting gifts. For instance, an institution may announce that it has attained the campaign's overall dollar goal even though it has not achieved all the purposes. It may have received more than enough support for three purposes, not quite enough for a fourth, and not nearly enough for a fifth. Is it ethical for the institution to proclaim the campaign a success? Or is the campaign truly successful if it attains the dollar goal because purposes were so loosely defined that almost any gift could be counted toward one purpose or another or because the rules allowed counting gifts whether or not they addressed a particular campaign purpose? The institution might be tempted to count gifts toward the overall goal that were received during the campaign but earmarked for wholly separate purposes. Would it be ethical to do so? Would it be more ethical to add these purposes to the original campaign purposes instead and increase the total campaign goal by the amount of these gifts?

The counting of *nucleus* gifts, major donations secured during the campaign's crucial but quiet first phase, before it "goes public," also raises issues. Campaign strategists may differ over percentages, but

## Comprehensive Fund-Raising Campaigns

there is almost universal agreement that the institution should raise a substantial portion of the overall goal before officially announcing that the campaign is under way. The recognized purpose of the "nucleus" phase is to test donors' responses to the campaign's objectives. At the same time, a successful nucleus phase permits kicking off the campaign publicly with good news on gifts already committed. This assures prospective donors that the campaign enjoys important support and has a full head of steam.

Absent clear rules, especially when the campaign's purposes are broad or loosely defined, the temptation can be strong to count as nucleus gifts whatever donations are received during the preannouncement period, whether or not they are in response to campaign solicitations or even relate to campaign purposes. Suppose a wealthy alumnus just happens to die during the nucleus phase of the campaign and leaves a bequest of several million dollars. The bequest was not solicited as a campaign gift. Indeed, at the time he wrote the bequest into his will, neither the alumnus nor the institution had any idea that his death would occur at the outset of a major campaign. Still, should the institution count it as a nucleus gift toward the campaign goal?

In fact many campaigns incorporate in their goals a projected dollar amount for bequests that will be realized and counted during the campaign. But what if a particular realized bequest is for a specified use that falls outside the campaign's purposes? Here again, can campaign strategists identify it as fulfilling a new campaign purpose and increase the campaign goal? It might likewise be tempting to count as nucleus support, if they are received during this phase, the final payments on a pledge commitment made several years earlier. The main ethical concern is that any particular gift amount should be counted only once and should be counted in the current campaign only if it helps meet a campaign objective.

The soliciting of bequests and life-insurance gifts, as well as what are known as planned or life income gifts, has become an increasingly widespread practice. What distinguishes such gifts is that the institution receives donor commitments of what may be substantial sums before—sometimes long before—it actually gains use of the funds. As campaign goals soar, such gifts represent a tempting source of big numbers to help meet those goals.

How institutions keep score on these gifts varies considerably.

Some only count realized bequests and the cash surrender value of contributed life insurance policies. Others count unrealized bequest commitments if the donors have reached a threshold age, normally sixty-five or seventy. Some institutions, as already noted, discount gifts to "present value" when they will not receive funds until a future date. Others count the full value of the gift without discounting. But even if a gift is discounted, the institution that includes the discounted amount toward the campaign goal may imply that the institution has the use of that money when in fact it will not for an indeterminate period.

Another issue involves the firmness of bequest commitments. Donors may inform the institution that they *intend* to leave a bequest; or they may commit themselves in writing to a bequest; or they may commit themselves not only concretely but *irrevocably* to leaving a bequest, specifying that the commitment will be binding on their estate. Including or excluding intended bequests in particular can be an ethical gray area. Inclusion may be tempting, but intentions can be tenuous—and subject to change.

Retained life interest gifts other than bequests are usually irrevocable commitments. And since the donor has actually transferred assets (rather than simply making a commitment for a future transfer of assets), the donor rightly believes that a gift has in fact been made. But should the institution count the total value of the gift or just the discounted amount? Many fund raisers favor counting deferred gifts at full face value, which not only puts the donors in the best light but also means larger figures in campaign totals.

Cautious institutions take into account the fact that a donor can make a bequest commitment and later change his or her will or that the donor's estate could be insufficient when the time comes to fulfill the bequest commitment. Such institutions may count only bequest and life insurance gift commitments that are irrevocable and legally binding—and not revocable commitments or mere expressions of intent.

There may be inherent ethical problems for any institution in announcing that it has raised so many millions of dollars toward its goal when it has not received actual proceeds and may not for years to come. Campaign progress reports based on counting these gifts raise expectations among faculty, for example, that the institution will not be able to fulfill for years. Is this not deceptive? The best solution is for the institution to clarify its gift-counting guidelines, as well as the nature and timing of these gifts, before and during a campaign.

Related questions may arise when campaign fund raisers count multiyear pledges. Under normal campaign rules, if a donor pledges near the start of a campaign a multiyear gift that will be fully paid by the conclusion of the campaign or within a set number of years, the institution can appropriately count the full amount as campaign support. But if three years into a five-year campaign a donor makes a pledge payable over the following ten years, such rules might prevent the institution from counting the full pledge. If the campaign is running out of time and is still short of its goal, and counting the full amount of this ten-year pledge would help it attain the goal, does the institution bend the rules? And, in any event, what about recognition for the donor? Why should a donor who makes a multiyear pledge of $1 million near the end of a campaign get credit for a smaller campaign gift than one who pledged $1 million at the very outset? The tensions between adherence to campaign gift-counting rules and equitable donor recognition can generate numerous dilemmas.

In sum, ethically as well as mathematically, scorekeeping for fund-raising campaigns can pose a host of thorny issues.

## Ethical Issues in Campaign Cost-Effectiveness

At the same time that campaign strategists are concentrating on building, managing, and deploying all the staff and volunteers engaged in gift solicitation and other campaign activities, they must also be concerned with the actual and perceived cost-effectiveness of these activities.

Donors in all areas of philanthropy, as well as the public, are increasingly insistent that organizations and institutions use gift dollars for intended purposes and not spend inordinate sums on the process of gift solicitation. They have read about alleged excesses in executive compensation and overhead expenses at some nonprofits and allegations that some charities spend large sums on fund-raising activities, leaving scant amounts for programs and services for which gifts are solicited.

The issue of spending on fund raising itself versus spending on intended purposes has been generating an increasingly heated debate throughout the philanthropic community, with obvious ethical considerations. One central issue involves accounting—how to distinguish between the costs of fund raising per se and the costs of educating the public about the purposes for which funds are being raised.

Aside from how costs are allocated, there are two sides to the question whether to hold fund-raising costs to an absolute minimum. Simple economics suggests that you should spend $1.00 if the expenditure brings a $1.01 contribution. While this means that more than 99 percent of the donation goes to covering the cost of soliciting it rather than to serving the donation's intended purpose, the institution still has a penny that it would not have had otherwise. But politically if not ethically, such a ratio raises a red flag and risks loss of credibility and trust.

On the other hand, while to hold fund-raising costs to the barest minimum so that the campaign leadership can proudly claim that they are spending only 10¢ for every $1.00 they raise may look good to donors and the public, it may do the institution a grave disservice if it means the campaign raises far less money than it might have. Some will argue that making only minimal investments in fund raising is itself unethical and that by spending 15¢ per $1.00 raised, the institution could generate a marginal return several times the incremental expenditure.

Here is an illustration: Institution A spends $1 million and raises $10 million; that is, it spends 10¢ per $1.00 raised. But Institution B spends $3 million and raises $20 million. That is it spends 15¢ rather than 10¢ per $1.00 raised, but by spending an additional $2 million it raises an additional $10 million. Thus, one can argue that being too conservative in fund-raising expenditures can shortchange the institution and that one is justified in spending more on fund raising when the results are a significant multiple of the investment.

It is important to remember, of course, that in the interests of trust and credibility, one should disclose these fund-raising costs accurately, and not try to hide or obscure them, lest there be suspicion about fund raisers' enriching themselves.

At some point campaign spending per gift dollar may reach a level that strains donor faith and confidence. Most educational institutions, however, are far from fund-raising spending levels that might be considered excessive in proportion to the returns in gift dollars that they generate. On the other hand, questions may arise concern-ing *how* campaign budgets are spent. Lavish salaries or entertain-ment allowances for senior fund raisers may well cause concern. Why serve filet mignon when chicken will suffice?

Inadequate staffing is a common problem when it comes to seek-ing the support of major donors. Take as a model the institution with about fifty thousand alumni, parents, and other supporters. Normal experience would suggest that about 10 percent of them (five thou-sand) would each have the capacity, if so inclined, to contribute at least ten thousand dollars over three to five years to an institutional campaign. How many major gifts officers would it take to cultivate these five thousand prospects and thus secure their maximum gift support?

Take as a rule of thumb that each of these prospects should be contacted at least four times per year. Assume that a major gifts offi-cer can reasonably manage sixteen contacts a week. Over fifty weeks that amounts to eight hundred contacts. At four contacts per pros-pect per year, that means each officer should have responsibility for periodic contacts with two hundred prospects. Most fund-raising professionals would agree that this is a *very* heavy load.

The institution with five thousand major-gift prospects would need a staff of twenty-five officers (at the very least) to maintain such a level of prospect contacts and ensure their loyalty and maximum support. Almost all institutions fall far, far short of this. Decision makers who do not provide staffing adequate to assure full coverage of prospects are shortchanging their institutions when.

## Ethical Issues in Donor Relations

Ethical ambiguities that sometimes surround relationships with donors take on larger dimensions in campaigns. Maintaining credi-bility with donors is essential. Adherence to clear ethical standards of truth telling, fairness, and respect for the individual can ensure it. The vast majority of campaigns follow the highest ethical standards in asking donors for their support. Fund raisers plan the solicitation of a gift with care and sensitivity. Whoever solicits the donor has done his or her homework and knows the donor's philanthropic in-terests, resources, and prior record of generosity. Conducted ethi-cally, such research has delved only into public records—no gossip or "personal" information—and thus has respected and protected the donor's privacy.

The volunteer solicitor, a trusted acquaintance, shares information with the donor in a straightforward way. Solicitor and donor discuss a specific gift figure and time frame. The solicitor makes a low-key, factual presentation, avoiding anything resembling "hype" or high-pressure "closing" tactics.

Moreover, while seeking as large a gift as feasible, the solicitor must keep the interests of the donor, and the donor's family and other dependents, paramount. It would be unethical to pressure donors to make gifts that are beyond their means or that disregard the welfare of donors or others. In cultivating donors, fund raisers risk developing personal relationships that could lead to awkward situations and conflicts of interest. There have been cases in which well-intended donors have asked fund raisers for advice on personal finances or estate matters, as well as cases in which donors have made personal gifts to fund raisers or left them substantial bequests in their estates. (These issues are explored in greater depth in chapters 6 and 7.)

The solicitor should not offer any special privileges or recognition for a gift to any particular donor that would not be available to any other donor making that gift; nor should the solicitor lead the donor to expect that the institution would provide special treatment if requested. Donor requests for special treatment might take various forms. A donor might want assurance that his or her gift will be counted toward the campaign goal even though the gift's purpose was not a campaign purpose. A donor might ask for waivers of rules that would otherwise require completion of a pledged gift within five years so that he can have eight years to complete his; or he might want his name on a facility, a bronze plaque, or an honorary degree; or he might want special campus privileges—when none of these forms of recognition would be available to other donors making similar gifts.

If the solicitor's paramount concern is to secure the donor's gift, the temptation to accede to such special requests can be compelling. Saying no to an insistent donor who has offered a generous gift can be one of a fund raiser's biggest challenges. Campaign rules may allow exceptions in special circumstances. If so, campaign leaders would do well to create a committee to review circumstances in particular cases and make judgment calls on whether exceptions are justified. Where such committees exist, those involved in the campaigns are responsible for referring special cases to them, providing them with thorough and accurate information, and then abiding by their rulings. One useful standard for dealing with many issues that may arise in relations with individual donors is to consider the impact on other donors and potential donors. Broader standards would include the potential impact on the campaign's success and, ultimately, on the institution's well-being and integrity.

Such decisions are not always easy. Fund raisers are responsible not only to donors seeking special consideration but to all the other donors and potential donors and to all of the institution's other present and prospective constituents. Those weighing an exception should consider how other stakeholders might perceive it. What if those stakeholders read about it on the front page of the local newspaper? What makes these decisions on exceptions so difficult is that often they require balancing of conflicting legitimate interests. Individual donor interests may pull one way, and institutional interests the other. The decision of a committee, however, will usually satisfy donors that they have received a fair hearing even though their requests may be denied.

## The Profession Steps In

With ethical questions about campaign design, marketing, score-keeping, and cost-effectiveness already stirring concerns in some quarters, Dr. Bornstein's survey became a catalyst for action. CASE launched what became a four-year project to develop standards that would improve consistency, accountability, and credibility in fund-raising campaigns. It formed the Campaign Reporting Advisory Group, a team of professionals chaired by Vance T. Peterson, vice president for institutional advancement at Occidental College, to draft these standards. The advisory group wrote numerous drafts and circulated them widely for comment, seeking broad consensus on standards allowing objective comparison of one campaign with another and rational measurement of any particular campaign's success in fulfilling intended goals.

In his preface to the final report, Peterson wrote that the standards were "rooted in two important convictions. One is that how well the campaign meets its objectives is far more important than the size of its dollar goal. The other is that success should be measured primarily in terms of how well the institution meets its own needs and fulfills its unique mission."[4]

The report comprises both campaign management guidelines and gift-reporting standards. The management guidelines include the following:

- Campaign design: "Care should be taken to design campaigns that reconcile the needs of the institution with the interest and capacity of its constituencies to fund them."[5]
- The campaign plan, which should be in writing, should cover a series of essential subjects (such as campaign gift-reporting policies) and should be reviewed and approved by the appropriate bodies.
- Campaign purposes, which extend well beyond attaining a dollar goal. Planners should "keep in mind that no campaign will be the last campaign."[6]
- Marketing: "While campaign case statements and other literature or presentations should be designed to inspire and motivate donors, such materials should not be used to distort institutional accomplishments, characteristics, or capabilities."[7]
- There should be recognition during a campaign for all donors, including those whose contributions cannot be appropriately counted toward the campaign itself.

The reporting standards cover campaign duration, including the nucleus phase; fundamental campaign-gift counting principles; what gift totals to report and how (including deferred gifts both at face value and discounted to present value); when and how to report various types of gifts; what types of funds (including government grants) to exclude from campaign totals; how to handle pledges; and standards for reporting particular types of gifts such as property, closely held stock, pooled income funds, various types of trusts, gift annuities, remainder interests, testamentary pledges, realized bequests, life insurance, and private grants.

CASE urged all institutions planning or already conducting campaigns to comply with the voluntary standards, which would take effect with the 1994–95 year. It asked institutions engaged in campaigns to submit reports by December 31 each year and said that it would assemble and annually publish information from these reports as a service to members and the public.

CASE President Buchanan set about securing endorsements of the standards among other education associations, and said CASE would provide training for professionals during 1994–95. "All of us who have contributed to these standards," Buchanan stated, "hope and expect that they will strengthen education and the philanthropic spirit that undergirds it, for the future benefit of society."[8]

## Professional Pressures and Temptations

Fund-raising professionals are in a position to serve as the campaign's conscience. With experience and proper training, they should be more familiar with the rules by which fund raising should be conducted than the presidents, deans, trustees, and volunteers, whose expertise normally lies in other areas. By remembering that they *are* professionals and always acting accordingly—in relations with donors as well as their campaign associates—fund raisers can set standards by their actions as well as their words.

In the heat of high-stakes campaigns, fund raisers themselves can face incredible pressures to condone or take part in behavior that may be unethical. Major campaigns with huge goals and finite deadlines can create a climate conducive to the bending of rules. Requests by major donors to "forget the rules" are difficult to ignore when the gifts in question are large. Fund raisers—and sometimes presidents of institutions too—get caught in a box: if they reject the request, the institution may lose an important gift; if they accede to it, they may perform a disservice to the institution's integrity.

Pressures may also arise within the campaign team. What does a fund-raising professional do, for example, when he or she is caught between an influential volunteer who insists that a large gift he secured be counted in the campaign and the fund raiser's interpretation of the rules, which tells him the gift should *not* be counted toward the campaign goal? What if an influential dean, or for that matter the institution's president, is the one applying pressure?

A special campaign committee whose purpose is to resolve donor requests for exceptions to gift-counting rules and make other judgment calls when required may play an invaluable role. Even the institution's president may be caught on the horns of a tricky dilemma, and the special committee may spare him or her, as well as fund raisers and others, a host of headaches. While a committee may not ensure total ethical correctness or consistency, the existence and use of such a process goes a long way toward ensuring fairness—and the perception of fairness. Thus it helps sustain the institution's credibility.

A special committee, perhaps involving members of the board of trustees, not only shares the decision-making burden but brings to bear the best collective analysis and judgment of top institutional leadership on serious ethical dilemmas encountered in campaign pressure cookers. After all, ownership of an effective fund-raising campaign is broadly institutional, and the ethical as well as the strategic decisions that it requires should be institutional too.

# 11

# *Employment*

## Richard F. Seaman

The rapid growth of educational institutions' financial needs and the accompanying heightened demand for effective fund raisers has resulted in a sharpened concern about ethical issues within the fundraising profession and an increased public awareness of the special issues associated with employment.

## Underlying Assumptions

Central to the success of all fund raising is the relationship between donor and institution. As the institution's representative, the fund raiser plays a critical role in the gift-making process. By its very nature, the fund raiser's interaction with donors and prospects involves highly confidential aspects of the donor's life. Simultaneously, the fund raiser is among the primary catalysts in helping to build trust, confidence, and a strong bond between the donor and the institution that will result in maximum institutional support. The fund raiser, therefore, inevitably has responsibilities in two directions—to the institution served and to the donor whose support is being sought—about which the fund raiser and the employing institution alike must be concerned. Institutional employment practices and policies affect the nature of the relationship between the fund raiser and the prospect and, thus, the relationship between the institution and the prospect. That is why institutions and professional fund raisers alike *must* be concerned about the framework within which employment policies and practices are developed and administered. Of central concern is the effect such employment policies and practices have on (1) the behavior of fund raisers, including the continuity of their service, and (2) the bonding between donor and institution.

Among the most trusted assumptions governing successful fund raising is this: contributions to institutions increase in direct relationship to the degree of bonding that develops between the donor or prospect and the institution. When donors develop a close relationship with an institution, they gain information about the institution and an understanding of the institution's case for support. Trust and commitment, two essential ingredients in any gift situation, are fostered, and bonding soon occurs. Such bonding is nurtured by caring fund raisers, who are the primary catalysts in maintaining continuity in such relationships. The impact of such bonding is clear: gift support is maximized. It is therefore in the institution's interest to encourage continuity of service by the institution's fund-raising representatives, because ultimately these representatives sustain the relationship between donors and the institution. An important by-product of positive employment policies is that fund raisers who have a long-term commitment to an institution are more likely to engage in behavior that fosters trust, commitment, and thus bonding among donors—and less likely to engage in questionable behavior that may do damage to such relationships.

Specifically, here I will look at *hiring;* the *continuity of service* by the fund-raising professional; professional *job mobility;* related issues associated with *presidential change* in an institution; the nature of *employment contracts;* and *compensation* policies and practices.

The advancement profession and educational, philanthropic, and other institutions are just beginning to identify and address ethical issues associated with employment policies and practices. Thus there is little professional and institutional consensus about which policies and practices are appropriate and which are not. At this point, the profession is beginning to raise the tough questions, but it is not yet capable of answering them. The primary focus of this chapter is to help institutions and individuals ask the right questions. For many of the questions raised, there are no unique "right" answers. But public statements known to the institution, fund raiser, and donor can reduce the occurrence of misunderstandings that give rise to charges of unethical behavior.

## The Dual Nature of the Fund Raiser's Responsibility

Unlike medical and legal professionals, who have in common that their primary responsibility is to the client, seasoned fund raisers would likely agree that the single most important rule governing their behavior and success as professionals is to foster relationships between donors and the institution and the institution's service of the donors' needs. The fund raiser's role is complicated: on the one hand, the fund raiser is employed and paid by a corporate third-party entity, and the professional's primary loyalty by definition of employment must be to an institution or agency that the professional serves, not to the donor. Yet that role is best accomplished when the fund raiser is primarily concerned with the donor's needs and interests, which will ultimately drive the gift decision. This complex relationship between the institution, the fund raiser, and the donor is fundamentally different from the client-centered relationship that is a basic characteristic of other professions.

A central ethical issue is one of *disclosure:* does the fund raiser have a duty to disclose anything in particular to donor prospects and volunteers? For example, the fund raiser may have the obligation to remind donors that his or her primary allegiance is to the institution. The fund raiser's responsibility to the institution can come into conflict with his or her need to protect aspects of the relationship with donors.

Developing close relationships with volunteers, prospects, and donors is fundamental to the process of fostering the essential bonding between the prospect and the institution. But at what point does it become appropriate and necessary for fund raisers to disclose to potential donors the essential institutional and personal self-interests that necessarily accompany their friendship?

Sometimes a prospect will want to make a significant gift to the fund raiser. Suppose, for example, that the donor approaches the fund raiser with a proposal to take out a retained life income gift, naming the fund raiser as the life income beneficiary and the institution as the ultimate beneficiary. The quick response of most would be to decline the gift. But it is not clear how this represents a conflict of interest. The institution, after all, has a primary responsibility to satisfy the *donor's* interest.

What about the donor who names the fund raiser the executor of her estate or leaves an outright legacy to the fund raiser? Or an offer by a donor to a fund raiser to provide, at a favorable interest rate, a mortgage for the fund raiser's purchase of a vacation cottage? Should the fund raiser accept a generous birthday gift? It is not clear where to draw the line. The fund raiser must be motivated to serve the donor, but the fund raiser is also obligated to serve the institution. Fund raiser self-interest surely comes last.

Calvin Mackenzie, a professor of government at Colby College, an ethics scholar, and a former advancement vice president at Colby, provides a helpful guideline:

> The conceptualization [of the dual nature of the fund raiser's role—as both independent broker and institutional representative] . . . is critical to the ethical burden the fund raiser carries into donor/prospect relationships. If the fund raiser were an independent broker, seeking to join a philanthropic prospect with a needy institution, he or she would bear a very high disclosure burden. It is no different from the burden that would fall upon a financial counselor who advised me to invest in a company in which he was a major stockholder: he would be ethically bound to disclose at the outset that he had a financial interest in the investment he was recommending.
>
> In reality, however, fund raisers are rarely independent brokers. More commonly they are employees of the institution seeking support, and the source of their employment is well-known to the potential donor. In that case, the disclosure burden is reduced because the fund raiser's loyalties and self-interest are more obvious. The fund raiser's principal responsibility is to clarify to the potential donor the impacts both to the institution and the donor of any specific gift formulation. Whenever appropriate as well, the fund raiser should advise the donor to seek independent legal or financial counsel.
>
> Fund raisers should never misrepresent themselves or their purposes. But potential donors must take responsibility for their own self-interest. They cannot rely upon fund raisers to know or protect donor self-interest. Nor should fund raisers bear obligation for that. Fund raisers should be fair and forthright and accurate. They should respond fairly to donor questions and concerns. But their primary responsibility is to get the best gift they can for their institutions within the parameters of fair and free negotiation.[1]

Relationships between institutions and donors are most likely to be fostered in support of the institution when no direct or implied components of the fund raiser-donor relationship inure to the fund raiser. Therefore, it is in the best interests of both the institution and the fund raiser for the fund raiser not to accept gifts, loans, testamentary executorships, and the like. The opportunities to do damage to the relationship between the donor and the institution and thus to the institution itself (its perceived integrity, for example) is too great a risk to run.

## Hiring

A recognition of the range of ethical issues related to the employment process is critical both for the institution and for the employee. Making them clear to an employee at the outset may help both employer and employee avoid difficulties later.

Of initial concern in the employment process is *the authenticity of the professional fund raiser's credentials.* The tendency in résumé writing is to claim credit for productivity that has, in the end, been sharply influenced by factors not in the control of the professional. An institution wins a NCAA sports championship, donations to the institution's sports program increase, and athletic fund raisers claim on their résumés that "gifts to the athletic program rose 30 percent in the past year." The fund raiser's credentials are most honestly represented by describing the *behavior* in which the fund raiser engaged rather than by making productivity claims, for example, "conducted athletic annual fund, which increased 15 percent in a year in which the university's basketball team won the NCAA championship." The reader of the résumé can then draw appropriate conclusions.

Institutions also face *dilemmas in conducting searches* for new employees. Should institutions, for example, intentionally avoid pursuing a rising professional star at a predominantly African-American institution on the ground that such raiding will do too much harm to that institution and compromise national and institutional social objectives? What is the appropriate balance between national, institutional, and personal interests? Similarly, what are the ethical implications in hiring of turning to one's professional friends and colleagues at an institution previously served? of *not* turning to them? Reasonable people can disagree about what is morally required here, but it is up to each college or university to be clear about its own policy. Only then can professional norms begin to form.

Institutions are best served when they commit to one hiring principle, especially when hiring at more senior levels of management (the director level and above): hire the candidate with the best professional training, talent, and experience in advancement work that you can find and do so without regard to any other factors, such as institutional affiliation (e.g., alma mater or minority institution) or personal friendship. If one truly believes that advancement work is indeed a profession, then seeking such professionalism on an open and freely competitive basis should be the guiding standard.

Finally, as one looks at the full range of ethical issues in hiring, it is appropriate to mention the *dilemmas in seeking or giving references* on employees, which are among the most difficult dilemmas associated with all hiring regardless of profession. Supervisors or employers sometimes must respond to requests for performance evaluations by prospective employers about employees whose performance has been substandard and whose continued employment is not desired or is only marginally acceptable. What responsibility does the supervisor have to the employee? to the present employer? to the considering institution or agency? Again, individuals and institutions alike are best served by openness and honesty. To behave otherwise is to compromise the integrity of relationships, which is so essential in the fund-raising profession and in education.

An associated guiding principle in employment—again, a principle not peculiar to the fund-raising profession—can provide assistance in avoiding problems in giving and obtaining references. Supervisors and institutions alike should insist on regular performance reviews under a system that is well understood and publicized in advance of the rating period. This will assure a full understanding between employer and employee of how employee performance is judged, thus setting a common basis for later employment references. Such reviews also hold the potential to correct errant performance or, at worst, provide the documentation for dismissal. In the review process, insist on truth, accuracy, full disclosure, and proper documentation. Discuss this with employees long before being confronted with outside requests for performance evaluations. This way, the employees are given primary responsibility for their performance.

## Assuring Continuity of Service

As so often emphasized, successful fund raising is dependent on the development of effective relationships with donors and prospects, and these relationships take time to build. The hard-boiled realities of a job market in which the supply of able fund raisers is substantially below demand complicates this crucial process. It is imperative for institutions to develop employment practices that assure continuity of employment. Each institution has a responsibility to itself and to its constituents to assure such continuity. Such continuity contributes critically to effective stewardship and to the development of trust and commitment between donor and institution—to the "bonding" that is so important in fund raising. The dedicated and concerned professional will then feel an *equal* professional responsibility to provide both the institution and its constituency with continuity of service.

One way to help assure institutional continuity of service is to govern such employment with a long-term and enforceable contract. In the contract, the institution must protect itself from mediocre performance. Likewise, the aspiring professional can reasonably expect to protect his or her opportunities for professional growth. A fixed-term contract for, say, three, four, or five years can do both: assure institutional continuity and also enable aspiring professionals to move upward. Escape clauses for both the professional and the institution can be built into the contract. For example, the contract could be nullified after a minimum of two years if the employee gains a truly superior job; or the employee could be released if substandard performance is demonstrated. Continuity of service can also be encouraged by a contract provision that calls for a bonus for satisfactory work performed over time. Or an institution could provide for a compensation incentive through mortgage support, the forgiveness of which is dependent solely on the time on the job (however, the tax implications of such arrangements deserve careful consideration).

## Professional Mobility

The mobility of the fund-raising profession raises a whole different set of ethical issues. How can institutions and potential employees alike avoid completing a search only to have the employee "back out" at the last minute because he or she receives a better offer? Should institutions collectively develop and administer employment standards that are subscribed to by all potential employees and institutions alike?

Additional issues are raised by outside employment agencies or professional headhunters seeking assistance in identifying potential employees, a problem not unique to the fund-raising profession. In responding to such requests, a very common, genuine, and positive motive of professionals is to be helpful to talented friends and colleagues and needful sister institutions. Pragmatic realism also tells us, however, that it is not uncommon for practitioners to want to keep themselves in the network by responding to requests for the nomination of candidates. Some may report that although they are not on the market themselves, they owe it to themselves to take a look at any opportunities that may be available. Here, pragmatic need is clearly in conflict with professing the importance of continuity of service to institutions and to prospects.

The mobility within the fund-raising profession raises yet another common dilemma. A fund raiser's knowledge of prospects and established prospect relationships necessarily accompany the fund raiser when he or she moves from one institution to another—sometimes within the same city. Such moves raise appropriate questions regarding the fund raiser's behavior toward the prospect after joining the new institution, as well as the new institution's expectation in this regard. There are presently no guidelines to govern fund raisers' behavior in such situations. Institutions can work to create such guidelines through contractual understandings with new fund-raising hires.

Relations with corporate and foundations prospects are least likely to be compromised, since they tend to be more formal and distant. Moreover, most corporations and foundations have quite clear gift guidelines or policies, thus sharply reducing the likelihood of an ethical breach. Relationships with individuals, however, are more complex. Here, the principle of honoring and serving the donor's needs is paramount. Respecting that principle suggests that the fund raiser and the new institution *can*, reasonably and within certain limits, take advantage of the set of relationships that the fund raiser brings to the new institution.

Both the fund raiser and the new institution must respect the donor's allegiances. They must also respect the confidential components of the donor's relationship with the prior institution—a central limitation of the continuing relationships. Otherwise, it is reasonable to let future relationships take their own course, relying for correctness on the principle that gift decisions are ultimately the responsibility of the donor.

## Employment Contracts

Employment contracts at the time of hire have the potential to clarify and define employment conditions that embrace a set of professional values that are important both to the institution being served and to the potential employee. Employment contracts might deal with such provisions as continuity of service; conditions for permissible outside consulting; rules for the acceptance of personal gifts by employees; joint affirmation of the ethical principles expressed by CASE and other professional societies' codes of ethics; compensation conditions and processes to foster ethical behavior by the advancement professional; and the like. By enhancing such principles and values, the institution ultimately encourages the fund-raising professional to perform more effectively. This, in turn, solidifies relationships with donors and prospects, which in turn enhances the level of gift support. Clearly, the value of such contracts to the professional and the institution alike increases as the level of responsibility of the professional increases.

## Compensation

It is not surprising that there are serious employment issues associated with compensation. Perhaps foremost among them is the appropriateness of salaries, job perks, and life style on the job. These matters were given national visibility by the recent Aramony controversy at United Way headquarters in Washington. The salary (reportedly $463,000) and job perks and lifestyle (limousines and the Concorde jet were mentioned) of the chief officer of a very visible charitable organization drew national ire and caused considerable damage to the fund-raising capability of the national United Way organization.[2] A full-fledged investigation followed national disclosure of the behavior of Mr. Aramony, who resigned his position in face of the criticisms. Local United Way chapters withheld their membership dues in protest. This is indeed a clear example of how compensation practices can affect the fund-raising function. One guiding principle that might serve both the institution and fund-raising professionals associated with charitable organizations is to engage in no behavior related to your employment that you are not willing to have reported on the front page of the nation's most respected newspaper! Potential public disclosure of institutional and fund-raising employment practices and the behavior of individual fund raisers helps to sustain ethical behavior among institutions and professionals alike.

Most institutions and individual practitioners are also concerned with institutional salaries and offers that come from other would-be employers. The shortage of good fund raisers has driven salaries up. This raises issues for institutions that want salary equity among all administrative positions but cannot ignore market realities within the advancement profession. The tendency at most institutions is for professionals, including faculty, to receive increases in their salaries at a slower rate than in the profession itself; that is, national salaries for the top people increase at a rate faster than any single institution increases its salaries. How often has it been necessary for institutions to provide "equity" increases to other employees when a new staff member from outside was hired? Or to make a salary "response" to keep a valued employee from being wooed by another institution?

What, then, does the ethically conscious fund-raising employee do in this competitive and pragmatic salary environment? The professional commitment carries with it an associated commitment and loyalty to the employer and to donor prospects to provide continuity of service; yet reasonable self-interest deems it appropriate to demand competitive compensation. The wise institution will incorporate competitive salary practices that take account of national compensation practices and trends to assure building compensation programs that help to create and sustain employee continuity. But what about the employee who is aware that national trends are outpacing personal compensation or learns from the network that a friend in the profession just moved to a similar job at substantially more money?

There are presently no professional guidelines to serve either individual professionals or concerned institutions. Individual professionals are not well served by "shopping," largely because such inquiries have the potential to damage the trust, commitment, and continuity of service that are so important to institutions' fundraising success. But the institution should update its information about competitive compensation and act on such information earlier rather than later, thus discouraging such "shopping" and encouraging continuity of service.

A different kind of concern surfaces when one considers the desirability of paying commissions for work performed. Why should fund-raising professionals and educational managers not take advantage of a well-proven marketing and performance incentive?

The primary answer rests with the ethical principles that govern the relationships between the donor and the institution and between the fund raiser and the donor. Enlightened institutions know that their interests are long-term and that individual donor decisions and future donor relationships are also governed by long-term interests. An incentive for short-term performance carries with it the risk that long-term relationships will be compromised in the seeking of short term performance rewards. Moreover, an incentive program carries with it the risk of destroying that precious trust and integrity so essential to the productive relationship between the fund raiser, the donor or prospect, and the institution. What donor or prospect wants to be seen essentially as an object of manipulation by a fund raiser whose interest is stimulated by the promise of a proportion of each gift raised? What institution wants to present itself as being so greedy and insensitive to donor or prospect needs?

The fact that the fund raiser is a salaried employee of the institution does not carry the same implications, because the salaried person's performance is reviewed in the context of a full year of interaction with many donors and many prospects. Such a review may reward decisions to defer asking for a gift rather than run the risk of paying a commission on a gift prematurely sought and obtained (probably at a level less than might otherwise be the case).

The problem with employing the commission system in educational fund raising is that it rewards behavior that does not serve the best interests of the institution. The fund raiser is well advised to avoid programs that are commissioned-based; institutions are well served by avoiding such programs, including the payment of consultant fees that are based on funds raised rather than on per diem rates.

Bonuses are also a problem if they are based on individual performance, for the potential to earn a bonus may alter the wisest behavior of fund raisers as they interact with prospects. Such competitive bonuses can lead to adverse competition among staff members, who may vie for "credit" for a gift, for example, or be overly aggressive in dealing with a prospect. Furthermore, there are usually many events and people associated with gift situations. How does one evaluate the relative contributions of each person?

The case can be made that collective bonuses—for the performance of an entire unit, for example—may actually stimulate performance without harmful consequences. Properly administered, this kind of bonus can increase prospect contacts and encourage teamwork in a division, thereby contributing constructively to the institution's relationship with prospects. An example would be a bonus to an entire annual-fund team that exceeded its goal by a wide margin. Nonetheless, a caution is in order: bonuses for development units can cause resentment within other divisions of an institution whose own activities may have had substantial impact on the relationship between the prospect and the institution, such as alumni relations and public relations. How does one measure and reward the contributions of so many contributors to the process? And should effective results not be the common norm on which compensation is based?

A new practice among some individuals and business institutions is to offer a "finder's fee" for helping to "place" a gift for a specific charity. Responding to this concern and related concerns about a seeming overemphasis on the tax aspects of charitable gifts, the CANARAS Group, a group of fifteen planned giving officers, adopted a statement of standards called *The CANARAS Convention* in June 1989 (see chapter 10).

Individuals or business institutions that find themselves in a third-party position between donors and institutions argue that they are providing compensable services for the institution and the donor and thus should be rewarded for that service. Educational institutions would return the argument, as the CANARAS Group did, that a charitable gift is just that—a gift—and that the relationship between donor and charity should not be encumbered by actions that ultimately diminish the charitable impact of the donor in an unreasonable way. Clearly, the principles of fairness and balance are at play. Institutions are not served by the promotion of gifts by third parties if the gifts are not consistent with the institutional mission. However, legitimate expenses associated with the consummation of a gift by the donor (e.g., the costs of drawing a trust instrument by a third party) are clearly within bounds. Compensation solely for the act of referral is what is being disputed. Surely one helpful guideline is to insist that the donor be made aware of any provisions of such an arrangement in advance.

## Presidential Change

A number of issues affecting the institution and its advancement function, and the chief advancement officer in particular, are associated with presidential change at an institution. For the record, and to provide an appropriate context, I should mention that during my twenty-five years in advancement work I have been privileged to serve five institutions. During that time I served no less than nine different presidents (and one acting president) and experienced firsthand the transitions associated with four changes of presidents. Common to all of these changes were subsequent major management reorganizations that in varying degrees directly affected the institution's advancement organization and programs and the professionals associated with each.

It is not surprising that new presidents want to shape their own administrations. It is especially critical that the relationship between the chief advancement officer and the president be an effective one, characterized by mutual professional and personal respect and open and free communication. Most would argue that it is the new president's prerogative to select his own team and to organize the advancement function to his liking. However, acting on that perspective can have potentially harmful implications for advancement. If important institutional values and positive fund-raising results are associated with the concept of continuity of relationships with donors and prospects, then any new president must move with care and sensitivity in deliberately changing those relationships. For example, the "chemistry" between the president and the chief advancement officer may not be ideal, but that between the chief advancement officer and major volunteers and donors important to the new president may be quite solid. Difficulties for an institution's long-term advancement program may result from too frequent changes in either presidents or chief advancement officers, whether by personal election, retirement, or mandate. The close donor and prospect relationships, built over a long period of time, cannot quickly be reestablished. There is also risk of a serious adverse impact on the institution from a breakdown in trust between the institution and the donor or prospect that could accompany such change. The academy is both enormously resilient over the long term and very fragile over the short term. The advancement function critically serves both time frames.

If the employment norm within the academy becomes one of expectation of major administrative organizational change with each new president, then it is likely that that expectation itself will contribute to more mobility among chief advancement officers, which conflicts with the institutional need for continuity, trust, and bonding in the relationship with prospects or donors and the associated institutional success in fund raising. Presidential change, then, necessarily involves a balancing of short-term and long-term interests, some of which necessarily compete with each other in terms of their desirability and institutional impact.

To provide at least some assured institutional continuity and to forestall potentially unnecessary "employment shopping" by valued senior staff, those with the power to make such decisions have the option to provide a "rolling" employment contract to senior officers that guarantees the employee a specified employment period associated with his or her new job at an institution or a similar arrangement specially made in anticipation of presidential transition. For example, the retirement of a president is anticipated and the continued institutional service of a valued employee is desired, yet no one wishes to tie the hands of the new president. The employee could be given a rolling two-year appointment, which could be "bought out" after the new president has had an appropriate period to undertake a firsthand, full and fair evaluation of the employee's performance. Such an employment "guarantee" would likely encourage continued service by the employee and discourage potentially needless and distracting "shopping."

At play in these situations is the need to balance the competing interests of the institution, the employee, and the new president, and to do so in a sensitive fashion. This is extremely important both with respect to observing the very best employment practices for the institution and the individuals affected by them and with respect to upholding the requirements essential to the successful conduct of an effective institutional advancement program. The trust, commitment, and bonding developed over the years between donors and institutions, which are so essential to effective fund raising, can all too easily be upset by rapid, careless, or capricious change.

## Summary

Ethical concerns within the fund-raising profession have traditionally focused primarily on matters of privacy and confidentiality and on the relationship between the donor and the institution. The growth in the size, complexity, and sophistication of the profession raises a host of ethical issues associated with employment practices and employment lifestyles and the complex relationships between institutions, fund raisers, third parties, and donors or prospects.

There is a dearth of ethical guidelines for such relationships. Professional associations like CASE, fund-raising professionals, donors and prospects who care both about the institutions they wish to support and how they are treated, and the institutions served by the profession and donors alike are all equally challenged to help create new and commonly accepted ethical guidelines that will serve their mutuality of interests and thus our society.

# Appendixes:
# Codes of Ethics and
# Statements of Principles

*Statement of Ethics (CASE, 1982)*

*The CANARAS Code (1990)*

*The CANARAS Convention (1989)*

*Code of Ethical Principles and Standards
of Professional Practices (NSFRE, 1992)*

*Ethics Statement (NEDRA, 1990)*

*Model Standards of Practice for the Charitable
Gift Planner (NCPG, 1991)*

*Code of Ethics (APRA, 1992)*

*Principles and Practices for Effective
Grantmaking (Council on Foundations, 1980)*

# Statement of Ethics

Institutional advancement professionals, by virtue of their responsibilities within the academic community, represent their colleges, universities, and schools to the larger society. They have, therefore, a special duty to exemplify the best qualities of their institutions, and to observe the highest standards of personal and professional conduct.

In doing so, they promote the merits of their institutions, and of education generally, without disparaging other colleges and schools.

Their words and actions embody respect for truth, fairness, free inquiry, and the opinions of others.

They respect all individuals without regard to race, color, sex, sexual orientation, marital status, creed, ethnic or national identity, handicap, or age.

They uphold the professional reputation of other advancement officers and give credit for ideas, words, or images originated by others.

They safeguard privacy rights and confidential information.

They do not grant or accept favors for personal gain, nor do they solicit or accept favors for their institutions where a higher public interest would be violated.

They avoid actual or apparent conflicts of interest and, if in doubt, seek guidance from appropriate authorities.

The follow the letter and spirit of laws and regulations affecting institutional advancement.

They observe these standards and others that apply to their professions and actively encourage colleagues to join them in supporting the highest standards of conduct.

Council for the Advancement and Support of Education, 1982. Reprinted by permission.

# The CANARAS Code:
# A Code for Gift Planners

*For all individuals and organizations engaged in soliciting, planning, rendering advice with respect to, accepting and administering charitable gifts.*

The solicitation, planning and administration of a charitable gift is a complex process involving philanthropic, personal, tax and financial considerations.

This Code is intended to assure that the process is conducted in a professional and ethical manner that achieves a fair and proper balance between the personal interests of the donor and the purposes of the charitable institution. We recommend its adoption and observance by all Gift Planners.

1. In any solicitation or planning of a charitable gift, the Gift Planner shall give primary emphasis to the philanthropic nature of the gift; tax considerations should not be the primary focus of the gift. Any investment considerations should reflect the fact that the gift is being invested, at least in part, for and on behalf of the charity.

2. The Gift Planner shall explain all aspects of a proposed charitable gift fully, fairly and accurately to the donor during the gift planning process. This explanation should include:

- the charity's proposed use of the gift;
- all fees and costs of planning and management;
- valuation issues and procedures;
- tax consequences and reporting requirements;
- alternative arrangements for making the gift;
- financial and family implications; and
- any other information which is relevant to the donor's decision to make the gift.

## *The CANARAS Code*

3. A Gift Planner shall not act or purport to act as a representative of any charity without the express knowledge and approval of the charity and shall not, while in the employ of a charity, act or purport to act as a representative of the donor.

4. A Gift Planner acting on behalf of the charity shall encourage the donor to discuss the proposed gift with a competent lawyer or accountant of the donor's choice; a Gift Planner acting on behalf of the donor shall, where appropriate, encourage the donor to discuss the proposed gift with the charity to whom the gift is to be made.

5. Fees charged by Gift Planners shall be reasonable in relation to the services provided and shall be charged to the person to whom, or on behalf of whom, the services are provided. A Gift Planner shall not solicit, and a charity shall not pay, any fee, directly or indirectly, for the right to receive a gift.

*Drafted and adopted by The CANARAS Group, member council of The National Committee on Planned Giving:*

*Bruce Bigelow*
  *(Hood College)*
*Deborah H. Blackmore*
  *(University of Pennsylvania)*
*Donald L. Blunk*
  *(Skidmore College)*
*Joseph Cofield*
  *(Boston College)*
*Gary Dicovitsky*
  *(University of Virginia)*
*Richard W. Johnson III*
  *(Clarkson University)*
*Marvin L. Kelley*
  *(Wesleyan University)*
*Jack Kreckel*
  *(University of Rochester)*

*John G. Lewis, Jr.*
  *(Brown University)*
*Benjamin P. Madonia III*
  *(Hamilton College)*
*Donald Martin*
  *(Colgate University)*
*Ronald E. Sapp*
  *(Johns Hopkins Institute)*
*Peter J. Ticconi, Jr.*
  *(Williams College)*
*Alex Velto*
  *(St. Lawrence University)*

*August 15, 1990*

—*With appreciation to David M. Donaldson and Jonathan G. Tidd*

# *The CANARAS Convention*

As planned giving professionals, we appreciate that a thorough understanding of the tax aspects of a charitable contribution can be crucial to the proper structuring of a charitable gift, but we believe that the *only* legitimate basis for making a charitable gift is a genuine desire to support the work of the donee organization.

We affirm that the principal rationale underlying the Federal tax deduction for charitable contributions is that they assist charitable organizations to work for the public good and thereby meet public needs which would otherwise have to be met with direct governmental expenditures. We are deeply concerned about what we perceive as growing abuse of the charitable contribution deduction by persons or organizations who view that deduction primarily as a means to make money or avoid taxes.

We are appalled by recent promotions which appear to be "selling" charitable gift arrangements as tax shelters or commercial transactions (with significant profit for the promoter) without any appreciation of the true nature of a charitable contribution. Such an approach is, in our judgment, totally inconsistent with the basis of philanthropy.

In order to reinforce our concept of charitable giving, we have, acting as individual professionals rather than the representative of any particular institution, agreed on the following statement of position:

1. We express strong disapproval of, and disassociate ourselves from, any effort to represent charitable gifts as tax shelters rather than as thoughtful contributions to the work of charity.
2. While we recognize and appreciate that there are many organizations and individuals who provide valuable services at legitimate charges to both donors and charitable organizations, we express strong disapproval of, and disassociate ourselves from, promoters of charitable gifts who charge unreasonable fees or commissions for arranging or managing charitable gifts, or who, without our knowledge or ap-

proval, undertake to negotiate gifts on behalf of our charitable institutions.

3. We will not cooperate with any person or organization which charges a "finder's fee" for arranging a charitable gift; and we will recommend that the charitable organizations which we represent decline to accept any gift which, in our judgment, involves an unreasonable fee or commission for establishing or managing the charitable gift.

4. We urge that, whenever possible, the donee institution be directly involved with any potential donor in helping to plan any gift to that institution in order to ensure that the gift is in keeping with genuine philanthropy and is truly sensitive to the needs and interests of the institution.

We urge all of our fellow fund-raising professionals, and others who are concerned about these issues, to subscribe to the foregoing statements of position. Unless these issues are addressed by the charitable community in a prompt and constructive fashion, the misguided efforts of those for-profit promoters who seek to subvert the charitable tax deduction as a tax shelter could cause a congressional and public opinion backlash which will seriously undermine the future of philanthropy.

*Deborah H. Blackmore*
*(University of Pennsylvania)*
*Donald L. Blunk*
*(Skidmore College)*
*Gary Dicovitsky*
*(University of Virginia)*
*Paul Harkess*
*(Union College)*
*Richard W. Johnson III*
*(Clarkson University)*
*Marvin L. Kelley*
*(Wesleyan University)*
*Jack Kreckel*
*(University of Rochester)*
*John G. Lewis, Jr.*
*(Brown University)*

*Frank A. Logan*
*(Dartmouth College)*
*Benjamin P. Madonia III*
*(Hamilton College)*
*Donald Martin*
*(Colgate University)*
*W. Richard Park*
*(Amherst College)*
*Ronald E. Sapp*
*(The Johns Hopkins Institute)*
*Peter J. Ticconi, Jr.*
*(Williams College)*
*Alex Velto*
*(St. Lawrence University)*

*June 23, 1989*

*—With appreciation to David M. Donaldson, Esquire of Ropes and Gray, Boston, Massachusetts*

# Code of Ethical Principles and Standards of Professional Practices

Statements of Ethical Principles
*Adopted November 1991*

The National Society of Fund Raising Executives exists to foster the development and growth of fund-raising professionals and the profession, to preserve and enhance philanthropy and volunteerism, and to promote high ethical standards in the fund-raising profession.

To these ends, this code declares the ethical values and standards of professional practice which NSFRE members embrace and which they strive to uphold in their responsibilities for generating philanthropic support.

Members of the National Society of Fund Raising Executives are motivated by an inner drive to improve the quality of life through the causes they serve. They seek to inspire others through their own sense of dedication and high purpose. They are committed to the improvement of their professional knowledge and skills in order that their performance will better serve others. They recognize their stewardship responsibility to ensure that needed resources are vigorously and ethically sought and that the intent of the donor is honestly fulfilled. Such individuals practice their profession with integrity, honesty, truthfulness, and adherence to the absolute obligation to safeguard the public trust.

*Furthermore,* NSFRE members

- serve the ideal of philanthropy, are committed to the preservation and enhancement of volunteerism, and hold stewardship of these concepts as the overriding principle of professional life;
- put charitable mission above personal gain, accepting compensation by salary or set fee only;
- foster cultural diversity and pluralistic values and treat all people with dignity and respect;

## Code of Ethical Principles

- affirm, through personal giving, a commitment to philanthropy and its role in society;
- bring credit to the fund-raising profession by their public demeanor;
- recognize their individual boundaries of competence and are forthcoming about their professional qualifications and credentials;
- value the privacy, freedom of choice, and interests of all those affected by their actions;
- disclose all relationships which might constitute, or appear to constitute, conflicts of interest;
- actively encourage all their colleagues to embrace and practice these ethical principles;
- adhere to the following standards of professional practice in their responsibilities for generating philanthropic support:

## Standards of Professional Practice

*Adopted and incorporated into the NSFRE Code of Ethical Principles November 1992*

1. Members shall act according to the highest standards and visions of their institution, profession, and conscience.
2. Members shall comply with all applicable local, state, provincial, and federal civil and criminal laws. Members should avoid the appearance of any criminal offense or professional misconduct.
3. Members shall be responsible for advocating, within their own organizations, adherence to all applicable laws and regulations.
4. Members shall work for a salary or fee, not percentage-based compensation or a commission.
5. Members may accept performance-based compensation such as bonuses provided that such bonuses are in accord with prevailing practices within the members' own organizations and are not based on a percentage of philanthropic funds raised.
6. Members shall neither seek nor accept finder's fees and shall, to the best of their ability, discourage their organizations from paying such fees.
7. Members shall disclose all conflicts of interest; such disclosure does not preclude or imply ethical impropriety.
8. Members shall accurately state their professional experience, qualifications, and expertise.

9. Members shall adhere to the principle that all donor and prospect information created by, or on behalf of, an institution is the property of that institution and shall not be transferred or removed.
10. Members shall, on a scheduled basis, give donors the opportunity to have their names removed from lists which are sold to, rented to, or exchanged with other organizations.
11. Members shall not disclose privileged information to unauthorized parties.
12. Members shall keep constituent information confidential.
13. Members shall take care to ensure that all solicitation materials are accurate and correctly reflect the organization's mission and use of solicited funds.
14. Members shall, to the best of their ability, ensure that contributions are used in accordance with donors' intentions.
15. Members shall ensure, to the best of their ability, proper stewardship of charitable contributions, including: careful investment of funds; timely reports on the use and management of funds; and explicit consent by the donor before altering the conditions of a gift.
16. Members shall ensure, to the best of their ability, that donors receive informed and ethical advice about the value and tax implications of potential gifts.

# E

# *Ethics Statement*

NEDRA was formed to promote professional status among development researchers, to provide educational information focusing on, but not limited to, research skills exchange; and to foster networking support.

NEDRA's membership is open to individuals who seek a positive association with the development research community and whose terms of affiliation shall not be contrary to the goals of the Association, and who shall uphold the responsibilities and integrity of the Association without conflict of interest. NEDRA encourages its member to recognize the responsibilities concomitant with their professional duties and to conduct these duties in an ethical manner:

Members will avoid activities that may damage the professional reputation of researchers, their employers, or of those from whom we gather information

Members' methods should comply with the legal guidelines set forth by their organization's legal department and the ethical guidelines set forth by the institution.

Members will not misrepresent themselves of their purpose in order to obtain information that a source would ordinarily withhold.

Members shall respect the confidentiality of all information gained and refrain from divulging or using this information for other than its intended purpose.

Members shall exercise due care in gathering and evaluating data and strive to ensure that the research is accurate.

Members will seek to advance the skills and methods of our profession. We will share our advances in skills and methods with others in the association.

New England Development Researchers Association (NEDRA), 1990. Reprinted by permission.

# Model Standards of Practice for the Charitable Gift Planner

## Preamble

The purpose of this statement is to encourage responsible charitable gift planning by urging the adoption of the following Standards of Practice by all who work in the charitable gift-planning process, including charitable institutions and their gift-planning officers, independent fund-raising consultants, attorneys, accountants, financial planners and life insurance agents, collectively referred to hereafter as "Gift Planners."

This statement recognizes that the solicitation, planning and administration of a charitable gift is a complex process involving philanthropic, personal, financial and tax considerations, and as such often involves professionals from various disciplines whose goals should include working together to structure a gift that achieves a fair and proper balance between the interests of the donor and purposes of the charitable institution.

*I. Primacy of Philanthropic Motivation.* The principal basis for making a charitable gift should be a desire on the part of the donor to support the work of charitable institutions.

*II. Explanation of Tax Implications.* Congress has provided tax incentives for charitable giving, and the emphasis in this statement on philanthropic motivation in no way minimizes the necessity and appropriateness of a full and accurate explanation by the Gift Planner of those incentives and their implications.

*III. Full Disclosure.* It is essential to the gift-planning process that the role and relationship of all parties involved, including how and by whom each is compensated, be fully disclosed to the donor. A Gift Planner shall not act or purport to act as a representative of any charity without the express knowledge and approval of the charity, and shall not, while employed by the charity, act or purport to act as a representative of the donor, without the express consent of both the charity and the donor.

*IV. Compensation.* Compensation paid to Gift Planners shall be reasonable and proportionate to the services provided. Payments of finder's fees, commissions or other fees by a donee organization to an independent Gift Planner as a condition for the delivery of a gift are never appropriate. Such payments lead to abusive practices and may violate certain federal and state regulations. Likewise, commission-based compensation for Gift Planners who are employed by a charitable institution is never appropriate.

*V. Competence and Professionalism.* The Gift Planner should strive to achieve and maintain a high degree of competence in his or her chosen area, and shall advise donors only in areas in which he or she is professionally qualified. It is a hallmark of professionalism for Gift Planners that they realize when they have reached the limits of their knowledge and expertise and, as a result, should include other professionals in the process. Such relationships should be characterized by courtesy, tact and mutual respect.

*VI. Consultation with Independent Advisers.* A Gift Planner acting on behalf of a charity shall in all cases strongly encourage the donor to discuss the proposed gift with competent independent legal and tax advisers of the donor's choice.

*VII. Consultation with Charities.* Although Gift Planners frequently and properly counsel donors concerning specific charitable gifts without the prior knowledge or approval of the donee organization, the Gift Planner, in order to ensure that the gift will accomplish the donor's objectives, should encourage the donor, early in the gift-planning process, to discuss the proposed gift with the charity to whom the gift is to be made. In cases where the donor desires anonymity, the Gift Planner shall endeavor, on behalf of the undisclosed donor, to obtain the charity's input in the gift-planning process.

*VIII. Explanation of Gift.* The Gift Planner shall make every effort, insofar as possible, to ensure that the donor receives a full and accurate explanation of all aspects of the proposed charitable gift.

*IX. Full Compliance.* A Gift Planner shall fully comply with and shall encourage other parties in the gift-planning process to fully comply with both the letter and spirit of all applicable federal and state laws and regulations.

*X. Public Trust.* Gift Planners shall, in all dealings with donors, institutions, and other professionals, act with fairness, honesty, integrity and openness. Except for compensation received for services, the terms of which have been disclosed to the donor, they shall have no vested interest that could result in personal gain.

Board of Directors, National Committee on Planned Giving, April 30, 1991; Committee on Gift Annuities, May 2, 1991. Reprinted by permission.

# Code of Ethics

As representatives of the profession, American Prospect Research Association (APRA) members shall be respectful of all people and organizations. They shall support and further the individual's fundamental right to privacy. APRA members are committed to the ethical collection and use of information in the pursuit of legitimate institutional goals.

In their work, prospect researchers must balance the needs of their institutions/organizations to collect and record information with the prospects' right to privacy. This balance is not always easy to maintain. However, the following ethical principles apply:

## I. Fundamental Principles

A. *Relevance.* Prospect researchers shall seek and record only information that is relevant to the fund-raising effort of the institutions that employ them.

B. *Honesty.* Prospect researchers shall be truthful with regard to their identity, purpose, and the identity of their institution during the course of their work.

C. *Confidentiality.* Confidential information pertaining to donors or prospective donors shall be scrupulously protected so that the relationship of trust between donor and donee and the integrity of the prospect research professions upheld.

D. *Accuracy.* Prospect researchers shall record all data accurately. Such information must be verifiable or attributable to its source.

## II. Procedures

*A. Collection*
1. The collection and use of information shall be done lawfully.
2. Information sought and recorded may include all public records.
3. Written requests for public information shall be made on institutional stationery clearly identifying the sender.
4. When requesting information in person or by telephone, neither individual nor institutional identity shall be concealed

*B. Recording*
1. Researchers shall state information in an objective and factual manner.
2. Documents pertaining to donors or prospective donors shall be irreversibly disposed of when no longer needed (e.g., by shredding).

*C. Use*
1. Non-public information is the property of the institution for which it was collected and shall no be given to persons other than those who are involved with the cultivation or solicitation effort or those who need that information in the performance of their duties for that institution.
2. Only public or published information may be shared with colleagues at other institutions as a professional courtesy.
3. Prospect information is the property of the institution for which it was gathered and shall not be taken to another institution.
4. Prospect information shall be stored securely to prevent access by unauthorized persons.
5. Research documents containing donor or prospective-donor information that are to be used outside research offices shall be clearly marked "confidential."
6. Special protection shall be afforded all giving records pertaining to anonymous donors.

## Recommendations

1. Prospect researchers shall urge their institutions to develop written policies based upon the laws of their states defining what information shall be gathered and under what conditions it may be released and to whom.
2. Prospect researchers shall urge the development of written policies at

their institutions defining who may authorize access to prospect files and under what conditions.

3. Prospect researchers shall urge their colleagues to abide by these principles of conduct.

American Prospect Research Association, 1992. Reprinted by permission.

# Principles and Practices
# for Effective Grantmaking

*In subscribing to this statement, members of the Council affirm their belief
in the principles and practices and willingness to move toward implementing them.*

1. Whatever the nature of the entity engaged in private grantmaking,
   and whatever its interests, it should seek to establish a set of basic
   policies that define the program interests and the fundamental objective to be served.
2. An identifiable board, committee or other decision-making body
   should have clear responsibility for determining those policies and
   procedures, causing them to be implemented, and reviewing and
   revising them from time to time.
3. The processes for receiving, examining and deciding on grant applications should be established on a clear and logical basis and should
   be followed in a manner consistent with the organization's policies
   and purposes.
4. Responsive grantmakers recognize that accountability extends beyond the narrow requirements of the law. Grantmakers should establish and carry out policies that recognize these multiple obligations for accountability: to the charter provisions by which their
   founders defined certain basic expectations, to those charitable institutions they serve, to the general public, to the Internal Revenue
   Service, and to certain state governmental agencies.
5. Open communications with the public and with grantseekers about
   the policies and procedures that are followed in grantmaking is in
   the interest of all concerned and is important if the grantmaking
   process is to function well, and if trust in the responsibility and accountability of grantmakers is to be maintained. A brief written

## Principles and Practices for Effective Grantmaking

statement about policies, program interests, and grantmaking practices, geographic and policy restrictions, and preferred ways of receiving applications is recommended. Prompt acknowledgment of the receipt of any serious applications is important. Grantseekers whose programs and proposals fall outside the interests of the grantmakers should be told this immediately and those whose proposals are still under consideration should be informed, insofar as is possible, of the steps and timing that will be taken in reaching the final decision.

6. Beyond the filing of forms required by government, grantmakers should consider possible ways of informing the public concerning their stewardship through publication and distribution of periodic reports, preferably annual reports, possibly supplemented by newsletters, reports to The Foundation Center and the use of other communications channels.

7. The preservation and enhancement of an essential community of interest between the grantor and the grantee requires that their relationship be based on mutual respect, candor, and understanding with each investing the necessary time and attention to define clearly the purposes of the grant, the expectations as to reports related to financial and other matters, and the provisions for evaluating and publicizing projects.

   Many grantmakers, going beyond the providing of money, help grantees through such other means as assisting in the sharpening of the objectives, monitoring the performance, evaluating the outcome, and encouraging early planning for future stages.

8. It is important that grantmakers be alert and responsive to changing conditions in society and to the changing needs and merits of particular grantseeking organizations. Responses to need and social conditions may well be determined by independent inquiries, not merely by reactions to requests submitted by grantseekers. In response to new challenges, grantmakers are helpful if they use the special knowledge, experience and insight of individuals beyond those persons, families, or corporations from which the funds originally came. Some grantmakers find it useful to secure ideas and comments from a variety of consultants and advisory panels, as well as diversified staff and board members. In view of the historic underrepresentation of minorities and women in supervisory and policy positions, particular attention should be given to finding ways to draw them into the decisionmaking processes.

9. From time to time, all grantmaking organizations should review their program interests, basic policies, and board and staff composition, and assess the overall results of their grantmaking.

10. Beyond the legal requirements that forbid staff, board members and their families from profiting financially from any philanthropic grant, it is important that grantmakers weigh carefully all circumstances in which there exists the possibility of accusations of self-interest. In particular, staff and board members should disclose to the governing body the nature of their personal or family affiliation or involvement with any organizations for which a grant is considered, even though such affiliation may not give rise to any pecuniary conflict of interest.

11. Grantmakers should maintain interaction with others in the field of philanthropy including such bodies as regional associations of grantmakers: the Foundation Center, the Council on Foundations and various local, regional, and national independent sector organizations. They should bear in mind that they share with others responsibility for strengthening the effectiveness of the many private initiatives to serve the needs and interests of the public and for enhancing general understanding and support of such private initiatives within the community and the nation.

Council on Foundations, 1980. Reprinted by permission.

# Notes

## 1 Law and Regulation

1. Thomas Blackwell, *College Law: A Guide for Administrators* (Washington, D.C.: American Council on Education, 1961), 194.

2. Frederick Pollock, *Principles of Contracts*, 3d ed. (New York: Voorhis, 1906), 186; Blackwell, *College Law*, 223.

3. See, for example, *Trustees of Farmington Academy v Allen*, 14 Mass. 172 (1817); *University of Vermont v Buell*, 2 Vt. 48 (1829); and *Colorado Women's College v Bradford-Robinson Printing Co.*, 114 Colo. 237, 246, 157 P2d 612, 616 (1945).

4. The definition of the term *charitable* in this context includes not only educational, scientific, and religious organizations as embraced by IRS par. 501(c)(3) of the U.S. Tax Code but also other categories of nonprofit organizations.

5. Other agencies administer laws that impact on the fund-raising process (such as the U.S. Postal Service), but the IRS is the sole federal agency to regulate the process itself.

6. Application for Recognition of [Tax] Exemption (form 1023), question 3, pt. 1; Bruce Hopkins, *The Law of Fund-Raising* (New York: John Wiley & Sons, 1991), ch. 6, n. 6, par. 5.

7. Form 990, pt. 1, line 1, and pt. 2, line 30 and col. D; Hopkins, *Law of Fund-Raising*, ch. 6, n. 7, par. 6.

8. See, in general, Hopkins, *Law of Fund-Raising*, ch. 6, n. 7, par. 10.

9. See, in general, ibid., par. 11.

10. See, in general, ibid., pars. 1 and 2.

11. Rev.Rul. 67-246,1967-2 CB. 104.

12. Department of the Treasury, Internal Revenue Service, *Deductibility of Payments Made to Charities Conducting Fund-Raising Events*, Publication 1391 (Washington, D.C., 1988), 6–88.

13. Terry L. Simmons, "Higher Education and the Revenue Reconciliation Act of 1993: Substantiation and Other News," *Charitable Gift Planning News* 11, no. 7 (1993).

14. The term *abusive fund raising* appears in *Internal Revenue Manual Supplement* 7(10)G-59(Rev.2), a supplement to the *Internal Revenue Manual* distributed late in 1991 for the benefit of examining agents.

15. *Internal Revenue Manual Supplement*, par. 1.07.

16. Rev.Rul. 86-63.

17. IRS Technical Advice Memorandum 9147007 (1991).

18. IRS Announcement 92-15, 1992-4 I.R.B.40.

19. *Village of Schaumburg v Citizens for a Better Environment* 444 US 620 (1980).

20. *Secretary of State of Maryland v Joseph H. Munson Co., Inc.*, 467 US 947 (1984).

21. *Riley v National Federation of the Blind of North Carolina, Inc.*, 108 S.Ct. 2667 (1988).

22. See, e.g., *Telco Communications, Inc., v Carbaugh*, 885 F2d 1225 (4th Cir 1989).

23. Ill. Ann. Stat. ch. 23, par. 5117, § 17(b).

24. Arkansas Code, Act 1177 (1991).

25. The states that have no such statutory or other regulatory law are Delaware, Idaho, Montana, and Wyoming.

26. See, in general, Hopkins, *Law of Fund-Raising*.

27. Arizona, California, Florida, Hawaii, Iowa, Louisiana, Mississippi, New Hampshire, New Mexico, North Dakota, and Tennessee.

28. Connecticut, Georgia, Illinois, Kansas, Maine, Michigan, Minnesota, Missouri, New Jersey, New York, North Carolina, Oklahoma, Oregon, Pennsylvania, Rhode Island, South Carolina, Utah, Virginia, and West Virginia.

29. N.C. Gen. Stat. § 131c-5(d).

30. Kansas, Maryland, New Jersey, New York, Ohio, Oklahoma, Oregon, Virginia, and Wisconsin.

31. Code of Va. § 57-60(1).

32. Hawaii, Kentucky, and Mississippi.

33. Arizona, Hawaii, Illinois, Kansas, Mississippi, Missouri, North Carolina, Oregon, Pennsylvania, Rhode Island, Tennessee, Virginia, and West Virginia.

34. Kansas, Minnesota, Missouri, New Jersey, and New York.

35. The rationale for exempting educational institutions from state charitable solicitation laws is developed in an internal report prepared

by Bruce Hopkins in January 1987 for CASE, "The Case for the Exemption of Schools, Colleges, and Universities from State Charitable Solicitation Acts."

36. Ill. Ann. Stat. ch. 23, pars. 5117, 5115 §§ 15(b)(5) and 15(a).

37. Revised Statutes Annotated § 7:28-f(I)(h).

38. Code of Va. § 57–57(H)(1).

39. If this provision is read literally, a charitable organization would commit a prohibited act under Connecticut law if it engaged in an unrelated business activity (and paid the tax).

40. Conn. Gen. Stat. Ann. § 21a-190e.

41. R.S.A. § 7:28-f(I)(b).

42. Conn. Gen. Stat. Ann. § 21a-190e.

43. Ann. Code of MD Subtitle 5, § 6-501.

44. Mass. Gen Laws ch. 68 § 22.

45. Ill. Ann. Stat. ch. 23, par. 5115 § 15(b)(6).

## 2 The Moral Context of Fund Raising

Sections of this chapter appeared in Bernard Gert, "Morality, Moral Theory, and Applied and Professional Ethics," *Professional Ethics* 1, nos. 1 and 2 (1992): 5–24.

1. The terms *moral* and *ethical* are used synonymously here.

2. Much of what follows is based on the work of philosopher Bernard Gert. See his *Morality: A New Justification for the Moral Rules* (New York: Oxford Univ. Press, 1988).

3. The moral obligation of the fund raiser to support the institution rests, of course, on the assumption that the mission of the institution is itself moral.

4. Henry A. Rosso, "A Philosophy of Fund Raising," in Rosso et al., *Achieving Excellence in Fund Raising: A Comprehensive Guide to Principles, Strategies, and Methods* (San Francisco: Jossey-Bass, 1991), 3–7; S. Ostrander and P. Schervish, "Giving and Getting: Philanthropy as a Social Relation," in *Critical Issues in American Philanthropy*, ed. Jon Van Til (San Francisco: Jossey-Bass, 1990); Robert L. Payton, *Major Challenges to Philanthropy: A Discussion Paper for Independent Sector* (New York: Independent Sector, 1984).

5. Robert L. Payton, Henry A. Rosso, and Eugene R. Tempel, "Toward a Philosophy of Fund Raising," in Dwight Burlingame and Lamont J. Hulse, *Taking Fund Raising Seriously: Advancing the Profession and Practice of Raising Money* (San Francisco: Jossey-Bass, 1991), 9.

6. Consent is one kind of justification for deception. I consent to be deceived when I go to a magic show; thus, deception in this case is not immoral. Other forms of justification include public acceptance (e.g., for unmarked police cars) and the prevention of greater evil, coupled with the requirement that all of the people being deceived have failed to meet a moral requirement. One would be hard-pressed to justify deceiving a prospective or actual donor, whose basic act is one that is morally encouraged rather than required. For more analysis of deception, see Deni Elliott, "On Deceiving One's Source," *International Journal of Applied Philosophy* 6, no. 1 (summer 1991): 1–8; Deni Elliott and Charles Culver, "Defining and Analyzing Journalistic Deception," *Journal of Mass Media Ethics* 7, no. 2 (spring 1992): 69–84; and Deni Elliott, "What Counts as Deception in Higher Education Development," in Burlingame and Hulse, *Taking Fund Raising Seriously*, 73–82.

7. Bobbie Strand, "Prospect Research Is Spelled R-e-s-p-e-c-t," in Bobbie Strand and Susan Hunt, eds., *Prospect Research: A How-To Guide* (Washington, D.C.: CASE, 1986).

8. On psychological motivations for giving, see, for example, Ernest Dichter, "Why People Give," in *Some Aspects of Educational Fund Raising*, ed. Jean D. Lineham (Washington, D.C.: American Alumni Council, 1962), 45–49; and Kathleen Teltsch, "The Ultimate Gift," *New York Times*, Educational suppl., Apr. 10, 1988, 22–24. On economic motivations, see, for example, Lynn Gatozzi, "Charitable Contributions as a Condition of Probation for Convicted Corporations: Using Philanthropy to Combat Corporate Crime." *Case Western Reserve Law Review* 37 (1987): 569. And on social motivations, see, for example, Letty Cottin Pogrebin, "Contributing to the Cause," *New York Times Magazine*, Apr. 22, 1990, 22–24.

## 3 The Language of Fund Raising

For their insightful comments on an earlier version of this chapter, I am indebted to Jacqueline Dunaway, Deni Elliott, and Terry Price, as well as to all of the discussants at a colloquium at which I spoke on this topic.

1. Barbara E. Brittingham and Thomas E. Pezzullo, *The Campus Green: Fund Raising in Higher Education*, ERIC Document Reproduction Service No. ED 321 706 (Washington, D.C.: George Washington University, School of Education and Human Development, 1990).

2. Karlyn Kohrs Campbell, *The Rhetorical Act* (Belmont, Calif.: Wadsworth Publishing, 1982), v.

3. Brittingham and Pezzullo, *The Campus Green*, v.

4. Mal Warwick, "The Art of Asking," *Warwick File* 5, no. 1 (1991): 2.

5. Wellesley College, *Work in Progress: The Campaign for $150 Million* (Wellesley, Mass., Jan. 1992), 4.

6. Debbie Goldberg, "How the Other Half Gives: Alumnae Are Coming into Their Own—and Giving Some of It Back," *CASE Currents*, Mar. 1989, 27.

7. Brittingham and Pezzullo, *The Campus Green*, iii.

8. Council for Advancement and Support of Education, *Winning Words: A Volunteer's Guide to Asking for Major Gifts* (Washington, D.C., 1984), 5.

9. "Are Direct Mail Donors Really Environmentally Conscious? Part II," *Warwick File* 5, no. 1 (1991).

10. Philip T. Drotning, *Putting the Fund Raising* (Chicago: Contemporary Books, 1979), 70.

11. *Direct Mail for Fund Raising*, CASE Answer File (Washington, D.C.: CASE, 1989), 9.

12. Council for Advancement and Support of Education, *Reach Out and Raise More Funds: An Administrative Guide for Planning and Conducting a Successful Phonathon* (Washington, D.C.: CASE and AT&T, 1986), 3.

13. Toni L. Lehtinen, "Money by Mail," *CASE Currents*, Nov.–Dec. 1982, 9.

14. Deni Elliott, "My Search for the Charitable Impulse" (paper presented to the Task Force on Ethics and Higher Education Advancement, Washington, D.C., Sept. 20, 1990).

15. Lee Royce, "Divide and Conquer: Segmentation Can Help Raise More Money through Direct Mail," *CASE Currents*, May 1988, 22–25.

16. Bartley P. Cardon, University Campaign Chairman, University of Arizona Foundation, to the campus community, Jan. 21, 1992. Appealing to a person's sense of obligation bears some resemblance to stimulating a preference, but the two are different. In the latter, the appeal is to self-interested motivation; in the former, it is to a conception of duty that requires certain actions, even if they are contrary to one's self-interest. Insofar as the exchange model assumes purely self-interested motivation, the appeal to the sense of obligation does not fit under it.

17. This explanation of offering an opportunity was presented to me by the dean of a major business school. My discussions with a number of fund raisers and with individuals who study philanthropy and are not

persuaded by the "opportunity for self-interested gain" model have led me to conclude that this is not as unusual a view as the proponents of that model make out.

18. CASE, *Winning Words*, 1.

19. Noel W. Johnston, "The Art of Asking," *CASE Currents,* Apr. 1982, 41.

20. "Are Direct Mail Donors Really Environmentally Conscious? Part II." *Warwick File* 5, no. 1 (1991).

## 4 Funding Raising as a Profession

1. For helpful overviews of the salient issues in the sociology of the professions, see Andrew Abbott, *The System of Professions* (Chicago: Univ. of Chicago Press, 1988); Magali Sarfatti Larson, *The Rise of Professionalization* (Berkeley: Univ. of California Press, 1977); and Robert Dingwall and Philip Lewis, eds., *The Sociology of the Professions* (New York: St. Martin's, 1983).

2. This definition is based on the distinctions made by Dennis Campbell in *Doctors, Lawyers, Ministers: Christian Ethics in Professional Practice* (Nashville: Abingdon, 1982).

3. The basic structure for this section relies in large measure on the work of Robert E. Carbone. See his *Fund Raising as a Profession* (College Park, Md.: Clearinghouse for Research on Fund Raising, 1989). In this chapter I use somewhat different criteria for making the case for fund raising as a profession. My primary focus is on the ethical significance of the professional status of fund raisers. I am indebted to his work, as is obvious, for many methodological and substantive ideas.

4. For an extended discussion of this issue, see Michael Novak, ed., *Democracy and Mediating Structures: A Theological Inquiry* (Washington, D.C.: American Enterprise Institute, 1980).

5. See Carbone, *Fund Raising as a Profession.*

6. For an analysis of the difference between strongly and weakly differentiated moral norms for professionals, see Alan Goldman, *The Moral Foundations of Professional Ethics* (Totowa, N.J.: Rowan & Littlefield, 1981).

## 5 Handling Prospect Research

1. Jeanne B. Jenkins and Marilyn Lucas, *How to Find Philanthropic Prospects* (Ambler, Pa.: Fund-Raising Institute, 1986), 2–3.

2. Sissela Bok, *Secrets: On the Ethics of Concealment and Revelation* (New York: Vintage Books, 1983), 93.

3. Mike McNamee, "Privacy and the Prospect Researcher: How to Draw the Line between Uncovering Useful Donor Data and Digging Up Dirty Little Secrets," *CASE Currents,* June 1990, 10–17.

4. Bok, *Secrets,* 94 (quotation), 11.

5. Ibid., 119.

6. Ibid., 112.

7. *CASE Advisory on Advancement Practice: Principles and Recommendations Regarding Ethics and Confidentiality in Development Research* (Washington, D.C.: CASE, 1991).

8. Michael J. Worth, "Prospect Research: A Tool for Professionalism in Fund Raising," *Fund Raising Management,* June 1991.

## 7 Gifts and Donors' Expectations

1. Barbara E. Brittingham and Thomas E. Pezzullo, *The Campus Green: Fund Raising in Higher Education,* ERIC Document Reproduction Service No. ED 321 706 (Washington, D.C.: George Washington University, School of Education and Human Development, 1990), 5–7, 33.

2. Maurice G. Gurin and Jon Van Til, "Understanding Philanthropy: Fund Raising in Perspective," *Giving USA Update,* May/June–July/Aug. 1989, 3, cited in Brittingham and Pezzullo, *The Campus Green,* 6.

3. Brittingham and Pezzullo, *The Campus Green,* 34–35.

4. Jerald Panas, *Mega Gifts: Who Gives Them, Who Gets Them* (Chicago: Pluribus Press, Division of Teach 'em, 1984), 87.

5. A cautionary note may be in order. Benefits offered or given to donors, whether used as a formal or informal incentive to induce a gift, are considered "premiums" by the Internal Revenue Service. Premiums are not prohibited; however, if the value of premiums given to donors exceeds certain legal limits—the lesser of fifty dollars or 2 percent of the gift value—donors are required to reduce by the amount of that value the tax deduction they claim for their gift. This is an issue for which clear legal guidelines exist. To the extent that institutions engage in "returning benefits" to donors, they have a responsibility to alert donors about the worth of the premiums being offered, its value, and its effect on the donor's tax deduction.

## 8 Planned Giving

1. Norman S. Fink, "Issues and Ethics for Non-Profit Executives and Institutions" (paper presented to the Chicago Planned Giving Roundtable, Feb. 6, 1990), 14.

2. "The State of Planned Giving in America," *Planned Giving Today* 3, no. 1 (1992): 1–3.

3. Janet Novack, "Tax Dodges Begin at Home," *Forbes*, Nov. 16, 1990, 170–71.

4. *The CANARAS Convention* is presented in full in the Appendix.

5. Robert I. Brauer, IRS Assistant Commissioner, to members of the CANARAS Group, May 15, 1990.

6. *The CANARAS Code* is presented in full in the Appendix. Neither the *Convention* nor the *Code* could have been written without the invaluable assistance of attorney David M. Donaldson and attorney-consultant Jonathan G. Tidd.

7. Frank A. Logan, remarks delivered at the opening plenary session of the annual conference of the National Conference on Planned Giving, Oct. 14, 1990, Indianapolis.

8. *Model Standards of Practice for the Charitable Gift Planner* is presented in full in the Appendix.

9. A great deal of credit for the safe passage of *Model Standards* through a thicket of political and professional obstacles can be ascribed to consultant Frank Minton, who served as NCPG president in 1991.

10. The NSFRE *Code of Ethical Principles and Standards of Professional Practices* is presented in full in the Appendix.

11. Robert F. Sharpe, Jr., Barlow T. Mann, and Jonathan Tidd, "Is There 'Security' in Planned Giving," *Trusts and Estates*, Aug. 1990, 20, 24, 26–31.

12. Robert F. Sharpe, Jr., quoted in "Views and Counsel from Seven Consultants," *Planned Giving Today* 3, no. 1 (1992): 4.

13. Alan Farnham, "The Windfall Awaiting the New Inheritors," *Fortune*, May 7, 1990, 72.

## 10 Comprehensive Fund-Raising Campaigns

The authors wish to acknowledge their use of certain information and ideas from an unpublished manuscript prepared for this book by Frederick Nahm and Marilyn Lucas of the University of Pennsylvania and entitled "Recording Gifts and Reporting Campaigns. Nahm has since become president of Knox College in Galesburg, Illinois.

1. Peter McE. Buchanan, "Some Blunt Talk about Fund Raising," *CASE Currents*, Oct. 1991, 10–19.

2. Rita Bornstein, "Adding It Up," ibid., Jan. 1989, 12–17.

3. Ibid.

4. Vance T. Peterson, preface to *CASE Campaign Standards: Management and Reporting Standards for Educational Fund-Raising Campaigns* (Washington, D.C.: CASE, 1994), iii.

5. Ibid., 1.

6. Ibid., 2.

7. Ibid.

8. Ibid., 1.

## 11 Employment

1. Calvin Mackenzie, memorandum to the author, Mar. 18, 1991.

2. Baltimore *Sun*, Apr. 10, 1992, 12A.

# Selected Bibliography

Abbott, Andrew. *The System of Professions.* Chicago: Univ. of Chicago Press, 1988.

Addams, Jane. 1982. *Philanthropy and Social Progress.* New York: Thomas Y. Crowell, 1982.

Aman, Kenneth, ed. *Ethical Principles for Development: Needs, Capacities, or Rights?* Upper Montclaire, N.J.: Institute for Critical Thinking, 1991.

"Are Direct Mail Donors Really Environmentally Conscious? Part II." *Warwick File* 5, no. 1 (1991).

Bailey, Anne Lowrey. "Every Excuse in the Book and How to Avoid Them." *CASE Currents,* Nov.–Dec. 1984, 39–41.

———. "More Scholars, Colleges Taking an Interest in the Study of Philanthropy and Non-Profit Organizations." *Chronicle of Higher Education,* Sept. 21, 1988, A34–A36.

———. "Sexual Harassment: Growing Issue for Fund Raisers." *Chronicle of Philanthropy,* July 30, 1991, 17–18.

———. "Today's Fund-Raising Detectives Hunt 'Suspects' Who Have Big Money to Give." *Chronicle of Higher Education* 34, no. 41 (1988): A1, A25–A26.

Bash, Roger. "Fundraising in Career Development Services." *Journal of Career Development* 12, no. 3 (1986): 231–39.

Bergan, Helen. *Where the Money Is: A Fund Raiser's Guide to the Rich.* 2d ed. Alexandria, Va.: BioGuide, 1992.

Berke, Richard L. "A Crusader Tilts at the Ivory Towers Looking for Old-Fashioned Corruption." *New York Times,* Apr. 21, 1991.

Beyers, Bob. "In Public Relations and Fund Raising, Colleges Should Remember: Candor Pays." *Chronicle of Higher Education,* Aug. 8, 1990, B1, B3.

## Selected Bibliography

Blackwell, Thomas. *College Law: A Guide for Administrators.* Washington, D.C.: American Council on Education, 1961.

Bok, Derek. "Accepting Gifts." In Bok, *Beyond the Ivory Tower,* 266–79.

———. *Beyond the Ivory Tower: Social Responsibilities of the Modern University.* Cambridge: Harvard Univ. Press, 1982.

Bok, Sissela. *Secrets: On the Ethics of Concealment and Revelation.* New York: Vintage Books, 1983.

Bornstein, Rita. "Adding It Up." *CASE Currents,* Jan. 1989.

Bowyer, J. Barton. *Cheating.* New York: St. Martin's 1982.

Brittingham, Barbara E., and Thomas E. Pezzullo. *The Campus Green: Fund Raising in Higher Education.* ERIC Document Reproduction Service No. ED 321 706. Washington, D.C.: George Washington University, School of Education and Human Development, 1990.

Broce, Thomas E. "Characteristics of a Successful Fund Raiser." In *Professionalization in Fund Raising: Guide to Raising Money from Private Sources,* 42–43. Norman: Univ. of Oklahoma Press, 1979.

Brown, William. "Ethics for Survival: Constructing Commission Rates for University Development Officers." *Journal of College and University Personnel Association* 37, no. 2 (1986): 20–23.

Buchanan, Peter McE. "Some Blunt Talk about Fund Raising." *CASE Currents,* Oct. 1991, 10–19.

Burlingame, Dwight, and Lamont J. Hulse. *Taking Fund Raising Seriously: Advancing the Profession and Practice of Raising Money.* San Francisco: Jossey-Bass, 1991.

Camenisch, Paul. "Gift and Gratitude in Ethics." *Journal of Religious Ethics* 9, no. 1 (1981): 1–34.

Campbell, Dennis. *Doctors, Lawyers, Ministers: Christian Ethics in Professional Practice.* Nashville: Abingdon, 1982.

Campbell, Karlyn Kohrs. *The Rhetorical Act.* Belmont, Calif.: Wadsworth Publishing, 1982.

Carbone, Robert. *Fund Raising as a Profession.* College Park, Md.: Clearinghouse for Research on Fund Raising, 1989.

Carnegie, Andrew. "The Gospel of Wealth." In *The Gospel of Wealth and Other Timely Essays,* 14–49. Cambridge: Harvard Univ. Press, Belknap Press, 1962.

Clotfelter, Charles. "Tax-Induced Distortions in the Voluntary Sector." *Case Western Reserve Law Review* 39 (1988): 663–94.

Coon, Horace. *Money to Burn: Great American Foundations and Their Money.* New Brunswick, N.J.: Transaction Books, 1990.

Cordes, Colleen. "Stanford U. Embroiled in Angry Controversy on Over-

## Selected Bibliography

head Charges." *Chronicle of Higher Education* 37, no. 21 (Feb. 6, 1991): A1, A20–A21.

Council for Advancement and Support of Education. *CASE Advisory on Advancement Practice: Principles and Recommendations Regarding Ethics and Confidentiality in Development Research* (Washington, D.C.: CASE, 1991).

———. *Reach Out and Raise More Funds: An Administrative Guide for Planning and Conducting a Successful Phonathon.* Washington, D.C.: CASE and AT&T, 1986.

———. *Winning Words: A Volunteer's Guide to Asking for Major Gifts.* Washington, D.C., 1984.

Critz, Doris. "Women as Senior Development Officers." In *Handbook for Educational Fund Raising,* edited by Francis Pray, 285–89. San Francisco: Jossey-Bass, 1981.

Cutlip, Scott. "The Cheats in Fund Raising." In *Fund Raising in the United States,* 441–73. New Brunswick, N.J.: Rutgers Univ. Press, 1965.

Daniels, Lee A. "Potential Donors Figure in Entry to Vermont U." *New York Times,* Nov. 8, 1989.

DeFazio, Frank. "Commercial Appeal: How Advertising Can Help Your Institution Meet Its Goals." *CASE Currents,* July–Aug. 1988, 16–27.

DeMott, Benjamin. "A Fund Raising Success Story But With a Vexing Aftertaste." *Change,* Sept.–Oct. 1986, 11.

Desruisseaux, Paul. "Conservative Foundations to Turn Attention to Philanthropy Itself." *Chronicle of Higher Education,* Sept. 2, 1987, A72–A77.

———. "Guidelines for Those Who Give Away Money for a Living." *Chronicle of Higher Education,* Apr. 15, 1987, 31, 34.

Dichter, Ernest. "Why People Give." In *Some Aspects of Educational Fund Raising,* edited by Jean D. Lineham, 45–48. Washington, D.C.: American Alumni Council, 1961.

Dingfelder, William. "Non-Profits Must Consider Ethics in Soliciting Gifts." *Fund Raising Management,* Dec. 1982, 36–37.

Dingwall, Robert, and Philip Lewis, eds. *The Sociology of the Professions.* New York: St. Martin's, 1983.

Drotning, Philip T. *Putting the Fund Raising.* Chicago: Contemporary Books, 1979.

Elliott, Deni. "My Search for the Charitable Impulse." Paper presented to the Task Force on Ethics and Higher Education Advancement, Washington, D.C., Sept. 20, 1990.

## Selected Bibliography

———. "On Deceiving One's Source." *International Journal of Applied Philosophy* 6, no. 1 (summer 1991): 1–8.

———. "What Counts as Deception in Higher Education Development." In Burlingame and Hulse, *Taking Fund Raising Seriously*, 73–82.

Elliott, Deni, and Charles Culver. "Defining and Analyzing Journalistic Deception." *Journal of Mass Media Ethics* 7, no. 2 (spring 1992): 69–84.

Elliston, Frederick. "Development Ethics." Paper presented at the CASE 5 District Conference, Chicago, Dec. 12, 1983.

Fadiman, Jeffrey. "A Traveler's Guide to Gifts and Bribes." *Harvard Business Review*, July–Aug. 1986, 122–32.

Farnham, Alan. "The Windfall Awaiting the New Inheritors." *Fortune*, May 7, 1990.

Fawcett, John R., Jr. "Is It Folly for Businesses to Support Any But Pro-Business Universities?" *Chronicle of Higher Education*, Jan. 28, 1974, 17.

Fink, Norman S. *Ethics for Fund-Raisers*. Chicago: Research Institute of America, 1993.

———. "Issues and Ethics for Non-Profit Executives and Institutions." Paper presented to the Chicago Planned Giving Roundtable, Feb. 6, 1990.

Fisher, James. "The Growth of Heartlessness: The Need for Studies on Philanthropy." *Educational Record*, winter 1986, 25–28.

Flint, Anthony. "Chasing a Billion Dollars: Endowments Seen Path to Stability." *Boston Globe*, Dec. 23, 1990.

Gatozzi, Lynn. "Charitable Contributions as a Condition of Probation for Convicted Corporations: Using Philanthropy to Combat Corporate Crime." *Case Western Reserve Law Review* 37 (1987): 569–88.

Gauker, Christopher. "The Principle of Charity." *Synthese* 69 (1986): 1–25.

Gert, Bernard. *Morality: A New Justification for the Moral Rules*. New York: Oxford Univ. Press, 1988.

———. "Morality, Moral Theory, and Applied and Professional Ethics." *Professional Ethics* 1, nos. 1 and 2 (1992): 5–24.

Gewirth, Alan. "Private Philanthropy and Positive Rights." *Social Philosophy and Policy* 4, no. 2 (1987): 55–78.

Giltenan, Edward. "Giving So It Doesn't Hurt." *Forbes*, Oct. 3, 1988, 181–82.

Goldberg, Debbie. "How the Other Half Gives: Alumnae Are Coming into

*Selected Bibliography*

Their Own—and Giving Some of It Back." *CASE Currents,* Mar. 1989, 10–15.

Goldman, Alan. *The Moral Foundations of Professional Ethics.* Totowa, N.J.: Rowan & Littlefield, 1981.

Goss, Kristen. "Fund Raisers, Criticized for Altering Ethics Code, Draft a New Version." *Chronicle of Philanthropy,* Mar. 20, 1990, 4, 10.

———. "Fund-Raising Executives Pass First Part of New Ethics Code." *Chronicle of Philanthropy,* Nov. 27, 1990, 29.

———. "A Guide for Counting Gifts." *Chronicle of Philanthropy* 4, no. 4 (Dec. 3, 1991): 21–23.

———. "Independent Sector Urges Non-Profits to Develop Codes of Ethical Conduct." *Chronicle of Philanthropy,* Oct. 30, 1990, 25, 27.

———. "Internal Misconduct Leads Non-Profits to Look to Their Missions to Resolve Ethical Questions." *Chronicle of Philanthropy* 3, no. 18 (July 2, 1991): 31, 34.

———. "Public's Perception Worries Fund Raisers: They Fear They Are Viewed as Salespeople or Beggars, in Spite of Growing Professionalism." *Chronicle of Philanthropy,* June 26, 1990, 19–21.

———. "Should Charities Pay for a Donor's Ill-Gotten Gains?" *Chronicle of Philanthropy* 3, no. 18 (July 2, 1991): 25–26.

Greene, Stephen. "Should More Grants Fail?" *Chronicle of Philanthropy* 2, no. 21 (Aug. 7, 1990): 1, 10–11.

Gurin, Maurice G. "A Fair Practice Code." In *What Volunteers Should Know for Successful Fund Raising,* 131. New York: Stein & Day, 1981.

———. "Many Colleges Do Have Courses on Philanthropy." *Chronicle of Philanthropy,* Apr. 17, 1990, 32.

Gurin, Maurice G., and Jon Van Til. "Understanding Philanthropy: Fund Raising in Perspective." *Giving USA Update,* May/June–July/Aug. 1989, 3–10.

Hall, Holly. "Choosing the Right Consultant." *Chronicle of Philanthropy,* Feb. 26, 1991, 22–24, 26–27.

———. "For Clients, the Tactics of Fund-Raising Consultants Often Spur Complaints." *Chronicle of Philanthropy,* Feb. 26, 1991, 25.

———. "For Consultants, Frustrations Arise from Ways That Some Charities Pick Advisers." *Chronicle of Philanthropy,* Feb. 26, 1991, 25.

———. "Head of College Fund Raiser Group Calls for End to Protracted Capital Campaigns With Huge Goals." *Chronicle of Philanthropy,* July 28, 1992, 20.

————. "Non-Profits Seen Facing a Variety of Ethical Issues." *Chronicle of Philanthropy*, July 10, 1990.

Harris, Seymour. "Gifts." In *The Economics of Harvard*, 279–91. New York: McGraw-Hill, 1970.

————. "Gifts and Their Uses, 1636–1900." In *The Economics of Harvard*, 292–95. New York: McGraw-Hill, 1970.

————. "Methods of Raising Money." In *The Economics of Harvard*, 296–303. New York: McGraw-Hill, 1970.

————. "Sources of Money." In *The Economics of Harvard*, 304–10. New York: McGraw-Hill, 1970.

Harvey, Phillip D. "Donors Are Too Often Guided by Their Hearts and Not Their Heads When They Give." *Chronicle of Philanthropy*, Mar. 26, 1991.

Heard, Alex. "Embarrassment of Riches." *Spy Magazine* 34 (Jan. 1990): 81–87.

Helyar, John. "To Keep Prep School in Chips, 'Mr. Chips' Courts the Wealthy." *Wall Street Journal*, Sept. 5, 1980.

Hixson, Richard. *Privacy in a Public Society: Human Rights in Conflict.* New York: Oxford Univ. Press, 1987.

Holton, Felicia. "In a Secular Society, How Can We Teach People about Philanthropy? A Conversation with Robert L. Payton." *University of Chicago Magazine*, fall 1985, 2–7.

Honan, William. "Endowment Embattled over Academic Freedom." *New York Times*, Dec. 17, 1989.

Hooker, Michael. "Moral Values and Private Philanthropy." *Social Philosophy and Policy* 4, no. 2 (1987): 128–41.

Hopkins, Bruce. *The Law of Fund-Raising.* New York: John Wiley & Sons, 1991.

Howard, John A. "A Legitimate Quid Pro Quo in Corporate Philanthropy for Higher Education." *Prospect*, May 15, 1977, 15–17.

Jenkins, Jeanne B., and Marilyn Lucas. *How to Find Philanthropic Prospects.* Ambler, Pa.: Fund-Raising Institute, 1986.

Johnston, David. "Looking for an Honest Answer." *Foundation News*, Jan.–Feb. 1988, 54–56.

Johnston, Noel W. "The Art of Asking." *CASE Currents*, Apr. 1982, 41–42.

Joseph, James. "The Council in the 1980's." Address delivered at annual meeting of Council of Foundations, Boston, Apr. 1990.

————, ed. *The Charitable Impulse.* New York: Foundation Center, 1989.

## Selected Bibliography

Josephson, Michael. *Ethics in Grantmaking and Grantseeking.* Nashville: Josephson Institute, 1992.

Kelly, Kathleen. *Fund Raising and Public Relations: A Critical Analysis.* Hillsdale, N.J.: Lawrence Erlbaum Associates, 1991.

Kidder, Rushworth. "To Solve Today's Problems, Foundations Must Look at the Underlying Issues: Ethics and Values." *Chronicle of Philanthropy,* Aug. 7, 1990, 28–29.

Krukowski, Jan. "The Passionate Philanthropist." *CASE Currents,* Apr. 1979, 38.

Larson, Magali Sarfatti. *The Rise of Professionalization.* Berkeley: Univ. of California Press, 1977.

Lefever, Ernest. *Scholars, Dollars, and Public Policy.* Washington, D.C.: Ethics and Public Policy Center, 1983.

Lehtinen, Toni L. "Money by Mail." *CASE Currents,* Nov.–Dec. 1982.

Lenkowsky, Leslie. "Performance, Not a Code of Ethics, Is the Key to Ethical Behavior for Non-Profits." *Chronicle of Philanthropy* 3, no. 3 (Nov. 13, 1990): 37–38.

————. "What's the Difference between a Beggar and a Fund Raiser?" *Chronicle of Philanthropy,* Mar. 6, 1990, 31–32.

Levine, Art, and Jo Ann Tooley. "The Hard Sell behind the Ivy." *U.S. News and World Report,* Apr. 11, 1988, 54–55.

Levy, Charles. *Education and Training for the Fundraising Function.* New York: Bureau for Careers in Jewish Service, 1973.

————. "The Fundraising Function." In *Professional Components in Education for Fundraising,* edited by Frank M. Loewenberg, 16–39. New York: Council on Social Work Education, 1975.

Lucas, Robert. *The Grants World Inside Out.* Urbana: Univ. of Illinois Press, 1992.

Magarrell, Jack. "Businesses Advised to Support Universities Friendly to Them." *Chronicle of Higher Education,* Mar. 8, 1976, 1, 12.

————. "Colleges Seen Threatening Capitalism." *Chronicle of Higher Education,* Nov. 7, 1977, 5.

————. "Princeton Alumni Unit Pushes Conservative Views." *Chronicle of Higher Education,* Mar. 15, 1976, 7.

Martin, James. "Institutional Investment and the Development Officer." In *Handbook for Educational Fund Raising,* edited by Francis Pray, 310–12. San Francisco: Jossey-Bass, 1981.

Marts, Arnaud. *Philanthropy's Role in Civilization: Its Contribution to Human Freedom.* New Brunswick, N.J.: Transaction Books, 1991.

## Selected Bibliography

McIntyre, Jim. "The Good, the Bad, and the Ethical: How Can Business Officers Tell the Difference?" *NACUBO Business Officer*, Nov. 1991, 32–35.

McMillen, Liz. "College Fund Raisers Criticize Promotion of Gifts as Tax Shelters." *Chronicle of Philanthropy*, Oct. 11, 1989, A36.

———. "Frostburg State's Fund-Raising Foundation Continues to Draw Criticism; Misuse of a Bequest Is Alleged." *Chronicle of Higher Education*, Nov. 21, 1990, A25–A26.

———. "Trouble May Await Colleges That Accept Money from Donors With Questionable Records." *Chronicle of Higher Education*, Apr. 6, 1988, A23–A25.

McNamee, Mike. "A Closer Look at the Law." *CASE Currents*, Apr. 1990, 18–19.

———. "Privacy and the Prospect Researcher: How to Draw the Line between Uncovering Useful Donor Data and Digging Up Dirty Little Secrets." *CASE Currents*, June 1990, 10–17.

———. "The Problem with Premiums." *CASE Currents*, Apr. 1990, 13–16.

Miner, T. Richardson. "The Ethics of Fundraising." *Hospital News* (N.H.), Oct. 1990, 14.

Moody, Michael. "Why Don't Colleges Teach Students How Philanthropy Works?" *Chronicle of Philanthropy*, Mar. 20, 1990, 32.

Moore, Jennifer. "Fund Raisers Debate Where to Draw the Line in Digging Up Personal Data on Potential Donors." *Chronicle of Philanthropy*, Sept. 8, 1992, 23.

Muller, Steven. "The Definition and Philosophy of Institutional Advancement." In *Handbook of Institutional Advancement*, edited by A. Wesley Rowland, 1–9. San Francisco: Jossey-Bass, 1977.

Munger, John. "Packaging Student Financial Assistance: The Case for the Private Donor." *Journal of Student Financial Aid* 13, no. 2 (1983): 19–24.

Murningham, Marcy. *Moral Values, Philanthropy, and Public Life: Recasting the Connections*. Washington, D.C.: Lighthouse Investment Group for Council on Foundations, 1989.

Murphy, Mary K., ed. *Cultivating Foundation Support for Education*. Washington, D.C.: CASE, 1989.

Natale, Samuel. "Ethics, Morality, and Marketing." *Nonprofit World Report*, July–Aug. 1984, 20–21, 29.

———. "Organizational Ethics: What Is It and What Does It Mean for Nonprofits?" *Nonprofit World Report*, May–June 1984, 27–29.

New, Anne. "Ethical Standards for Fund-Raising." *Philanthropy Monthly,*
Aug. 1978, 31–32.

Nielsen, Waldemar A. *The Golden Donors: A New Anatomy of the Great
Foundations.* New York: E. P. Dutton, Truman Talley Books, 1985.

Novack, Janet. "Tax Dodges Begin at Home." *Forbes,* Nov. 16, 1990.

Novak, Michael, ed. *Democracy and Mediating Structures: A Theological
Inquiry.* Washington, D.C.: American Enterprise Institute, 1980.

O'Connor, Thomas W. " 'Offensive Snooping' by Prospect Researchers."
*Chronicle of Higher Education,* July 27, 1988, B5.

Odendahl, Teresa. *Charity Begins at Home: Generosity and Self-Interest
among Philanthropic Elite.* New York: Basic Books, 1990.

Olsson, Gunnar. *Lines of Power: Limits of Language.* Minneapolis: Univ.
of Minnesota Press, 1991.

O'Neill, Michael, ed. *Ethics in Nonprofit Management: A Collection of
Cases.* San Francisco: Institute for Nonprofit Organization Management, 1990.

Panas, Jerold. *Mega Gifts: Who Gives Them, Who Gets Them.* Chicago:
Pluribus Press, Division of Teach'em, 1984.

Parsons, Talcott. "Professions and Social Structures." In *Social Structures and Social Action.* Chicago: Univ. of Chicago Press, 1963.

Payton, Robert L. "Essential Qualities of the Development Officer." In
*Handbook for Educational Fund Raising,* edited by Francis Pray, 282–
84. San Francisco: Jossey-Bass, 1981.

———. "The Ethics and Values of Fund Raising." In *The President and
Fund Raising,* 33–45. New York: Macmillan, 1989.

———. *The Ethics of Corporate Grantmaking.* Occasional Paper No. 5.
Washington, D.C.: Council on Foundations, 1987.

———. *Major Challenges to Philanthropy: A Discussion Paper for Independent Sector.* New York: Independent Sector, 1984.

———. "Philanthropy in Academia: Making the 'Non-Subject' Real." *Giving USA Update,* Mar.–Apr. 1988, 4–5.

———. *Philanthropy: Voluntary Action for the Public Good.* London: Col-
lier Macmillan, 1988.

———. "Tainted Money." *Change,* May–June 1987, 55–61.

Payton, Robert L., Michael Novak, Brian O'Connel, and Peter Hall Dob-
kin. *Philanthropy: Four Views.* New Brunswick, N.J.: Transaction
Books, 1988.

Payton, Robert L., Henry A. Rosso, and Eugene R. Tempel. "Toward a
Philosophy of Fund Raising." In Burlingame and Hulse, *Taking Fund
Raising Seriously,* 3–36.

*Selected Bibliography*

Peavey, Marion. "Ethical Standards and Guidelines for Practice." In *Handbook for Educational Fund Raising,* edited by Francis Pray, 306–9. San Francisco: Jossey-Bass, 1981.

Philips, Michael. "Bribery." *Ethics,* July 1984, 621–36.

Pitchell, Robert J. "Corporate Donors." *Wall Street Journal,* Jan. 30, 1978.

Pollock, Frederick. *Principles of Contracts.* 3d ed. New York: Voorhis, 1906.

Pogrebin, Letty Cottin. "Contributing to the Cause." *New York Times Magazine,* Apr. 22, 1990, 22–24.

Rabinowitz, Alan. "The Philanthropic Universe." In *Social Change Philanthropy in America,* 13–24. Westport, Conn.: Quorum Books, 1990.

Rainbolt, William. "Gifts That Can't Be Matched." *CASE Currents* 13, no. 1 (1987): 12–18.

Reinert, Paul. "The Spiritual Dimensions of Giving and Getting." *Momentum,* no. 3 (Sept. 1985): 6–9.

Richards, Glenn. "How and When to Refuse a Gift." *Private School Quarterly,* winter 1984, 35–37.

Roche, Robert P. "Huge Fund Drives May Not Be Worth the Cost in Ill Will and Unfulfilled Expectations." *Chronicle of Philanthropy,* Mar. 12, 1991, 40–41.

Rosenzweig, Robert M. "The Debate over Indirect Costs Raises Fundamental Policy Issues." *Chronicle of Higher Education,* Mar. 6, 1991, 40.

Rosovsky, Henry. *The University: An Owner's Manual.* New York: W. W. Norton, 1990.

Rosso, Henry A., et al. *Achieving Excellence in Fund Raising: A Comprehensive Guide to Principles, Strategies, and Methods.* San Francisco: Jossey-Bass, 1991.

Rowland, A. "Perspectives on Institutional Advancement." In *Handbook of Institutional Advancement,* edited by A. Wesley Rowland, 522–33. San Francisco: Jossey-Bass, 1977.

Royce, Lee. "Divide and Conquer: Segmentation Can Help Raise More Money through Direct Mail." *Case Currents,* May 1988, 22–25.

Ryan, Ellen. "The Good, the Bad, and the Money: An Expert Offers Advice on the Ethics of Planned Giving." *CASE Currents,* Oct. 1989, 11–13.

Schooler, Dean. "Fund Raising's Future Shock Requires Look at Alternatives." *Fund Raising Management,* Sept.–Oct. 1978, 34–39.

Selected Bibliography

———. "Rethinking and Remaking the Nonprofit Sector." *Foundation News,* Jan.–Feb. 1978, 17–23.

———. "Understanding Fund Raising." *Philanthropy Monthly,* Nov. 1979, 18–23.

Scully, Malcolm G. "Corporations' Unrestricted Gifts to Universities Stir New Debate." *Chronicle of Higher Education,* Nov. 12, 1973.

———. "Packard Urges Corporations to Stop Unrestricted Gifts." *Chronicle of Higher Education,* Oct. 29, 1973.

Shakely, Jack. "Ethics of Charitable Solicitation." *Grantsmanship Center News,* Feb.–Mar. 1975, 14–19.

Sharpe, Robert F., Barlow T. Mann, and Jonathan Tidd. "Is There 'Security' in Planned Giving?" *Trusts and Estates,* Aug. 1990.

Simmons, Terry L. "Higher Education and the Revenue Reconciliation Act of 1993: Substantiation and Other News." *Charitable Gift Planning News* 11, no. 7 (1993).

Smith, Ginger. "Preventing Misuse in Matching Gifts." *Matching Gift Notes* 3, no. 1 (fall 1985): 1–2.

Smith, Joel. "Professionals in Development: Dignity or Disdain?" *CASE Currents* 7, no. 3 (Mar. 1981): 10–13.

Smith, Page. *Killing the Spirit: Higher Education in America.* New York: Viking, 1990.

"The State of Planned Giving in America." *Planned Giving Today* 3, no. 1 (1992): 1–3.

Stehle, Vince. "Arts Groups Debate Propriety of Accepting Philip Morris Money." *Chronicle of Philanthropy,* Sept. 18, 1990, 5, 15.

———. "Code of Standards for Fund Raisers and Planners Adopted by Two National Planned-Giving Groups." *Chronicle of Philanthropy* 3, no. 16 (June 4, 1991): 17, 19.

———. "Debate Rages over Financial Consultants' Role in Gifts." *Chronicle of Philanthropy,* Feb. 20, 1990, 4–5, 8.

———. "Fund Raisers Assail Planners Who Push Gifts as Tax Shelters and Take Big Finder's Fees." *Chronicle of Philanthropy,* Oct. 3, 1989, 11–12.

———. "Planned-Giving Officials Vote to Revise Draft of Ethics Code." *Chronicle of Philanthropy,* Oct. 31, 1989.

———. "Prospect Researchers Are Pressed to Develop Code of Ethics and Head Off Controversy for Profession." *Chronicle of Philanthropy,* Sept. 4, 1990, 8–9.

———. "Prospect Researchers, Who Collect Confidential Information about Potential Donors, Are Divided over Ethical Questions." *Chronicle of Philanthropy*, Sept. 5, 1989, 5, 11.

Sterne, Larry. "NSFRE Deletes Ban on Soliciting for a Percentage." *Non-Profit Times*, May 1989, 1, 13–14, 54.

Strand, Bobbie. "Prospect Research Is Spelled R-e-s-p-e-c-t." In *Prospect Research: A How-To Guide*, edited by Bobbie Strand and Susan Hunt. Washington, D.C.: CASE, 1986.

Stringfellow, William. "Money and Idolatry." *Witness*, Mar. 1992, 19.

Swasy, Alecia. "Dead Horse Breeder Raises a Ruckus with a Beneficiary." *Wall Street Journal*, Apr. 25, 1990.

Sykes, Charles J. *The Hollow Men*. Washington, D.C.: Regnery Gateway, 1990.

Tardio, Robert. "New Giving Guidelines from Maryland: University of Maryland's Foundation Sets an Ethical Standard." *Matching Gifts Notes* 3, no. 4 (summer 1986): 1–2.

Teltsch, Kathleen. "Studying Philanthropy." *New York Times*, Nov. 18, 1986.

———. "The Ultimate Gift." *New York Times*, Educational suppl., Apr. 10, 1988.

Thompson, Kenneth, ed. *Private Means, Public Ends*. Lanham, Md.: Univ. Press of America, 1987. Vol. 4.

Van Til, Jon, ed. *Critical Issues in American Philanthropy*. San Francisco: Jossey-Bass, 1990.

"Views and Counsel from Seven Consultants." *Planned Giving Today* 3, no. 1 (1992).

Warner, Irving. "Fund Raisers Who Don't Know What They Don't Know." *Chronicle of Philanthropy*, Mar. 10, 1992, 41–42.

Warwick, Mal. "The Art of Asking." *Warwick File* 5, no. 1 (1991).

———. "Your Donors May Know More than You Think." *Nonprofit World* 11, no. 6 (1993): 8–9.

Wellesley College. *Work in Progress: The Campaign for $150 Million*. Wellesley, Mass., Jan. 1992.

Wheeler, David L. "NIH Office That Investigates Scientists' Misconduct Is Target of Widespread Charges of Incompetence." *Chronicle of Higher Education*, May 15, 1991, A5, A8–A9.

———. "President of Rockefeller U. Retracts Scientific Paper That NIH Office Says Contains Fabricated Data." *Chronicle of Higher Education*, Mar. 27, 1991, A1, A11.

Whitaker, Ben. "The Gift Horses under Scrutiny." In *The Foundations:*

## Selected Bibliography

*Anatomy of Philanthropy and Society,* edited by B. Whitaker, 11–28. London: Eyre Methuen, 1974.

Williams, Grant. "Charities Face Renewed Scrutiny by State Regulators." *Chronicle of Philanthropy,* 3, no. 3 (Nov. 13, 1990): 31, 34.

Wilshire, Bruce. *The Moral Collapse of the University: Professionalism, Purity, and Alienation.* Albany: State Univ. of New York Press, 1990.

Wineburg, Bob. "Robin Hood School of Fund Raising: Take Tainted Money." *Chronicle of Philanthropy,* Sept. 4, 1990.

Worth, Michael J. "Prospect Research: A Tool for Professionalism in Fund Raising." *Fund Raising Management,* June 1991.

Wright, Robert. "The Foundation Game." *New Republic,* Nov. 5, 1990, 21–25.

Zweibel, Ellen. "Looking the Gift Horse in the Mouth: An Examination of Charitable Gifts Which Benefit the Donor." *McGill Law Journal* 31 (1986): 417–55.

# Contributors

*Allen Buchanan* is the Grainger Professor of Business Ethics, professor of philosophy, and professor of medical ethics at the University of Wisconsin, Madison. He is the author of numerous articles on political philosophy and applied ethics and of the following books: *Marx and Justice* (1982), *Ethics, Efficiency, and the Market* (1985), *Deciding for Others* (with Dan J. Brock, 1989), and *Secession: The Morality of Political Divorce* (1991).

*James A. Donahue* is dean of students at Georgetown University and associate professor of theological ethics in the Department of Theology there. Donahue also serves as a consultant on ethics in institutional advancement for CASE. He lectures on ethical issues relating to fund raising and writes broadly in the field of applied ethics.

*Marilyn Batt Dunn* is president of the University of Washington Foundation and vice president for development of the University of Washington, Seattle. Dunn is active in CASE both regionally and nationally and currently serves as a member of the CASE Philanthropy Commission (1993–96).

*Deni Elliott* is Mansfield Professor of Ethics and Public Affairs and professor of philosophy at the University of Montana. She served as director of the Ethics Institute at Dartmouth College from 1988 through 1992. Her work includes publications and videodocumentaries in various area of applied ethics, including journalism ethics and academic research ethics.

*Contributors*

*Bernard Gert* is the Eunice and Julian Cohen Professor for the Study of Ethics and Human Values at Dartmouth College and adjunct professor of psychiatry at the Dartmouth Medical School. He has been studying, teaching, and writing about philosophy for more than thirty years and holds the view that philosophy, especially moral philosophy, should not only be understandable to nonphilosophers but be useful to them as well. He is the author of *Morality: A New Justification for the Moral Rules* (1988) and co-author, with Charles Culver, of *Philosophy in Medicine* (1982).

*Judith M. Gooch* has been involved in fund raising for more than twenty-five years as a volunteer and, since 1977, as a professional. She spent four years as director of grants at Mount Holyoke College, followed by four years as director of development at Lake Forest College and three years as director of development for the School of Science at The Massachusetts Institute of Technology. Since 1990 she has been a fund-raising consultant; her clients have included hospitals, social service agencies, museums, and arts organizations. She has led workshops and lectured extensively on various aspects of development, and her book *Writing Winning Proposals* was published by CASE in 1987.

*Bruce R. Hopkins,*, a lawyer in private practice with the law firm of Powers, Pyles & Sutter, in Washington, D.C., specializes in the areas of corporate law and taxation, with emphasis on the representation of nonprofit organizations. He is the author of *The Tax Law of Charitable Giving* (1993); *The Law of Tax-Exempt Organizations* (6th ed. 1992, suppl. 1993); *Charity, Advocacy, and the Law* (1992, suppl. 1993); and *The Law of Fund-Raising* (1991, suppls. 1992, 1993) and winner of the first annual National Society of Fund Raising Executives/Statley/Robeson/Ryan/St. Lawrence Research Award (1991).

*Frank Logan* is a planned giving consultant based in Hanover, New Hampshire. From 1973 to 1993 he served as a planned giving officer at Dartmouth College and was the director of the program from 1984 until his early retirement in 1993. He was the chair of the CANARAS planned giving group in 1989–90.

## Contributors

*Richard F. Seaman* is vice president for institutional advancement at Western Maryland College, a private, independent liberal arts college near Baltimore. He has spent his entire professional life in higher education, more than twenty-five years of which have been devoted to advancement work at, in addition to Western Maryland, Oberlin, Brown University, Skidmore, and Bowdoin. He has held major leadership roles in six comprehensive fund-raising campaigns that raised a total of nearly $350 million. He is a past member of the board of trustees of CASE.

*Mary Lou Siebert* has devoted her work at the University of Washington to stewardship of endowment donors and to corporate and foundation relations since 1992. In addition, she volunteers with several nonprofit organizations in the Seattle area. From 1987 to 1992 she was manager of prospect research during the University of Washington's successful $250 million capital campaign. Prior to living in Seattle, Siebert worked with the University of Illinois Foundation in Urbana, Illinois, and The Procter & Gamble Fund in Cincinnati, Ohio.

*Holly Smith* is professor of philosophy and dean of social and behavioral Sciences at the University of Arizona. She has also taught at Tufts University and the Universities of Pittsburgh, Michigan, Illinois at Chicago, and North Carolina. She has published widely on ethical theory and applied ethics.

*Eric B. Wentworth*, special assistant to the president at CASE, has had various duties in fifteen years there. He heads CASE's National Clearinghouse for Ethics in Educational Fund Raising. Previously a journalist, he worked for newspapers in Oregon as well as for the *Wall Street Journal* and the *Washington Post*.

# Index

Library of Congress Cataloging-in-Publication Data

The ethics of asking : dilemmas in higher education fund raising /
edited by Deni Elliott.
p.   cm.
Includes bibliographical references (p.   ) and index.
ISBN 0-8018-5049-5 (alk. paper)
1. Educational fund raising—United States—Moral and ethical
aspects. 2. Universities and colleges—United States—Finance.
I. Elliott, Deni.
LB2336.E84   1995
378'.02—dc20                                       94-47444

LB2336 .E84 1995

The ethics of asking :
dilemmas in higher